"The Coach Partnership ontological coaching certification programme provided in-depth knowledge and first-hand experience of how my emotions, my body, and the language I use impact my daily life. Seeing is the first step, learning how to shift my behaviours is opening up a new world of possibilities for me and for those I now have the privilege of working with as a coach."
> — **Tina Doran, PCC**
> **Senior Vice President, Finance, Payments & Corporate**

"I jumped into the programme to learn how to nurture a more engaged team. This beautifully crafted learning journey, delivered by a dedicated team of experts, far surpassed all expectations. My fabulous cohort and I were taken on a deep exploration into the domain of 'being' that was both challenging and enlightening. I not only achieved my goal, I gained a much greater level of self-awareness and discovered a new world of new possibilities. Thank you!"
> — **Chris Curtis, ACC**
> **Senior Vice President, Customer Success, DigitalRoute**

"Ontological coaching has helped me unlock limiting beliefs that held me back and revealed the importance of our body, emotions, and language in well-being. It has taught me when the 'magic' happens for my coachee."
> — **Tan Chew May**
> **Organisational Culture & Behaviour Shaper and Head,**
> **Downstream Culture Excellence, PETRONAS**

"Habituated in prescribing and mentoring, my advent into the realm of the 'being' during the foundations course was a retrospective introspection. Thanks to The Coach Partnership team, this awakening of sorts in the art of co-creating has been transformative. I offer a non-judgemental space to question who you are and what you commit to for embodying who you want to be."

— **Shazib Pervaiz, MBBS, PhD**
   Professor, Department of Physiology, Yong Loo Lin School of Medicine; Theme Lead, NUS Centre for Cancer Research (N2CR); National University of Singapore; National University Cancer Institute, National University Health System (NUHS)

"My journey to become a Certified Coach with The Coach Partnership began in May 2021. Taking time to understand and appreciate that I am a unique observer during The Foundations Program was refreshing. Learning the skills to coach others using the ontological model of coaching during The Art and Practice of Ontological Mastery programme was exhilarating. I cannot thank the team at The Coach Partnership enough."

— **Marie-Veronique 'Marie' Clement, PhD**
   Academic and Newfield Certified Coach, Yong Loo Lin School of Medicine, Department of Biochemistry, National University of Singapore

"The Coach Partnership ontological coach training programme experience went far beyond my expectations. The excellent coaching, mentoring, and support I received from the trainers, coaches, and friends set the foundation for the shifting, the growing, and the change that I now embrace as crucial to leading both myself and others. Thank you to everyone at The Coach Partnership!"

> **— Melanie Martens**
> **Academy Principal, Physical Education and**
> **Sports Teacher Academy, Academy of Singapore Teachers,**
> **Ministry of Education**

"When I made up my mind to go through the coaching certification programme back in July 2020, I was in the midst of a transformational journey in my life—facing uncertainty, ambiguity, vulnerability, and continuing to search for the authentic 'me' that had been lost somewhere along the way.

The Coach Partnership ontological coaching programme was so much more than a coach certification programme. It created a psychologically safe place for me to reconnect with myself, rediscover 'RINA', and form an intimate relationship with her again, or even for the first time.

I am grateful for the inspirational humans I met in the programme— the master coaches, mentor coaches, my study group members, and cohort classmates—who liberated me and dared me to step forward into the new chapter of my life as a coach.

With lots of love... Always a Beginner, the 'White Belt' Rina."

> **— Rina Sakuraba, PCC**
> **Founder and CEO of 35 CoCreation LLC**

"The Coach Partnership ontological coaching programme found me at a pivotal point of life. I learnt new distinctions around language, emotions, and the body that enabled profound self-discovery. I also gained confidence as a coach and was equipped with tools to help others live with purpose. Thank you to The Coach Partnership team for the guidance!"

 — **Melissa Tiro Park, ACC**
  HR Leader, Certified Coach

"I have gained extensive knowledge and personal growth through my attendance at The Coach Partnership's ontological coach training programme. The experience has not only been valuable in guiding my personal decision-making but also in enhancing the abilities of my team."

 — **Arifa Tan**
  Founder of IDStar Cipta Teknologi

"The Coach Partnership ontological coach training programme unlocked my superpowers! The somatic component was transformative, shifting me from a human doing to a human being. I am excited and empowered for this journey ahead. Thank you to the team at The Coach Partnership."

 — **Dr Pramilah Streram**
  Dentist; Founder of GetThrively

"#LifeAltering. That is the first phrase (with associated emotions) that comes to mind when I think of my (ongoing) journey with Marcus and The Coach Partnership team, both as a student and a practitioner of this exciting space.

When I started the journey several years ago, I expected that I would benefit as a coach and as an organisational leader. What I did not anticipate is the impact that I experienced in my life as a whole. The impact was not just intellectual but also physical and emotional, I look back with gratitude and look ahead in anticipation of what else awaits to be explored."

    — D.N. Prasad, PCC
    Founder & Executive Coach, Noetic Step Pte Ltd

"The Coach Partnership ontological coaching programme has opened up a whole new world of possibilities for me. The ontological approach goes far beyond actions and results and has profoundly transformed, not just my way of teaching and thinking about education, but also my perspective on life itself. The team at TCP are world-class coaches, trainers, and facilitators who bring exceptional expertise and unwavering support. My experiences with them have been above and beyond what I ever imagined possible. I highly recommend their programmes and am deeply grateful for the remarkable impact they've had on my life."

    — Sarah Cole
    Health Coach, Educator, Founder of Cole Coaching

"What is unique about ontological coaching training with The Coach Partnership is the holistic approach to learn about ourselves through, not only language, but also emotion and body. Its ontological coaching sheds light on beliefs, mood, somatic patterns, etc. that are mostly transparent to human beings; as a result, allowing you to see life newly. The only way you can get this is using yourself as an instrument. I'm now able to access the wisdom of my emotions and my body to expand my awareness and help my clients to do the same so that we can have new choices in life."

    — Duyên Lê
    Co-founder, TheBlossomCoach

THE PURPLE BOOK OF Coaching

Curated Wisdom and Practice for the Ontological Approach to a Meaningful Life

THE COACH PARTNERSHIP

Candid Creation Publishing

Candid Creation Publishing books are available through most major bookstores in Singapore. For bulk order of our books at special quantity discounts, please email us at enquiry@candidcreation.com.

THE PURPLE BOOK OF COACHING

CURATED WISDOM AND PRACTICE FOR THE ONTOLOGICAL APPROACH TO A MEANINGFUL LIFE

Editor	: Marcus Marsden
Publisher	: Phoon Kok Hwa
Copy editor	: Patricia Ng
Cover designer	: Danijela Mijailovic
Layout	: Corrine Teng
Published by	: Candid Creation Publishing LLP
	167 Jalan Bukit Merah
	#05-12 Connection One Tower 4
	Singapore 150167
Website	: www.candidcreation.com
Facebook	: www.facebook.com/CandidCreationPublishing
Email	: enquiry@candidcreation.com

National Library Board, Singapore Cataloguing in Publication Data

Name(s): Marsden, Marcus, 1967- editor.
Title: The purple book of coaching : curated wisdom and practice for the ontological approach to a meaningful life / editor, Marcus Marsden.
Description: Singapore : Candid Creation Publishing LLP, 2024.
Identifier(s): ISBN 978-981-17560-4-7 (paperback)
Subject(s): LCSH: Leadership. | Self-actualization (Psychology)
Classification: DDC 658.4092--dc23

Contents

Acknowledgements xiii

Foreword xvii

Introduction xxiii

1   The Context of Ontological Coaching in the 21st Century:
Making the Invisible Visible
Marcus Marsden 1

2   Ontological Leadership and Beyond:
A New Understanding of Language, Leadership, and
the Power of Conversations
Chalmers Brothers 24

3   What's Love Got to Do With It:
The Power of Productive Relationships for a Life
Well Lived
Tini Fadzillah 46

4   Becoming a Maestro of Emotional Agility:
The Essential Art of Intentional Emotional Shifting
Carol C. Courcy and Amanda Duarte 66

5   Playing at the Edge:
Why 30 Years of Studying Successful Leadership Has
Made Me Dead Serious About Play
Chris Balsley 89

6   The Interplay of Body and Emotions in
    Ontological Coaching:
    Movement and Dance in Ontological Exploration
        Beatriz Garcia 109

7   Mind Over Body or Body Over Mind:
    Unleashing the Ultimate Gift that Lies Within Us
        Rina Ho 137

8   Parenting Coaching:
    Nurturing Growth and Fostering Connection
        Dr Katrina Gisbert Tay 153

9   A Quest for Passion:
    What Are You Willing to Struggle For?
        Sari Marsden 177

10 Happiness:
    Harnessing the Power of Coaching for a Happier Life
        Clémence Blondel 201

11 Creating Ecosystems for Exceptional Results:
    Maximising the Power of Diverse Perspectives
        Eya Pagdanganan
        with Roxanne Angela Pagdanganan Sicat 223

12 Coaching as a Gateway to Our Consciousness:
    Opening the Door to Conscious Living Through Coaching
        Nabil Mattar 243

13 Coaching for Life's Big Questions:
    Creating a Transformational Space for New Thinking
        Terrie Lupberger 259

Closing Thoughts   277

The Works Partnership (TWP)   281
The Coach Partnership (TCP)   283
Suggestions for Further Reading   285

"Real generosity toward the future lies in giving all to the present."
Albert Camus
(*from* L'Homme révolté *[The Rebel]*)

Acknowledgements

In a book such as this, with so many contributors, the acknowledgements could take the form of a chapter in itself. All the authors would be quick to acknowledge that they did not get to this place in life on their own. This is also true for The Coach Partnership, the company. Individuals and companies exist both as separate entities and as parts of a greater whole.

The company, and by extension this book, would not even exist if it were not for Mark Hemstedt. Having founded the parent company (The Works Partnership) with Tini Fadzillah (one of our authors) in the late 1990s, Mark was the driving force behind bringing ontological coaching to Asia, and the creation of The Coach Partnership in 2009. Such passion and vision were two of the defining characteristics of Mark Hemstedt, as anyone who met him will surely attest. 2024 marks the fifth anniversary of his tragic and untimely death. He is still very much missed by the thousands of people he has impacted across the globe.

Not every member of The Coach Partnership team is represented as an author in this book. Without the following three members, however, the book would never have seen the light of day.

Joylynn Seetoh has been the rock of The Works Partnership and The Coach Partnership for 20 years. Her fierce determination and commitment to excellence are the heartbeat of the company, but don't be fooled, there is a very sensitive heart under that tough outer shell.

Sarah Gong has been single-handedly managing the company finances for 17 years. Mark's background was as an internal auditor and Finance Director at Unilever. That's a tough boss to work for as the company Finance Manager! Sarah's quiet, understated reliability is what allows everyone else in the company to focus on our coaching, facilitation and training.

Jenice Chua joined the company in 2021 and has quickly become indispensable as our company ninja. Initially employed to help with technical support, Jen has now expanded her role to include account management, where her passion to support other people shines brightly.

The Coach Partnership is also blessed to be in partnership with a veritable army of ontologically trained coaches and trainers from around the globe. It would be invidious to single out any individuals here, so I will settle for a universal 'thank you' to them: You play a role in supporting us to extend the reach of ontological coaching into more and more countries every year. It would not be possible without your dedication and desire to contribute to the growth of human beings.

A special thanks to our publisher, Kok Hwa, owner of Candid Creation, and his editor Patricia Ng. Your sharp eyes and detailed feedback has helped to pull these separate chapters into a coherent book. This is our third dance together. Thank you for continuing to believe in us.

Foreword

In the early 1990s, I landed my dream job—confidante to a people-centred CEO, co-architect of a cultural transformation, and Chief Human Resources Officer. On day one, my boss gave me a new bestselling business book, *The Fifth Discipline: The Art & Practice of the Learning Organization*, by Peter Senge, and said, "Let's make Systems Thinking our core change philosophy."

A Systems Thinking mindset views all organisational systems and processes as highly connected and interdependent and considers organisations and communities living entities. Systems Thinkers not only study individuals in those organisations but constantly ask, "What's happening at a system level? How is this system learning/not learning?" At the heart of Systems Thinking lies the concept of Double-Loop Learning[1], a theory explaining human nature and behaviour in systems.

In Single-Loop Learning, a person who fails will try again, looping through a finite list of known options for 'fixing' that problem. In Double-Loop Learning, the individual steps back and considers numerous other factors,

---

1   Argyris, Chris. "Double Loop Learning in Organisations." *Harvard Business Review*, vol, 55, 1977, pp. 115–125.

including context and their own mindset. They might ask, for example: Where might the true source of this challenge lie? If I fix <this>, what consequences might occur elsewhere? What perspective am I holding, and is it real? A Double-Loop Learner will often change something about themselves and how they observe and analyse all future situations.

Applying the principles of *The Fifth Discipline*, our leadership team reimagined the company, growing it into a thriving Learning Organisation.

For the next decade, in addition to my day job, I taught Systems Thinking to MBA students at a local university. When I researched coach training schools, the ontological approach attracted me most because it offered something that felt vaguely familiar to what I already taught—that the best approach to many/most situations involve less 'solving a problem' and more stepping back to consider the whole system and the factors that impact how we define the challenge.

WHAT IS ONTOLOGY?

Ontology is defined as the study of Being and an inquiry into the nature of human existence, revolving around a central question: "What does it mean to be a human being?" And the core model of Ontology ...

The OBSERVER we are sees ACTIONS to take to achieve RESULTS

... still reminds me of Argyris's model, Mindset → Actions → Outcomes. As in Double Loop Learning, if the actions we're taking aren't getting us the results we want, instead of cycling through our known options for action, we pull all the way back to consider: Who am I as an Observer of this situation such that I'm seeing <these> options? What beliefs frame my observation? What mood/emotions am I holding that may affect what I can/cannot see as possible?

You can see why I fell in love with the ontological approach!

THE GROWING IMPACT OF ONTOLOGY IN THE WORLD

I've now been coaching for 30+ years, starting in the corporate space (with that CEO I spoke about earlier) and through decades of success as a solo entrepreneur. In those years, I've been part of the training team for coaching programmes in the US, Europe, South Africa, Canada, Southeast Asia, and India. I have nearly 20 years of experience in the ontological tradition and, in fact, was part of the original team when The Coach Partnership (TCP) launched their first coaching cohort in Singapore in 2010. I am proud to still be part of the team as our 17th cohort continues their learning journey.

All the schools I work with have a winning formula that they execute well. What sets TCP apart is their desire to both Execute on and Expand ontological tools and distinctions into new domains. For example, TCP offered the world's first ontologically-centric, board-certified health and wellness coaching programme, was one of the first to take ontological coaching into a major healthcare system and was the first to roll out a global certification in Team Coaching (ontologically based, of course) just months after the International Coach Federation established team coaching competencies. In late 2024, TCP rolls out the first ontologically centred Parent Coaching programme on the planet.

The TCP team has opened new frontiers in the ontological conversation, and it is this group of thought leaders and innovators who have written the chapters you are about to enjoy.

HOW WE SPEAK MATTERS. *THAT* WE SPEAK MATTERS

Alan Sieler, one of the pioneers in the ontological space says, in describing the phenomenon of speaking:

> As participants in the speech act game, how we engage in language is never an innocent act. Language is a social phenomenon that occurs between people. Speaking is a social action, which carries a social responsibility. We have a responsibility for the manner in which we speak— what we say, how we say it, and when we say it.

> Even though we cannot be held entirely responsible for the interpretations people make of our speaking, we cannot walk away from accepting that what we say, how we say it, and when we say it will impact on others. … Each of us has a social responsibility for the listening our speaking may generate. This is especially so in coaching. Our responsibility is to listen and speak in ways that support the coachee to generate different interpretations that open new possibilities and enhance the quality of their existence.[2]

That is the intention of offering this book to the world: To support you, the reader, in generating different interpretations that open new

---

2   Sieler, Alan. *Coaching to the Human Soul: Ontological Coaching and Deep Change, Volume 1.* Victoria, Australia, Newfield Institute, 2003.

possibilities and enhance the quality of your life, and—if you are a coach—of your coaching.

BRING CURIOSITY TO YOUR DISCOMFORT

What you read here may also challenge you in ways that cause you to squirm a bit. If that happens, I invite you to say, "Brilliant!" and to embrace that discomfort. I believe discomfort is the core promise of coaching, for it is only on the edge of our comfort zone where growth and learning can occur (and you will hear this again in the chapters). So, find the edge of your own comfort zone, lean over that edge while you embody your best curious self and ask, "What's here for me?"

In these pages, you will find things that may challenge the way you see the world—or affirm it. These stories and perspectives are being shared into the world for the sake of helping you, the reader, expand your world view, consider a new area of learning, or expand your understanding of what coaching is and how powerful it can be as a tool for building a better life and world.

THOUGHT LEADERS, INNOVATORS, AND TRUSTED COLLEAGUES

I previously described the writing team as thought leaders and innovators. In addition, they are valued colleagues and friends from whom I have learnt much.

I have personal experience with every author in this book. Some I have coached, some have coached me. Some I have taught as students and to others I have been a student in their classroom. My very first coaching mentor is one of the chapter writers, while others I have mentored. I have shared the stage with many of them, in both live and virtual environments, and at other times, I've sat at their feet as an eager learner.

With all of them, I have engaged in deep discussion about what coaching is and what it might yet become, the gift it is to the world, and our shared desire, always, to become better at our craft and help raise up others. These are people who deeply care about improving the world through the art and science and practice of ontological coaching and the use of ontological tools and distinctions

VARIATIONS ON A THEME

Because this is an anthology, I invite you to approach it as you might a potluck dinner or a chef's tasting event where every chef was invited to prepare a special dish built around a single common ingredient: ontology. Each chef has taken a different approach to what they prepared, and you may like some more than others, yet you'll want to sample everything. If you enjoy the variety of a potluck buffet, you are in for a treat!

Jim Smith[3]
Executive and Ontological Coach

---

3   Jim Smith, PCC, is The Executive Happiness Coach®, global executive coach, National Board-Certified Health & Wellness Coach, Newfield Certified Ontological Coach, Newfield Certified Team Coach, somatic coach, and senior human resources professional. He is the author of *Happiness at the Speed of Life: 13 Powerful Strategies for Finding Happiness at Home and on the Job*, multiple e-books, and 20 years of blogging essays on the topics of coaching, leadership, and happiness.

Introduction

THIS BOOK AND YOU

Here is a great question to ask yourself right now: What would be my purpose in reading this book?

If your answer is, "To find an answer to a question I am struggling with", then I'd recommend that you put the book down and log on to ChatGPT instead.

This book promises no easy answers, but it does promise challenging questions, provocation and exploration. Each chapter is written by a different author and the intention of each author is to pique your curiosity.

Each author has chosen an element of the ontological coaching methodology that is particularly meaningful to them. As they share their personal and professional journey with that topic, you are invited along for the ride. As you briefly travel alongside each of them, we further invite you to make connections with your own life. The authors are sharing their journey not because it highlights the *right* way or the *only* way to see the topic in question, but rather they are sharing it to provide a stimulus for you to apply in relation to your own life.

This is not a textbook or an instruction manual for life. It is a companion.

Whether you agree or disagree with what is contained here is less important than how it stimulates you to view your life from a different perspective.

Some subjects will no doubt appear to be of more relevance to you than others. Be prepared, however, for that to change over time. What may seem of little relevance today, could be extremely beneficial for you to explore next month. Life comes at you fast!

It is not an accident that this book is a compilation. Each author is part of The Coach Partnership global faculty. The Coach Partnership is part of a parent company, The Works Partnership, that has specialised in offering ontological development programmes for over 30 years.

While The Works Partnership specialises in offering leadership development, team, and 1–1 coaching to corporations, The Coach Partnership focuses on offering coach training to individuals.

In both companies, we live the fundamental ontological principle that in life, we are all unique 'observers' and that no single person, however smart they may be, has the answer or the *correct* approach to the complexities of life.

Some of our authors have worked in this field for more than 30 years; others have worked in it for less than five years.

Some of our authors are from what we might loosely refer to as 'the West' and some are from 'Asia'. Some are women, some are men. Some are married, some are not. Some are parents, some are not. One of them loves giraffes.

What all the authors have in common, however, is that they are human beings who are passionate about the capacity of human beings to grow, develop, and ultimately create fulfilling lives. All of us practise an ontological approach to life, not only with professional clients, but with each other, and in our own personal lives.

We see ontological coaching not as a job to be done or as a task to be carried out, but as a way of living a fulfilling and productive life.

In summary, this book is best seen as a potential catalyst for your own personal journey towards a life of fulfilment and satisfaction, whatever those words may mean to you.

WHY PURPLE?

If you have got this far, then you are probably also wondering about the title of this book.

Why *purple*?

Why any colour at all?

Colour itself is a fascinating subject and has been the subject of much research over the years.

In the 2010 book, *Color Ontology and Color Science*, the authors of the various chapters expound on the science of colour, about colour information, colour consciousness, and colour language. They explain that colour is not merely a physical phenomenon but a complex interplay of perception, emotion, and meaning. How each person experiences colour is subjective and this is shaped by individual perception and cultural context, making it as much a psychological construct as a physical reality. As colours carry different meanings across cultures, they reflect the diverse ways in which humans interpret their world and express their identities.[1]

You can immediately see connections with the concerns of an ontological coaching methodology: individual perception, culture, context, constructs, interpretations, and identities.

Purple itself is a colour steeped in symbolism and imbued with meanings that are closely aligned with the essence of ontological coaching. It has long been held to carry spiritual connotations in both Western and Eastern religious and secular tradition.

In Roman times, purple dye was used to signify status because of the high price it commanded. Emperors and high-ranking officials often chose to wear it to show their position in society. This tradition lives on in the West—where royalty often prominently features the colour purple in its heraldry and associated trappings—and in China, where purple is often linked to power, wealth, power, and good fortune.

Purple is often used in Christian liturgy, representing penance and humility and in many Buddhist traditions, it symbolises spiritual awakening and enlightenment. While in Hinduism, purple symbolises spirituality and devotion, as well as being associated with the crown chakra, representing higher consciousness and enlightenment.

---

1 Cohen, Jonathan, and Mohan Matthen, editors. *Color Ontology and Color Science.* Cambridge, MA, A Bradford Book, MIT Press, 2010.

To this day, purple retains a unique aura and mystique.

In contemporary psychology, purple is often linked to creativity, innovation and wisdom. As a synthesis of red and blue, purple is often linked with transformation and in particular, the necessary interplay of the emotional (red) and the rational (blue) in any genuinely transformational experience.

"Purple, residing between the warmth of red and the coolness of blue, embodies a duality that invites both introspection and inspiration."[2]

That's why purple.

THE CHAPTERS AND THE AUTHORS

When we began this project, the brief for everyone was simple: Choose a topic from within the ontological methodology that is personally meaningful to you and then write a piece on that topic that encompasses both the professional and personal impact it has had on your life.
That's it.

There was no requirement to fit the writing to a specific style or make each chapter consistent in message. We wanted you to hear the unique voice of each author as they share their authentic experience. As a result, you may spot moments when one author's experience or point of view diverges from another author's experience or point of view.

For example, does the concept of a 'self' exist, or not? You might see different points of view on that in this book. Remember, the book is

---

2   Cohen, Jonathan, and Mohan Matthen, editors. *Color Ontology and Color Science.* Cambridge, MA, A Bradford Book, MIT Press, 2010.

designed to serve as stimulus for your further thought, not provide you with advice or solutions to problems.

The chapters themselves cover some of the most fascinating areas of human growth and development.

We begin and then end with meta-views on coaching as a whole and ontological coaching in particular:

Chalmers Brothers

Following my own chapter is Chalmers Brothers, author of *Language and the Pursuit of Happiness* and a lead trainer in The Coach Partnership faculty. Chalmers offers his take on the powerful role ontological coaching has played, not only in leadership and corporations, but also in his own life:

> "Organisations may be understood as networks of interdependent conversations … networks of interdependent commitments. That is, the results that organisations produce are directly driven by the ways people talk and listen and coordinate action with each other within that organisation."

Terrie Lupberger

In the closing chapter, Terrie Lupberger—Master Certified Coach, author of the upcoming book *The Inner Work of Work*, and Director of Coaching at The Coach Partnership—outlines her take on ontological coaching and the role that coaching plays in today's world:

> "The most significant issues we face in our world
> today are not technological but deeply human.
> They require from us qualities we didn't learn in

school or haven't fostered, such as deep empathy (for self and others), vulnerability, ethical consideration, collaboration, and a focus on human values that technology cannot provide.

I believe that's one of the major reasons that coaching emerged—as a response to our longing for safe space and authentic connection to reflect on the big questions of our lives. Questions on the best way forward when our traditional ways of thinking and doing are exhausted and our go-to solutions aren't working as we'd like."

The remaining chapters all focus on a specific aspect of the ontological coaching model.

Tini Fadzillah

The Founding Partner of The Works Partnership is Tini Fadzillah who shares her own personal and professional experience to illuminate the generative power of relationships:

"Growing up, I swam in the relationship strength of my family. I grew up in a household where my father was a career diplomat. Looking back, one of the biggest observations is that relationship and challenge can and MUST coexist. Nation-building, as I learnt at the dinner table, was never just about being nice to one another; rather, it was about creating relationships that would allow challenge, task, difficult requests, and conversations to coexist."

Chris Balsley

Military veteran and long-time lead somatic facilitator for The Coach Partnership, Chris Balsley, has chosen to look at the important and yet often misunderstood role of play in the world of development:

> "Leaders who create a playful culture are bringing out the best in everybody. Playful leaders create curiosity around them, both individually and collectively, knowing full well that whatever you put in front of a curious brain goes straight into long-term memory."

Beatriz Garcia

Another long-time lead somatic facilitator for The Coach Partnership, Beatriz Garcia has chosen to focus on her speciality—the link between emotions and the body; two subjects that are often seen as taboo or too 'touchy-feely' in today's world. She ably outlines how critical they both are to anybody interested in sustainable growth and development:

> "Embodiment and emotional awareness play pivotal roles in shaping our daily lives, both personally and professionally. These concepts highlight the interconnectedness between our physical experiences and emotional states, influencing how we perceive, react to, and navigate through the world."

Dr Katrina Gisbert Tay

A partner in The Works Partnership, Dr Katrina Gisbert-Tay has chosen the subject dearest to her heart: Parenting. As a qualified medical doctor, mother of three, and certified coach herself, she brings a multifaceted approach to her subject:

> "The ontological approach emphasises the importance of the parent's context, as we all carry unresolved traumas and unmet needs from childhood, which can influence how we are currently 'being' in the world. Ontological parenting coaching helps parents gain awareness and empowerment, allowing them to parent from a place of wholeness and presence rather than reactivity."

Sari Marsden

A somatic trainer for The Coach Partnership, Sari Marsden has chosen a subject that she lives and breathes every day of her life: Passion. She combines the Javanese culture of her youth with her own subsequent personal and professional experience to shine a light on another often-misunderstood subject:

> "The intersection of skill-based and value-based passions can be described as a 'sweet spot' where personal fulfilment and professional contribution align. This is where you enjoy the work you do as well as feel that you are making a meaningful impact."

Carol C. Courcy and Amanda Duarte

Carol Courcy, Executive Coach and author of *Save Your Inner Tortoise*, joined forces with The Coach Partnership Program Manager/Executive Coach, Amanda Duarte, to illustrate the power of developing agility in the area of moods and emotions:

> "Becoming a maestro comes when you are able to add an emotional tune, return to it as needed for desirable results and ultimately be more daring in the emotions you wish to experiment with. Being able to ENTER and EXIT any emotion, generates trust of this learning process, allowing you 'to try on' unfamiliar or difficult emotions you tend to avoid."

Clémence Blondel

The Coach Partnership Team Coaching Program Manager and Executive Coach, Clémence Blondel, has chosen to focus on the area of Happiness. This is an area that is often taken for granted or overlooked in the rush to discuss more 'weighty' subjects. "Are you happy?", however, remains one of the simplest and yet most profound questions one can ask of others or, indeed, oneself.

> "I see coaching not as a promise of constant happiness, which is utopian, but as a support for our well-being in various aspects of our lives for a period, whether that is weeks, months, or even years."

Eya Pagdanganan

Executive Coach with The Coach Partnership, Eya Pagdanganan, focuses on the critical role an ecosystem plays in life. She draws upon her own personal experience as a mother, as well as her extensive experience in corporate life:

> "In coaching, just as in life with Marianne, it's essential to build and maintain environments where support is readily available, expertise is valued, and collaboration is the norm. This supportive framework accelerates progress and leads to more sustainable and impactful results."

Nabil Mattar

Executive Coach with The Coach Partnership, Nabil Mattar, has chosen to dive into the all-encompassing subject of Consciousness. What is it and what implications arise for humans as uniquely 'conscious beings'?

> "Every day offers an opportunity for me to practise ontological coaching by tuning into my inner observer and noticing my body, emotions, and language. This is where consciousness comes into play—being aware of how I think, feel, and act in every moment."

Rina Ho

A former corporate senior executive, Rina Ho—now Executive Coach with The Coach Partnership, and a sports enthusiast—has chosen to explore a subject of great personal impact in her own life: The relation between body and mind. How do they influence each other and what are the consequences of listening to one over the other?

> "While the mind can drive us to achieve great things, it is equally important to listen to our bodies and understand their signals. Intuition and gut feelings play a significant role in leadership and coaching, helping us build relationships, gain insights, manage risks, and facilitate growth."

THE NEXT STEP

So, the table is set. Where will you begin?

This is not a book that requires you to read the chapters in sequential order. In fact, there is much to be said for doing precisely the opposite, and turning immediately to the subject that grabs your attention.

Neither is it a book that requires you to read it in one go. It may well be that a chapter you read here today inspires you to pick up a different book on a similar subject, to have a different conversation with someone in your life, or even to go out and immediately be different in the world.

However you choose to navigate the chapters, I do recommend that you give yourself time to digest them thoroughly before you move on. Pause to consider how the observations in the chapter are impacting you. In particular, notice which thoughts and experiences are different to the ones that are currently alive in your life.

Approaching the book with this kind of curiosity (as opposed to judgement) will give you an insight into you, and the way that you are currently integrating and interacting with the world.

We offer this book and the ontological methodology as a companion and as stimulus on your path towards a meaningful life.

The first step in that journey begins with identifying your current operating context, because it is that context that determines everything else in your life.

The world is just out there 'worlding' and it will continue to do so long after you and I have departed.

Are you ready to get curious and explore?

CHAPTER 1

The Context of Ontological Coaching in the 21st Century

Making the Invisible Visible

Marcus Marsden

While all the chapters in this book offer different *content*, they share one thing, and that is the *context* in which they were written.

They were all written by human beings in the year 2024.

This may seem self-evident; it is, however, always important to illuminate the context, if we are to fully understand the content. The ontological approach to coaching always starts with the importance of context. Your 'observer' is a form of context.

(For more a more thorough explanation of this idea, please refer to Terrie Lupberger's chapter in this book as well as my earlier book, *Start With Who.*)

Throughout every chapter, you will see references to the context of being human—we all have a body and experience physical sensations, we all live in moods and experience emotions, and we all necessarily live in language and use it to create our reality and shape our personal identity. We all exist as individuals and yet necessarily live interdependently.

The context of being human, however, is not the only important one at play.

It is of equal importance to bear in mind that we live in the 21st century. Human beings writing in 1924 or 2124 would, no doubt, be writing differently. Some content might be similar, but a lot would be different.

As an example, the 1920s were labelled 'The Roaring 20s'. Led by Hollywood, it is easy to assume that this was the global context, but it wasn't. In much of the West, it certainly was 'roaring'—the 1920s were an era of post-war prosperity, innovation, and technological developments.

In many parts of Asia, however, it was anything but 'roaring'. Many countries remained under colonial rule, and while Japan was emerging as a major power, China was experiencing huge internal strife and revolution and civil war in Russia led to the formation of the Soviet Union.

You can, therefore, imagine how an author writing a chapter on 'happiness' in the 1920s might write very differently, based on time and location.

Similarly, recent advances in the field of neuroscience mean that someone writing on 'consciousness' or 'body and emotion' in 2024 would necessarily write differently to someone writing in 1924.

Writing this in 2024, I cannot even imagine how an author writing in 2124 would write. Can you?

It is, of course, notoriously difficult to pinpoint the key elements of one's own historical context. We are always the proverbial goldfish, swimming in our goldfish bowl, unable to comprehend the concept of water, because it is completely transparent to us. One of the reasons that context is so powerful is that it is invisible.

The closest human beings have ever really come to jumping outside their goldfish bowl and viewing their context was when the first astronauts went to the moon and sent back images of the earth. For the first time, we were able to see the totality of our planet from outside of it.

Immediately, viewed from outside the usual context, the same content looked very different. Most notably, national boundaries disappeared, individual human beings became invisible, and the interconnectedness of everything and everyone became apparent.

Your viewing point inevitably shapes your point of view. Once you fully grasp the implication of this, it's a complete game changer for your life.

You don't observe the **real** world.
You create and then interact with **your** world.

Rather than a detached observer, passively and neutrally observing an external world, you are an integrated and creative force, existing within a much larger and greater entity.

To illustrate what a game changer this point of view can be, consider this.

Most people believe that they exist in their own mind and that other people exist outside their mind, in the external world. Slow the tape down (as I like to say), however, and consider this alternative point of view: All the people in your life actually exist *inside* your mind, while you exist *outside* your mind, inside their minds.

How could this be true?

Consider what happens when you walk into a room of 30 people. Do they all see the same person? Superficially yes, but it is also true to say that they all have different knowledge, assessments, feelings, and beliefs about you.

It's as though they have all saved their own personal version of you to their hard drive. When you walk into that room, 30 different versions of you appear; 31, if you count your own.

Despite the difficulty associated with identifying one's own context, let's reflect for a moment on the current situation in which we find ourselves in 2024. It might be a fool's errand to do so, and it is certainly impossible to do so with any *certainty*. It is, however, important to at least make the attempt, because doing so can illuminate the important role that ontological coaching can and does play in today's world.

HUMAN CONTEXT IN THE 2020s

As a disclaimer, I am necessarily writing this from within my own context.

I was born in England in 1967 and I have always seen myself as the product of the celebrations that occurred there in 1966—England winning the World Cup and Bob Dylan's legendary tour that revolutionised popular music. (Knowing my parents, it had more to do with the on-field exploits of Bobby Moore than with the onstage performances of Bob Dylan.) My parents subsequently divorced, and I was fortunate to have three wonderful parents for the rest of my life. I learnt a lot from the way the three of them danced what must have been a tricky dance, especially during my teenage years.

Following a youth playing as much sport as I could, I attended Oxford University, where I studied Philosophy and Theology, something which I was turned onto by a fantastic schoolteacher. How he made that subject come alive for a rebellious schoolboy is another thing that made a huge impact on me, especially as many of the other teachers were advocating for me to leave the school early.

Fresh out of university, I went to work for Unilever in marketing. This was something that not only gave me a fantastic grounding in business, but also opened me up to the subjects of leadership and personal development, that have formed such a seminal part of my adult life. It was in Unilever that I met Mark Hemstedt and TWP. To all intents and purposes, my adult life really started in my 30s.

In 2002, I left the safe shores of my marketing career in England and arrived in Jakarta to join Mark and his co-founder of TWP, Tini Fadzillah, who you might recognise as a fellow contributor in this book. It was there that I met and married a young lady called Sari, another contributor in this book.

In 2019, we sadly lost Mark in a tragic accident, a brutal reminder of the fragility and absurdity of human life. Five years on, here I am, writing the introductory chapter to a book of which I believe Mark would be very proud. It was his vision that brought ontological coaching to Asia in 2010. The contributors in this book, together with many others—too many to mention here—continue to manifest and develop that vision in 2025.

So, just like everyone else, I see what I see based on my viewing point, and much of what I write is necessarily more applicable to certain parts of the world than it is to others.

That said, I offer my take on three of the key drivers in the contemporary context to illuminate the important role that I believe ontological coaching, at its best, can play in 2024. Note that ontological coaching is not practised in every corner of the world, and I do not believe that to be a coincidence. Ontological coaching shows up in the regions of the world where it is most needed and most valuable.

Freedom

From the moment World War II ended, there has been a move from centralised power to personal freedom. There was a breakdown in the traditional forces of servitude. Totalitarian systems (political and religious) faltered. In Europe, fascism was defeated, and communism retreated as the Berlin Wall fell. In Africa, apartheid was overturned, and globally, the unquestioning belief in governments and religious figures declined.

This phenomenon was not just evident at a political and religious level, but also a cultural level.

When Bob Dylan was inducted into the Rock 'n' Roll Hall of Fame in 1988, this was what Bruce Springsteen said:

> "Dylan was a revolutionary—the way that Elvis freed your body, Bob freed your mind. He showed us that just because the music was innately physical, it did not mean that it was anti-intellect."

(Interesting to note how the freeing of the body precedes the freeing of the mind. Something ontological practitioners might recognise.)

Individualism and independence have become the ultimate prize, essentially used as synonyms for the 'self-actualisation' at the top of Maslow's famous pyramid.

Equality

At the same time as there was a 'rush to freedom', there was an increased acknowledgement of the importance of 'equality'. Most obviously, the civil rights and feminist movements, both of which gained traction in the 1960s in the West, in particular.

That every human being deserves to be treated equal with regards to the law, suffrage, dignity, and opportunities might seem self-evident today, but it was not always so. Indeed, in some parts of the world, it is still not so.

You might notice that, in absolute terms, these two values are in conflict.

- Absolute freedom for everyone inevitably results in inequality.
- Absolute equality for everyone inevitably results in curtailed freedom.

This is one of the central paradoxes of a life lived in the 2020s.

Technology

This rush to freedom and the desire for equality has been fuelled by incredible technological advances over the same period. Machines were now doing the chores, there was low-cost travel and incredible advances in the medical field (e.g. consider how the contraceptive pill gave women control over their reproductive cycle, something that has had a massive impact on freedom, equality, and indeed, society as a whole, where it has had a raft of consequences, both intended and unintended). Of course, there is also the internet and social media. Amongst other things, the internet offers a step change in speed and reach. Instant gratification and worldwide communication are now in the hands of any individual with a connection.

The combination of these factors has been seismic and tumultuous. Suddenly, we are faced with a dizzying array of choices. Curtailed freedom and inequality equated to less choice and a simpler life. As freedom and equality surge, then so does complexity.

Curtailed freedom, inequality, and a simple life

or

maximised freedom, equality, and a complex life?

Which one offers the greater happiness or fulfilment? That's a question for *you* to consider in your own life.

Increasing levels of personal freedom, equality, and incredible technological advancement. This all seems to be a wonderful development for humankind ... and it is ... or at least it can be. The combination can certainly form a heady, intoxicating cocktail.

The massive rise of human freedom, with equal access to technology (internet) and people living and working behind screens and keyboards has led to certain key ramifications. Firstly, people are now one step removed from many of the real-world consequences of their new freedoms. This separation of freedom from consequence has important ramifications.

In earlier times, personal freedom and consequence were closely linked. As an example, if a person exercised their freedom of speech to walk up to a 6-foot-5-inch boxer and insult them, chances are that person would receive a punch on the nose.

Nowadays, one can do something similar anonymously, from half the world away and the comfort of one's sitting room, before logging off to safety.

Today, we all have the freedom to instantly communicate on a worldwide basis with (almost) zero consequences.

Paradoxically, and maybe even because of this development, we now also have the phenomenon of 'cancel culture' where the consequences of saying the 'wrong' thing can be severe. Every action has a reaction.

Grappling with 'freedom of speech' issues in this new context is one of the big pain points in the 2020s. In the 20th century, before the internet, there was a generally accepted axiom that while freedom of speech was paramount in democratic societies, shouting "Fire!" in a crowded theatre was not okay. That was the original 'fake news'.

In the 2020s, where someone can literally send a message around the world with one click, that example seems delightfully quaint. Today, the theatre has become the world and shouting "Fire!" has become the publication of fake news, which if believed, might start World War III. The stakes have risen exponentially.

In recent times, people in the UK have received prison sentences for their postings on social media. There is more than 'being cancelled' at stake here.

Secondly, this delinking of consequences and communication also extends to beliefs. When life is primarily viewed through a computer screen, it becomes easy to view individual human beings as fungible. They become interchangeable. One can replace another, at no cost to the system.

This belief is swiftly overtaken when one finds oneself face-to-face with other human beings. As soon as we actually meet, we are forcefully confronted by the personal physical, mental, and emotional distinctions that each unique human being inevitably carries.

Personally, I remember this very well from the period immediately following the Covid lockdowns, when I heard, "I'd forgotten how tall you are", on more than one occasion.

Human beings easily lose their individuality and uniqueness when viewed through the lens of a computer screen. It becomes far easier to become detached and to lose compassion and empathy when one's primary interaction is through a screen and a keyboard. We start to see real human beings in the same way that we view actors in a TV series.

As human beings, we are far more than our superficial classifications.

Every human being is not the same. Every man is not the same. Every woman is not the same. Every member of the same nationality or race is not the same. To treat everyone from within the same 'classification', socio-economic or demographic group as the same, or to expect them all to think or act the same, is to fundamentally misrepresent the individual beauty and complexity of human beings.

Which pairing is more similar: An English man/Singaporean man or an English man/English woman?

It's an impossible question to answer, but when viewed through a screen and from behind a keyboard, it becomes a lot easier, because individual characteristics fall away, and human beings become depersonalised concepts. This has been one of the key factors in the rise of what is sometimes referred to as 'cultural Marxism', where individualism is diminished for the good of the system.

When insulated from reality, from behind a screen, such thinking is seductive, but apply it directly in the real world and things begin to fall apart very quickly. Theory and practice are not the same thing, as Albert Einstein famously said: "In theory, theory and practice are the same. In practice, they are not."

ONTOLOGICAL COACHING IN THE 2020s

Human Beings as Unique Observers

So, in a context that prizes personal freedom, cherishes equality, and increasingly fuels both through incredible technological advances, what role can and does ontological coaching play?

The first element is simple. Ontological coaching places the 'unique observer' at its very heart. The chapters by Chalmers Brothers and Terrie Lupberger (Chapters 2 and 13, respectively) both underscore this element. Further detail on this subject can also be found in Chalmers' book

Language and the Pursuit of Happiness as well as my previous book, *Start With Who.*

While cultures inevitably exist and general classifications such as gender, race, and nationality can always be made, the ontological coaching methodology will always seek to work with the individual and to illuminate the hitherto invisible foundations that sustain the framework of the world that they have created and with which they interact.

(Note that in ontological *team* coaching, the team can be treated as a single entity at times.)

Ontological coaching is a powerful antidote to any perception of the fungibility of human beings.

Can I do everything a woman can do?
No. I cannot do what Serena Williams does.
Can I do everything a man can do?
No. I cannot do what Roger Federer does.

Human beings are not 'plug and play' figures in an on-screen drama, however it may appear from behind a screen and a keyboard.

Ontological coaching reminds us of the beautiful, paradoxical, messiness of being human.

"That's Where I Draw the Line"

The rise in personal freedom and equality, combined with technological advances, brings another consequence that ontological coaching can help to address.

Once personal freedom is prized, it is accepted that we all have an equal right to it, and it becomes easier to manifest, then there is a temptation (or even a perceived requirement) to keep pushing the boundaries: "If I/we can, then I/we should" or even "If I/we can, then I/we must".

This is the attitude that underpins the prevalent FOMO ('fear of missing out') mindset.

It also, however, often shows up in my coaching in a slightly different way. This is a common story that I hear in my coaching:

> "I do not really want to be doing this job, but my parents worked really hard for me to have this opportunity in life. Their generation never had this level of possibility and so I would have felt incredibly guilty if I hadn't taken it."

Freedom brings its own chains.
Equality affects people unequally.

In this era of technologically fuelled, seemingly ever-increasing freedom and equality, ontological coaching can therefore play another critically important role.

This role starts with an important fact. A fact that is easy to overlook or forget in a world drunk on the freedom to type whatever you want, and the airbrushed, idealised images of social media:

Everyone draws the line somewhere.

However 'liberal' a person might claim to be, no one lives a boundary-free life.

(It is interesting to note how 'drawing a line' and 'establishing a boundary' can be perceived very differently in this context. While the former is often seen as restrictive, the latter is generally seen as offering necessary protection.)

Everyone locks their car, front door, bicycle, or phone.
Even advocates of 'gentle parenting' don't generally let their young children experience freedom by running around busy streets on their own or wandering around dimly lit areas of town, late at night.

When we look at a societal level:
- We all have beliefs about a minimum age for things like alcohol consumption, sexual consent, and obtaining a driving licence.
- We have beliefs about who is eligible for financial assistance from the state and who is not.
- We have beliefs about when abortion and euthanasia are permissible and when they are not.

Right now, there are hot debates in the West about at what age sex-altering drugs should be made available, what constitutes an acceptable level of immigration, and whether 'Just Stop Oil' protestors should be allowed to hold up traffic and spray paint on valuable works of art.

As I write in 2024, there is a furious row erupting about whether boxers with X and Y chromosomes should be allowed to fight in the Women's Olympic Boxing event. For safety reasons, boxing has weight classes that are binary—there are weigh-ins and you are either inside the weight limit or you are outside it. There is a sharp dividing line.

For a long time in human history, sex was also considered as binary. Now people disagree.

While no one (that I know) wants to see biological men fighting biological women in an Olympic boxing ring (or anywhere else), society is struggling to agree on how and where to draw the line.

The three horsemen of the current apocalypse ride together. As technology fuels more scientific understanding, how do we balance freedom and equality?

What used to be simple has become complex.

When we look at a professional level:
- We have beliefs about how many hours a day/week someone should be asked to work, what constitutes a fair wage, or an acceptable ROI (return on investment).
- We have beliefs about which emotions are acceptable to show in a meeting and which are not.
- We have beliefs about which topics of conversation are acceptable at the office and which are not.

When we look at a personal level:
- We have beliefs about how to fairly split the household chores or the correct role of parents and grandparents in the upbringing of a child.
- We have beliefs about the correct age to give a child their first smartphone.
- We have beliefs about how much time/money to spend enjoying the present moment and how much to spend on preparing for the future.

We also have beliefs about what constitutes an acceptable amount of money to spend on a Bob Dylan collection in a calendar year.

Everyone draws the line somewhere.

When freedom is prioritised, however, and everyone has an equal right to their opinion (and can freely communicate it to the world, via technology to which everyone has equal access), how can we proceed?

The question is not simply: "Where do I draw *my* lines?" but "Where can I, and do I, draw lines for *other* people, and who do I allow to draw lines for me? Where do I have that authority and to whom do I give that authority?"

I know from many coaching conversations that people often fear to publicly or even privately acknowledge that they even draw lines at all.

They are worried about being seen as ungrateful or as lacking ambition (if they do it to themselves) or as a fascist/lacking empathy/old-fashioned (if they do it to someone else.) Then they wonder why they are experiencing burnout.

'Gentle managing' is just as prevalent as 'gentle parenting' in my experience.

Hierarchies have proven to be extremely useful in human systems (at a societal, organisational, and family level) but how can we establish and then maintain hierarchies, if everyone is to be free and equal?

As soon as we draw a line, some people are on the inside and some people are on the outside. Some people will experience more freedom and some people will experience less freedom. The situation will no longer be equal for everybody.

A parent with two children reading this will immediately recognise the situation as will a leader working with managers on different job grades, or with different levels of experience.

At a societal level, consider the question of free speech from earlier in the chapter. Who gets to decide what is okay to publish and what is not?

In previous times, this role generally defaulted to national governments, but the internet and social media has blown away national boundaries. Now that role seems to be defaulting to the owners of the social media companies (something that many people seem okay with, so long as those owners share their own personal views). A lot of people, however, are uncomfortable with a handful of extremely rich (unelected, but highly successful) men deciding these things.

As a human race, we are currently grappling with such issues and it's not an exaggeration to say that the very existence of our species is at stake.

Part of the problem here is the current term 'progressive'. After all, who would choose to be seen as 'regressive'?

'Progressive' implies that all developments are positive—'progressing' towards some kind of improved state or utopia. If I'm not 'progressive' and advancing the march to utopia, then I must be 'regressive' and holding back progress towards the promised land.

That is, however, not true at all. Pushing forward for its own sake and assuming that 'all change is progress', leading us to utopia, is a dangerous state of mind to adopt.

The concept of 'Chesterton's fence' is a good reminder: "Never tear down a fence until you fully understand why it was put there in the first place."

In fact, the very essence of life is the yin and yang of survival and evolution.

If our ancestors had stayed in the same place, safely and endlessly doing the same thing, over and over again, then we would never have adapted to new environments and evolved. As a result, we would have died out as a species.

On the other hand, if our ancestors had rashly run around every blind corner they had come to, or eaten every berry they found, then we would also have died out rather fast.

Not every change is 'progressive' (for the greater good). Change is simply change.

> **Just because you can, it doesn't mean you should.**
> **Choosing not to use a freedom is part of our freedom.**

Turning down a promotion or an opportunity is a perfectly valid choice and is not a betrayal of your parents, your gender, your race, or your personal worth.

This is where ontological coaching can support us all.

It reminds us that we all draw the line somewhere and that it is part of our very humanity that we do so. Where we draw the line, how we draw the line (is it a dotted line?), when we move the line, how thick that line is, how straight that line is … all of those decisions go towards establishing our unique, authentic way of being and, ultimately, our public identity.

It is *not* the role of an ontological coach to tell anyone where they should draw their lines or make judgements about where or how a person is drawing their lines.

It *is* the role of an ontological coach to support a client to see where they are drawing their lines for themselves and for others. To notice when and why they are moving the lines (or not), to where and what the consequence of those decisions are. Similarly, to help a client identify where, why, and how they are allowing someone else to draw lines for them.

Another element that often plays a huge role in my coaching conversations is how a client reacts to one of their lines being crossed (either by other people, or by they themselves). When this happens, the conversation turns towards the critical areas of forgiveness and then trust: Are you willing to forgive this person who has transgressed (knowingly or not) and crossed a line that you had drawn? Will you trust them again?

Similarly—and for many people more pertinently—how will you treat yourself when you cross one of your own lines or boundaries? Are you willing to forgive yourself or trust yourself again?

Questions such as these always lead to powerful conversations that enable clients to see their operating mindset and the lines they have drawn that make it up.

Ultimately, two things are inevitable:
- The drawing of lines; and
- The consequences of drawing those lines.

While there is no correct place to draw your lines, and no right time to choose to move your lines, there are always consequences associated with your choices.

An ontological coach can facilitate a conversation with their client that supports them to clearly see where they are drawing their lines and whether or not the resulting consequences are consistent with who they wish to be and their desired results.

> "The line it is drawn, the curse it is cast
> The slow one now will later be fast
> As the present now, will later be past
> The order is rapidly fadin'
> And the first one now will later be last
> For the times they are a-changin'"
> Bob Dylan, 1963

CONCLUSION

The offer of an ontological coach is, therefore, to support their client as they seek to navigate the increasing complexity of life in the 2020s.

I have set out and examined two particular elements of this offer that I believe to be particularly pertinent at this point in history:

- focusing on human beings as unique 'observers' rather than fungible categories; and.
- legitimising and recognising the inevitable drawing of lines in the face of the technologically fuelled rush towards unrestrained freedom and equality.

This exploration uncovers a third element where I believe an ontological coach is well placed to support a client, and that is dealing with paradox.

As you read the following chapters, you might notice the ubiquity of paradox:
- We are already whole and complete and we are constantly growing and becoming. (Chalmers)
- We are both unique observers and we are all the same. (Chalmers)
- Mind over body and body over mind. (Rina)
- The same object can appear both large and small. (Rina)
- I play when I'm safe and I feel safe when I play. (Chris)
- I support my children's growth and they support mine. (Kat)
- We are individuals who crave independence, and we necessarily exist as interdependent beings. (Eya)
- Numbing myself to avoid discomfort limits the emotional range that I require in order to create comfort. (Carol and Amanda)
- We can experience happiness and sadness at the same time. (Clemence)
- Trying too hard to be happy can limit well-being. (Clemence)
- Moving the body creates emotion and emotion has me move my body. (Beatriz)
- Freedom brings its own chains. (Marcus)
- Equality impacts people unequally. (Marcus)
- Life is about tending to our daily doings while also tending to our bigger questions of meaning and purpose; one doesn't deny the other. (Terrie)

This list goes on.

The ontological coach aims not to solve the mysteries of existence for their clients but rather to support them as they dance in the sweaty, messy and, ultimately, absurd existence that we call life.

Marcus Marsden
Managing Partner, TWP & TCP;
Senior Trainer & Executive Coach;
Author of *Start With Who*;
Co-Author of *Fit To Lead*

Marcus is a leadership development trainer and executive coach, based in Singapore, with clients throughout Asia. His work is informed by more than 30 years of business and management experience, developed in senior management roles in Europe and Asia.

Marcus specialises in experiential leadership development, top team dynamics, and coach training as well as coaching senior executives and teams in leadership, interpersonal excellence, engagement, and change.

Marcus is a certified ICF coach (PCC) and lead trainer for the ICF ACTP Newfield Coach Training programme.

After graduating from Oxford University in 1989, Marcus joined Unilever in London and went on to develop a career that progressed through Brand Management, to General Management and Change Management.

Arriving in Asia in 2002, Marcus quickly developed into one TWP's leading trainers and coaches. He has worked extensively with businesses throughout Asia and Europe, including Unilever, PETRONAS, Prudential, Danone, Shell, Aditya Birla Group, Sony, Makro, La Prairie, Live Ramp, AXA, Glenmark, Fonterra, Ipsos, Cipla, ZaloPay, and Syfe.

Marcus took on the role of TWP/TCP Managing Partner in 2019.

When not working, he is passionate about health, fitness, and nutrition. His wife, Sari, is a Nike Training Club trainer, ICF-certified PCC Coach and championship-winning fitness model. Together, in 2017, they published *Fit To Lead*, a book that emphasises the role of the body in leadership and performance.

In 2022, Marcus authored a second book, *Start with Who*, that discusses the power of identity and context via provocative questions such as: Who have you decided you are? When and why did you decide that? What evidence do you use to reinforce your beliefs about yourself? The book begins with his favourite quote from Bob Dylan: "All I can do is be me, whoever that is."

Marcus is a passionate fan of Liverpool FC and the Las Vegas Raiders, both of which have taught him a healthy relationship with failure.

CHAPTER 2

Ontological Leadership and Beyond

A New Understanding of Language, Leadership, and the Power of Conversations

Chalmers Brothers

My name is Chalmers Brothers and I'm pleased to be able to share a bit about my own background, how I found ontological coaching (or more accurately, how it found me!), and the ways in which this body of learning has become central to my life.

I was born in New Orleans, LA and raised in the town of Slidell, LA, about 40 minutes north. It was a relatively rural environment, and I spent a lot of time doing what many of my friends were doing: fishing, hunting, playing sports, doing schoolwork, and as we got older, thinking about the future and what life after high school would hold. We had a 'traditional' household in the sense that my dad worked and my mother was a stay-at-home mum, and I'd say my relationship with my parents—especially my dad—included many of the ups and downs that are part of many adolescents' experiences.

I ended up with an engineering undergraduate degree (although I didn't really enjoy and was never very good at engineering work!) and spent six months working as a field engineer in an oilfield in the Gulf of Mexico. I was relieved when, in 1982, the bottom fell out of the 'oil patch' in Louisiana and, being convinced that grad school was better than unemployment, I got my MBA at the Louisiana State University. This gave me a new 'non-engineering' path forward, and I accepted a job offer from Andersen Consulting (now Accenture) at the end of 1984.

Up until this point, I had had a very traditional, 'regular' educational and work path. I enjoyed consulting much more than engineering and working at Andersen Consulting (this is all before the Enron fiasco at Arthur Andersen) had some prestige attached to it, as the firm had a stellar reputation.

In 1987, my life changed, dramatically, for the better—although initially it didn't seem that way. My wife and I had been married for a year; she was a second-year medical student and I was in my second year at Andersen. Some friends attended a weekend programme in Baton Rouge and simply would not be quiet about it. Every time we were together, that's all they talked about.

Now, I don't know whether it was working at Andersen, or my DNA, or my periodic 'battles' with my dad, or some combination of these, but at that point in my life, I had developed what I now see as an utterly arrogant orientation. As our friends were imploring us to attend this programme that had so obviously impacted and benefited them, here was my thought process:

1. "I'm not really sure what a 'workshop' is …";
2. "I'm pretty sure I don't need one … "; and
3. "If I haven't heard of this company or body of work already, how good could it be?!"

At some point our friends said, "Look, we'll pay for y'all to go and if you don't think it's worth it, don't pay us back!"

That got my attention and we went.

By the time our three-day programme was over, after the cognitive, emotional, and physical 'dust' had settled a bit … I was left with the following observations and feelings and thoughts:

- "I came in here three days ago rock solid certain about many things. I can now identify three to four really important things (about myself, about other people, about 'how things are') that I am no longer certain about *at all*. So maybe … just maybe … there might be other things in my life, other aspects of my life, that I don't need to be so completely certain about!"

  I like to say now that I was walking around with 'terminal certainty', and in that workshop, it got cracked. There was a type of opening that occurred that I had not experienced before. The expression I use now to describe myself back then is "Sometimes wrong, but never in doubt!"

- Emotionally, for the first time in my life, I experienced two very different emotions, side by side: Regret and Ambition. I was sad and regretful about how I had been, things I had said and not said, things I had done and not done, things I had thought and not thought … and I was also immediately ambitious about and grateful for the brand new possibilities for change and growth that were suddenly in front of me!

This now reminds of a wonderful quote by Carl Rogers, because it very much applied to me at the time. He said: "The curious paradox is this: Once I accept myself as I am, then I can change!"

- The body of learning I was just introduced to was not available in traditional educational settings. Neither in my undergraduate engineering or graduate business education was anything remotely like this offered or available. Nor was it available in any corporate education or training programmes I'd ever been part of.

- At that time, not only did I not know this, but I didn't know that I didn't know this! I was unaware that this entire body of learning even existed, much less, any of the key distinctions and tools and practices within it. That new awareness—that I had been utterly blind to the existence of something so powerful, so helpful, so beneficial—was part of my shift away from 'terminal certainty' and toward being much more open to learning in the months and years that followed.

- I became aware of a wonderful paradox: We human beings are utterly unique, and we are also the same. That is, we are obviously unique, with individually valid expressions of what it means to be human, unique observers, unique beings. At the same time, we also share deeply some common traits and fundamental characteristics related to how we perceive, make meaning, and navigate in our worlds.

- On the last day, each participant made a public declaration, the type of which I had never done and the type of which I and other coaches now refer to as primary declarations. I still remember mine, and it is still a part of my 'come from', my personal context, as I go through my professional and personal life. My 1987 primary declaration was: "I am an honest, loving, understanding, and contributing man." I believe wholeheartedly that this declaration, at that point in my life, was a direction changer. It was a genuinely creative act, reorienting me toward a different future. It had the effect, not of describing but producing a tremendously different destination for me—different than the one I would have had without it—30 years down the road.

- During that weekend, I was introduced to the generative and creative power of language, to the ways in which we each 'speak ourselves into the world' … whether we are aware of this or not. Becoming aware of this, even in an introductory way, sparked something in me I had not anticipated and not experienced before. It energised me and excited me and I felt like blinders had been taken off and I was seeing myself, my possibilities, my relationships, and even the world in a new way. Again, reflecting on the power of language, I remember thinking this on that final day of that initial programme: "I don't know exactly what this is, but I'm absolutely going to learn more about it. I don't know exactly what this is, but I'm going to do this someday. I'm going to somehow, someday, do my version of this type of learning, teaching, and sharing."

My wife and I attended additional programmes in Louisiana through the early 1990s, and in 1995, I participated in Newfield Network's ontological coaching certification programme Mastering the Art of Professional Coaching. This was my springboard into bringing my version of what I had learnt into the business world.

By that point, I had left Andersen Consulting and was working as an independent consultant. Initially, when my new clients would request a strategic planning facilitation, a process improvement workshop, or a team-building programme, I would agree, with one requirement: that they give me half a day 'upfront' to do what I wanted to do to 'set the stage' for success in whatever programme we were doing. In this half day,

I shared what I considered to be the most helpful distinctions, practices, and tools that I'd learnt in my ontological coaching programmes. This was always framed as an investment in what was to come, an investment so that the conversations that were required for strategic planning, process improvement, or team building could be as productive as possible.

Gradually, that half day 'upfront' expanded to the point where I built a series of programmes that were composed entirely of these new distinctions, tools, practices and ways of seeing things. As I moved away from traditional consulting work, I moved into developing leadership and team development programmes—and providing coaching to participants involved in these programmes—entirely based on my new learnings.

I've also had the great privilege, for the past 27 years, of being part of a speaking network for Vistage International, a worldwide association of CEOs and business leaders. I have learnt so much from working with thousands of incredible leaders in peer groups around the world who challenge each other and who taught me one of the most helpful distinctions I've ever been taught: that of *Carefrontation*. As the name implies, *Carefrontation* is a conversational space in which we care enough about each other to initiate conversations which may have historically been considered difficult or challenging, and that we know in our hearts are important and need to be had! Given the central role of conversations for leaders and teams, this has been an integral addition to the 'tool kit' I now share with my clients.

In the sections that follow, I share with you some of the most important distinctions, tools, and practices that are included in my programmes with leaders and teams. A key thread you will notice is the claim that language is creative and generative, not merely descriptive. And it is this generative understanding of language that provides the basis for the effectiveness of the tools and practices involved.

MY STARTING POINT: SELF-AWARENESS AND BASIC CLAIMS

I begin every programme with a drawing of a big eye looking at a stick person, which is meant to indicate you taking a look at you … me taking a look at me … self-awareness. Self-awareness is my starting point and to me, may be understood as *the* necessary starting point for *any* purposeful, meaningful change. Right up front, I tell my clients that underneath everything else we will be doing, one of my primary objectives is to support them in becoming more powerful, more competent observers of themselves.

This foundational starting point is reinforced, I believe, by introducing some 'basic claims' or foundations for success, no matter what:

1. You cannot change another human being. The only person you can change is yourself. But you can't change what you don't see. You can't change what you don't notice. The first step is to notice.

2. We are not hermits, which means we are already interdependent. We already do huge amounts of our lives with and through people. So how we 'dance' with other people matters, and it matters a lot.

3. If you always do what you always did, you always get what you always got. New results require new actions, and many of the most important leadership actions aren't based primarily on arm strength, leg endurance, or hand-eye coordination. Something else is going on here.

4. We are always at choice. We always have choices, and we are constantly choosing every moment of our lives. And the degree to which we notice (see #1) dramatically impacts the choices we see as available in the first place!

5. How you see things matters, and it matters a lot. And many of us are not very powerful observers … of the ways we tend to observe! Developing the ability to take a look at how we look at things is a crucial part of this type of growth and development.

6. Change is perpetual, so get used to it. And because change is perpetual, learning had better be perpetual as well.

THE FUNDAMENTAL 'LANGUAGE ACTS'

In the ontological coaching framework, there are six fundamental 'language acts' or 'speech acts'. Every human interaction involves one or more of these, and only these. This is the 'universe set' of actions we human beings take in language:

- Declarations;
- Assertions;
- Assessments (a type of declaration);
- Requests;
- Offers; and
- Promises.

These are new distinctions, they are the actions we take in language. (Learning about these changed my life!) And we use them to produce results in our lives, both professionally and personally. Once we acquire them, we can see what we didn't see before and begin *doing* what we didn't do before, and then produce *results* we didn't produce before! In my work with leaders and teams, I initially focus on **Declarations, Requests,** and **Promises**. More on these to come.

KEY DISTINCTIONS, TOOLS, AND 'WAYS OF SEEING THINGS'

Let's start with a key claim: **Leaders 'get paid' to have effective conversations.** Leaders bring forth quantitative results (such as productivity, profitability, execution, achievement of measurable goals) and qualitative results (workplace culture, public identity, nature of relationships, levels of trust and cohesion), not by chopping down trees or operating levers of a bulldozer or hanging Sheetrock—but by engaging productively in certain types of conversations. And this is so close, we don't see it. It's so obvious, we can miss it. Leaders may be understood as 'conversational architects' and 'conversational engines' producing results via the power of language. This is crucial to understand and helps to orient leaders more explicitly toward specific conversations as levers for change and improvement.

Another key claim that's truly helpful for leaders: Organisations may be understood as **networks of interdependent conversations, networks of interdependent commitments.** That is, the results that organisations produce are directly driven by the ways people talk and listen and coordinate action with each other within that organisation.

A related key distinction I've found to be very valuable here is the distinction of **Missing Conversations.** I invite leaders to ask themselves this question when they see performance that is not—in their eyes— where it needs to be: "Is this performance the way it is because a previous conversation, that could have taken place, did not? If so, who would have led that conversation? Who would have participated? What would the conversation's outcome have been?" My experience is that looking at less-than-excellent performance through a conversational lens can bring much-needed clarity and can often spark ideas and solutions that other approaches don't yield.

Following the above understanding about the centrality of conversations for leadership and organisational effectiveness, I typically share what I consider to be five core competencies that I believe are required for success, for any and all organisations. These are:

- Functional;
- Technical;
- Conversational;
- Relational; and
- Emotional.

(Now, maybe there are six of these, maybe there are four; but something like this is going on!).

Functional and technical competencies have historically been what get most people *hired* into organisations, and they have now in many instances become 'threshold' competencies. That is, they have become the cost of admission, the basic requirements to even be in the game.

The higher up one moves in an organisation, the higher up the leadership ladder we progress, a shift takes place. At these levels, it's clear that *deficiencies* in conversational, relational, and emotional competencies will get you *fired*! These are the competencies required for leadership, teamwork, innovation, culture-building, healthy accountability, trust-building, relationship-building, customer service, successful problem solving, and a host of other important functions.

A key question: Why doesn't the best garage mechanic always make the best garage manager? And the answer always comes back: Because different competencies are required!

My work and the work of many of my colleagues contributing to this book focus squarely on conversational, relational, and emotional competencies as many of my clients are way above my pay grade regarding their functional and technical expertise.

FRAMEWORK FOR UNDERSTANDING AND WORKING WITH ALL ORGANISATIONS

I invite leaders to consider this foundational claim: **All organisations are unique, and all organisations are the same**. This is why leadership peer groups can be so productive! And the way all organisations are the same is represented by Fig. 2.1.

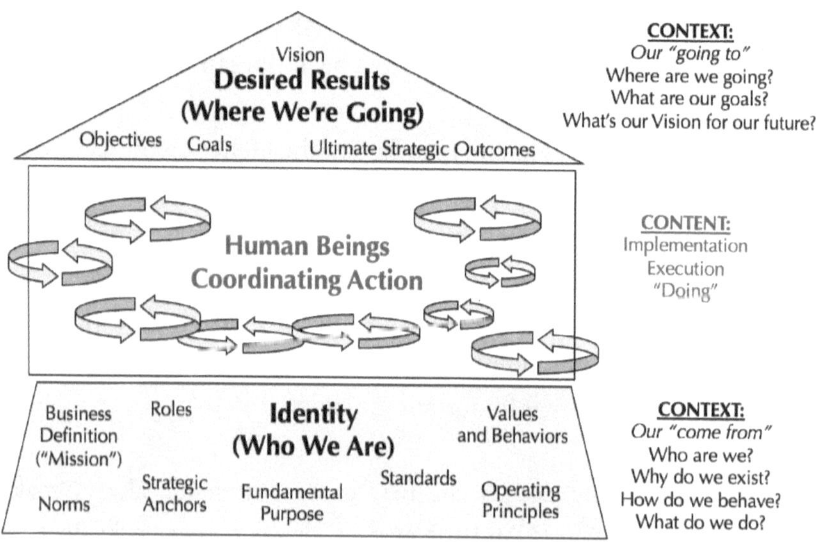

Fig. 2.1: The way all organisations are the same.

First, the 'roof'. All organisations have their version of Desired Results—where the organisation is 'going to'. Here we see organisational Vision, Goals, Objectives, Desired Strategic Outcomes.

Now, the 'basement'. All organisations have their versions of Identity, Purpose, Values, Standards, Principles—where the organisation is 'coming from' or what it's 'standing on' or 'standing for'.

The 'roof' and the 'basement' may be understood to be the **organisational context**, 'framing' and guiding the activities and interactions of employees. And this is where **Declarations** come into play.

Each organisation's 'roof' and 'basement' are declared into being by people with the authority to do so, namely leaders and leadership teams. These declarations are profoundly generative and creative—not passive and descriptive—and they serve as 'rudders' that orient and aim the organisation in certain ways and toward certain outcomes, and not others.

ORGANISATIONAL DECLARATIONS, SOCIAL COMMITMENTS, AND PUBLIC IDENTITY

Once made, public declarations bring social commitments into being; that is, once leaders make public their declarations about what the organisation is, where it's going, what it stands for, what we value, and how we're going to treat each other along the way, it is expected by those listening that:

- The leaders have the authority to make the declarations they are making; and
- That the leaders will act consistently with them!

Obviously, if we experience leaders making declarations they ultimately *don't* have the authority to make or if they act *inconsistently* with public declarations they've made, we begin to think differently about these people. We say that they are negatively impacting their public identities—how they 'show up', how they get perceived. In the first instance, we begin to view them as 'looney' or 'out of it' and in the second, we begin to assess them as 'hypocrites'. This is another way in which language creates and generates, as it has a direct impact on our public identity in the world. This is crucial for leaders and all of us to understand.

THREE KEY CONVERSATIONAL PROCESSES

There are three foundational 'conversational processes' that come into play when considering these organisational declarations and their role in purposeful culture creation. These are:
- The initial establishment of the 'roof' and the 'basement' to begin with;
- On-Boarding; and
- On-Going.

If leaders are indeed 'conversational architects', then it's clear that the design and convening of these conversations is crucial for purposeful and intentional culture-building—which is now almost universally understood to be an increasingly important aspect of organisational performance.

Certainly, leaders with authority must make the initial declarations of purpose, vision, goals, objectives, standards, principles, values, and behavioural norms.

And when new people join the organisation, it's required that they learn about these 'contextual' aspects along with their specific job duties and responsibilities. This takes place in what many organisations call On-Boarding. The weak version of On-Boarding we call osmosis, and it typically consists of "Let's sit the new person next to Phil, and just hope some of Phil's good habits rub off!" Nowadays, many organisations do a comprehensive, multifaceted, and much more effective version of On-Boarding in order to build shared understanding of and shared commitment to the behaviours, values, standards, and goals that the organisation considers to be of paramount importance.

But one-time On-Boarding is not sufficient to sustain these desired standards, behaviours and types of interactions over time. Many of my clients integrate key aspects of the 'roof' and the 'basement' into their *ongoing* processes, rituals and meetings, including performance reviews and regular correspondences. These On-Going, periodic reinforcements, reminders and refreshers—in the form of different types of conversations, messaging and incentives connected to the 'roof' and 'basement'—are essential for sustaining and stewarding the desired culture.

THE 'MIDDLE' OF THE HOUSE: A NETWORK OF INTERDEPENDENT COMMITMENTS

Now we turn our attention to the middle of the house and to what I consider to be a wonderfully helpful and beneficial way of understanding how organisations actually produce the most important results they produce. And we are now talking about two fundamentally important—and related—types of organisational results:

- **Quantitative** results, such as productivity, profitability, attainment of certain goals and numeric metrics; and

- **Qualitative** results, such as organisational culture, nature of key relationships, identity in the marketplace, impact in the community, levels of trust and cohesion and cooperation.

Let's start here. All organisations—from the largest and most complex to the smallest and simplest— may be understood, at their core, as human beings **coordinating action** in order to produce desired results. While this may seem at first obvious, it's important to look more closely at *how* employees coordinate action with one another. Employees are not coordinating action with magic, obviously. Rather, when we look closely we see that employees are coordinating action by making and managing promises (or commitments, or agreements) with each other. I use these terms—promises, commitments, agreements—interchangeably. So, at its core, each organisation may be understood as a network of interdependent commitments, happening at a variety of different levels throughout the organisation. And this network of nested *internal* commitments is ultimately in service to the *external* commitments the organisation is making to its clients and customers! In this way, we can see that our entire system of commerce may be understood to be promise-based.

Here's a key observation: We can make and manage commitments well, or we can make and manage commitments poorly. But we can't *not* do it! And we're already doing a version of this now, in every organisation. This is crucial to understand, as the ways we do the 'coordination of action dance' drives and influences both culture (which is qualitative) and execution (which is quantitative).

How do we get to a promise, commitment, or agreement? The starting point is someone making a request (or offer). And if that request gets accepted, a new commitment is now in place. But not all requests are created equal. Some requests do a great job of laying the foundation for shared understanding, a culture of healthy accountability and excellent and effective collaborative execution; and some don't. In my work with leaders and organisations, we focus directly on new distinctions in this area—specifically, distinctions involving Effective Requests.

ELEMENTS OF EFFECTIVE REQUESTS

Some requests are obviously more effective than others in establishing and sustaining a high-functioning, interdependent network of commitments that yield desired results. In my programmes, we include and discuss the following elements of effective requests:

- Committed Speaker;
- Committed Listener;
- Future Action and Conditions of Satisfaction;
- Time Frame;
- Context; and
- Mood.

Committed Speakers don't throw their requests over their shoulders, for example, as they're leaving the room! Committed Listeners aren't preoccupied with texting someone else, talking on the phone, watching TV, or otherwise multitasking. If the request is important, these first two elements are the starting points for success. We say it this way: You do not get to call yourself a Committed Speaker unless you take the actions required to elicit a Committed Listener!

Future Action may be relatively self-explanatory: What do you want me to do? And Conditions of Satisfaction include specific criteria or other aspects of the action that— if observed on the back end—would lead the requester to say, "I'm satisfied."

Time Frame is obviously a crucial aspect of an effective request. When do you want the Future Action to be done?

Now, Future Action and Conditions of Satisfaction, as well as Time Frame, are clearly impacted by something we call the 'Background of Obviousness'. This is a reminder that what's obvious to the speaker may not be obvious to the listener, and if we want genuinely shared understanding during this conversation, we need to take this into account. For long-term relationships, it's possible that the Background of Obviousness is super-thick and that people may reach shared understanding with very few words spoken. On the other hand, the relationship may be such that it's required to be very explicit and overt and specific in these areas in order to reach the level of shared understanding required for successful coordination of action. And that's the key.

The Context of the request is the front end, the first thing the requester says in order to 'paint the bigger picture' or share the 'why' or 'speak into their concerns' regarding what the forthcoming request is about, why it matters, what's at stake, and so on. I believe the cost/benefit of setting Context effectively on the front end of important requests is a very attractive one! What does it actually cost? A little bit of time and some intentionality. And the potential benefits related to shared understanding and shared meaning can be substantial.

The expression 'go slow to go fast' comes to mind here. Pay attention to Context. How many conversations are taking place within organisations that are only taking place because previous conversations did not produce the desired results?

Speaking of Context, I believe that leaders (and all of us) can benefit from thinking about the 3Cs in preparing for important conversations and important requests:

- What are you **Concerned** about?
- What do you **Care** about?
- What are you **Committed** to?

I invite you to use these 3Cs as you move forward with conversations that are important to you. Speak about these upfront to 'set the stage' and set the context for the content that is yet to come.

Finally, the Mood of the request is important—because the right conversation in the wrong mood is the wrong conversation!

Imagine the 'middle of the house'—all of the interconnected commitment cycles involving personal, phone, email, and texting interactions—attempting to be carried out with unclear or nebulous Conditions of Satisfaction, unspoken or assumed Time Frames, loose or non-existent Context, uncommitted listeners, and we can see that the impact on both quantitative and qualitative results is negative and significant!

VALID RESPONSES

Now, the 'front end' elements of Effective Requests are important but not sufficient for excellent coordination of action. The 'back end' is also key: How do you respond to requests, and how do you allow people to respond? Here, we claim that there are four and only four valid responses ... IF the results we seek are a sustained culture of healthy accountability (qualitative) coupled with clean and clear collaborative execution (quantitative). These responses are:

- **Yes**

  Yes = acceptance of Future Action, Time Frame, Conditions of Satisfaction—a new commitment is now in place.

- **No**

  No = a decline—no new commitment has been established.

- **Commit-to-Commit**

  Commit-to-Commit = "I understand what you're asking but I need to check my other calendar, as I think I have something that week. I'll check and have a Yes or a No for you by 5:00 p.m. today. Will that work?" Notice how this is not "I'll get back to you later" but includes a specific time frame by which the response will be provided.

- **Counter-Offer**

  Counter-Offer = "I understand that you want three locations up and running by 1st August. I can't do three, but I could do two. Or have three up and running by 15th August. Will either of these get us to a Yes here today?"

Notice: As different as these responses are, how are they similar? What do they have in common? They are definitive. They are not open-ended. What responses are conspicuously absent from our list? These do not make the list:

- "I'll try";
- "I'll do my best";
- "We'll see";
- "I'll get back to you later on that";
- "Possibly"; and
- A blank stare.

Again, build the 'middle of the house' in such a way that a great many conversations are allowed to end with "I'll get back to you on that" or "I'll do my best" or some other less-than-effective response and we can see that the results will be suboptimal at best and a train wreck at worst!

IN CLOSING

On a very personal note, I am now 100% convinced that had I not found this body of learning—or had it not found me!—that the 38-year marriage that I am so joyful about and grateful for now would have ended long ago. As many other contributors in this book have shared, the tools, distinctions, and practices within the world of ontological coaching are profoundly important in the domains of family and relationships. I live with ongoing gratitude that our friends were so persistent in the face of my arrogance in encouraging us to attend. (I now think that maybe—just maybe—they saw what I was blind to: how much I truly 'needed' that programme at that point in my life!)

On the organisational front, my work with leaders over these many years has evolved in many ways, but it still relies on and has always relied on the following fundamentals:

- Leaders 'get paid' to have effective conversations, and this bring us squarely to the topic of language and, specifically, to a new understanding of language.

- Language creates and generates; it does not simply describe. This new understanding is a crucial aspect of the shift in mindset required for leaders to fully embrace their role as 'conversational architects', and to understand that their conversations create new direction, new context, new energy, new relationships, and new possibilities for their organisations.

- Organisational context—and organisational direction and culture— are directly related to and dependent on Declarations made by leaders. These Declarations serve to 'orient' and 'move' the organisation into the future. Shared understanding of and shared commitment to declared values, behavioural norms, standards, goals and objectives are essential elements of intentional culture-building.

- Organisations—at their core—may be understood as networks of certain types of interdependent conversations. More specifically, organisations may be understood as human beings coordinating action by making and managing Commitments with each other. This is important to understand: We manage commitments, not time. We can do this well or we can do this poorly, but we can't not do it.

- The 'front end' of a Commitment is a Request; and not all Requests are created equal. The 'back end' of a Commitment is a response to a Request; and not all responses are created equal. Effective Requests and Valid Responses are essential elements for effective coordination of action.

- *How* organisations coordinate action—*how* the web of interdependent commitments actually plays out—drives two fundamental types of organisational results: quantitative results (such as productivity, profitability, and attainment of key goals) as well as qualitative results (such as workplace culture, public identity, nature of relationships, levels of trust, and cohesion) … and more.

* * *

It's a privilege to contribute to this book and I remain ever grateful for having been invited to participate, for having been introduced to this body of learning early in my life, as well as for the opportunities to teach and share this over the past (many!) years. I look forward to hearing from any of you interested in exploring more deeply in these areas and remember: Never Stop Learning!

Chalmer Brothers
Author, *Language and the Pursuit of Happiness* and *Language and the Pursuit of Leadership Excellence*, Speaker and Programme Leader

Chalmers is a certified executive coach, bestselling author and leadership development programme leader.

He is a former chair of a Vistage CEO peer group in Naples, FL and has been a top-rated speaker for Vistage groups throughout North America for 27 years.

Chalmers' two books—*Language and the Pursuit of Happiness: A New Foundation for Designing Your Life, Your Relationships and Your Results* (2005) and *Language and the Pursuit of Leadership Excellence: How Extraordinary Leaders Build Relationships, Shape Culture and Drive Breakthrough Results* (2015)—have been adopted by the leadership coaching and team development programmes at Georgetown University, George Mason University, Harley-Davidson Motor Company, the Newfield Network (US, Europe, Asia), The Coach Partnership and The Works Partnership (Singapore), and many others. His books have been translated into Japanese and Spanish, with Mandarin and Korean versions scheduled for 2024.

His 38-year career began with nine years at Andersen Consulting (Accenture) and since then has focused on helping leaders strengthen their influence and impact, shape powerful workplace cultures, build mutually productive relationships, and drive breakthrough results. He has clients in a variety of industries, large and small.

Chalmers and his wife of 37 years have three grown children and live in Naples, FL. He enjoys travelling with family and friends, fishing, hiking, golf, and kayaking.

CHAPTER 3

What's Love Got to Do With It

The Power of Productive Relationships for a Life Well Lived

Tini Fadzillah

Let's explore the importance of relationships.

Throughout this chapter, we will look at relationships and its importance through the ontological lens.

I will provide questions and distinctions that will challenge how you see and relate to people and relationships. To gain maximum value, read the content and apply the distinctions to your own life, to real situations and take an honest look into some of your own relationship successes and/ or failures.

I will take you on a deep exploration into your life and the relationships in it. I propose that a fulfilled life is one that is comprised of connected and productive relationships with others, with your community and with yourself.

I will offer my point of view around relationships and while this chapter is not designed to be a 'how to create better relationships' tutorial, it serves as an exploration of your own relationship with others, circumstances and yourself.

My wish is that you leave this section curious. Ask where and how you can expand who you are in your relationships and challenge your capacity to impact.

I provide examples that demonstrate that relationships are the foundation on which our successes sit on.

So, what comprises effective, productive and fulfilling relationships? Why do they matter? My premise, in this chapter, is that your capacity to cultivate healthy and productive relationships is critical to designing a life worth living.

By understanding its significance, you will have a better understanding of the forces that influence your impact with other people and ultimately the levels of fulfilment that you can design and weave into your life.

The following exploration may require courage, honesty, lightness, playfulness, and maybe irreverence. So, put on your seatbelt …

THE POWER OF STRONG RELATIONSHIPS

Executive Coach Laura McCafferty and author of the book *The Me I Didn't See* said in a recent personal communication:

> It is through relationships with others that we understand and learn ourselves. Development doesn't happen (only) through a cognitive or intellectual understanding of human beings. Development happens with and through others. We are constituted with and through others. Our way of being is experienced and felt through our interactions and relationships with others. Both our pain and our joy and everything in between is held in relationship to others. If there were no people with whom to be in relationship, our existence would simply be a matter of survival. Relationships bring meaning.

My name is Tini Fadzillah and I am the co-founder of The Coach Partnership. I have been an executive coach for the last 30 years, working with individuals and corporations globally. My focus has been on leadership and leadership presence through the ontological lens of self-awareness and helping to design lives that are fulfilled. I have learnt as much from my clients as they have from me.

In my work, I have noticed that the source of most breakdowns in life occur as a result of breakdowns in relationship(s). Here is an example. I once worked with John (not his real name) who ran a team. He was frustrated because one member of his team never delivered on specific expectations that John had. The expectation was for the team member to share real time data in detail. John's frustration showed in the quality of engagement and conversations that he had with his team overall and ultimately eroded the quality of their relationship.

My work with John was 'simply' to ask if he was explicit in his expectations and requests to the entire team and, specifically, with this particular person. John's response was no and that: "the team should know"; "it was their job"; "they were being paid to deliver on their job". This question allowed John to stop operating from his unspoken requests or assumptions and begin to develop trust and actually engage and develop his team. The tension between him and his team melted and a new level of engagement became possible—a level where honesty was welcome, where skills were developed, lack of clarity was highlighted, and feedback became a valuable source of information.

My clients are very ambitious and task-oriented men and women. In this context, many of them notice and wonder why their team members don't speak to them unless a crisis is about to explode. In such situations, my clients and I often explore the relationship habits that they have practised. Some common habits I saw were many going into their office first thing in the morning, shutting the door, and checking emails for two hours. Another observation was that leaders only had conversations with their team that focused solely on the task at hand with no concern or care for the person beyond the task.

Aside from the business examples stated above, at its most basic level are the relationships within families, within communities, and with friends who care about each other. The world is desperately in need of this. Imagine a household where communication, honesty, and genuine care exists. When young Jane knows that it is safe to state her opinion at the dinner table on general topics, imagine what impact that can have on who she eventually becomes as an adult. Imagine her level of confidence. Imagine what she will then encourage in her own family or in her teams at work.

The care I speak of may not look like the care of a parent to a child. Rather, it is recognising that when we operate for the greater good of one another, everyone wins.

Consider the tremendous power of the human spirit to connect, contribute, and thrive. This doesn't mean that arguments, disagreement, or conflict should not happen. Indeed, our capacity to push boundaries and challenge ideas is what impacts growth and evolution.

My colleague, Jim Smith, who is also The Executive Happiness Coach, said recently in response to my question on the importance of relationships in his work:

> Open, trusting relationships are, in my opinion, a core requirement for coaching work. Relationship building often helps clients move forward on the challenges they bring to coaching. I've lost track of how many times a client has wanted to focus on a 'difficult conversation' or a 'challenging direct report'. Their future actions often include sitting down with that individual to get to know them better and understand their thinking. Once that relationship has a broader base of common understanding, new options emerge that are more collaborative.

I offer six distinctions that will significantly impact your capacity to develop rich, productive, and meaningful relationships.

DISTINCTION 1: EVERYTHING HAPPENS IN RELATIONSHIP

I firmly believe that people are driven by their own ecosystem. Just like fish that swim in water, we too have designed the water that we swim in. In this water are the unique beliefs that we operate from—what you like, not like, what you have given yourself permission to do or not, what risks you take and the list goes on and on.

Let's begin with this distinction that EVERYTHING happens in relationship to something, someone else, or self. For example, if I want to ask someone out for dinner, this simple invite will only be accepted if there was some level of relationship already formed.

But let's stretch this idea. If I wanted to develop the capacity or skill of someone on my team, the person would need to trust that I have their best interests at heart, they need to trust my competence, that I was sincere in my offer to develop them, and ultimately, that I cared for their success.

If trust is built, there is a connection, and the other person receives my offer as sincere. In this situation, it is more likely that we will get more things done and experience a higher sense of fulfilment within that particular connection.

The examples I referred to above were having dinner with someone and developing someone on your team. The same thing can also be said for your family, your kids, your spouse, your siblings, your friends, etc.

How do you think you are doing in this domain? Where do you feel that your relationships are intact? With whom could you nurture and pay attention to the quality of that relationship? And for what reason would you nurture that particular relationship?

DISTINCTION 2: MY ASSESSMENTS DICTATE HOW I SEE MY WORLD

All of us are unique observers. You and I both see the world differently, just because we are different people. Not because I am better than you or you are better than me. Rather and simply because we are both just different—we have different parents, different friends, different environments, and the list can go on and on.

Based on this premise, one of the fundamental models that we use in the ontological approach to coaching is that the kind of OBSERVER I am leads to the ACTIONS that I see are available to me and ultimately, impacts the RESULTS that I achieve. The model can be read as Observer—Action—Results or OAR.

O leads to A which leads to R. This model reflects a double loop approach to learning, unlike many learning approaches which apply the single loop learning approach or A (Action) to R (Result) only.

Now, if I take a magnifying glass and hover it over the O, the coaching approach that I use sees people through three different lenses called BODY, EMOTIONS, and LANGUAGE respectively, or BEL. You can read more about this approach in the book by Chalmers Brothers titled *Language and The Pursuit of Happiness*.

Next, let me zoom in to the language portion of this model and of the many linguistic distinctions, let's focus on Assessment.

Human beings are assessment machines and make assessments of everything, such as situations, people, events, and self. No assessment is good, bad, right, or wrong. Rather, how you engage with it is what will determine whether the assessment is a productive one or not. Here is an example. I might assess myself to be incompetent in a particular situation. This assessment might freeze me so that no future action is taken or it might empower me to take significant action to learn what I need to learn.

Where we get tripped up is that we hold these assessments as facts and that limits us from seeing beyond the situation. Recognising this is where our freedom lies.

Imagine as a nine-year-old, you are asked to be the lead in a play. On opening night, however, you are wracked with nerves and you end up doing a really bad job. You are then told by your siblings that you should just play behind-the-scenes roles like handling the lights, camera, or costumes. If this statement to only play background roles is held as a fact, it could serve to be very unproductive and no growth will occur.

Fast forward to today. If playing only background roles was held as a fact, the actions of this adult would become quite predictable. For example, it's very likely that they would not take on lead roles to manage projects or take bold action or risks to impact situations. The possibilities of this person continue to be limited. So how can we work to limit the unproductivity that such assessments can have?

One of the fundamental places is to explore your assessments. Where did they come from? What do you gain by holding on to it? What do you gain were you to let them go?

The list of areas to explore your assessments are endless. And these assessments are what determines how you engage with the situation.

Imagine that I do not believe that my team at work can achieve a specific goal for this year. A productive relationship with this belief would have me start to develop my team so that we can succeed. An unproductive relationship with this assessment would have me give up before even starting on this goal. In this case, failure by the end of the year is more likely.

DISTINCTION 3: RELATIONSHIPS ARE CRITICAL TO PEAK PERFORMANCE

What I'm about to share is taken from the work that I've practised for the past 30 years with my own coach and designer of the models, Kelly Poulos. You can read more on these models in her book *Secrets To Winning*, written together with Emily Liu. These models and approach are easy and practical on paper, complex in execution, and fulfilling in its outcome.

So, imagine your life. How many of you can recall moments where there was so much tension in a relationship that you couldn't even see straight? The person may even be talking a lot of sense or even relaying a complement to you, but the message is received on deaf or resistant ears.

Yes, all of us would have had this kind of relationship before. In my work with thousands of executives, I have found that relationship tension is one of the biggest sources of unproductivity (especially in organisations). Here are some key distinctions organised around the power of relationship and productivity.

Let's begin with the components of a productive coach and player relationship. What will give this relationship the best chance of success? (Note that you can replace my reference to coach and player to leader and team member.)

When such a relationship begins, it's always about the other person. But if you are lucky enough to create a deep and/or long-standing relationship, the relationship morphs and will get to a point where there is shorthand in that relationship. As I make this real for myself, it is exactly reflected in the evolution of my relationship with Coach Kelly and frankly, many of my relationships with ex-clients and colleagues.

Such relationships build something. There has to be a strong enough relationship to trust and respect each other, enough to make something happen, together.

Such relationships are also not passive. As a coachee or team member, I am actively involved in the process. The coach or leader observes and inputs and the coachee engages with it. Imagine watching a tennis game— the dance of two people who navigate the ball can equate to the power of a truly effective relationship.

In any relationship there are two kinds of tensions that can occur:
- Relationship tension; and
- Challenge tension.

In simple terms, relationship tension means: I'm uncomfortable with you, I'm nervous or guarded. The person rubs me the wrong way. This is actually a big issue in productivity. Relationship tension is the enemy of productivity.

How many of you can relate? Imagine you have a boss or project manager who you cannot relate to and they had great ideas. You wouldn't be able to hear what the person is saying. This is the death of a productive relationship.

In China, the word *guānxì* (关系) means relationship. But it is deeper than just 'relating'. It means if there is no connection or ease, no one moves forward.

Task or challenge tension refers to 'let's get the job done'. But if I show you up to only be challenging and challenge you to get done what you said that you are committed to, all that creates is resistance. We will both just go back and forth and nothing gets done. Many bosses/leaders can't understand why and report to me that their team player simply resists or complies because they just couldn't wait for the conversation to be over.

Identifying our home base is useful as it makes us aware of which 'muscle' we are comfortable with and which we are not—relationship or task.

Consider this as a skill set. Whatever muscle that's weak, you can make it stronger.

So how can we develop these muscles?

First thing is to find a compelling reason to do so. When you begin to intentionally build muscles, it will be painful—just like in the gym.

Ask questions and listen!

It's also the tone. There is a **relatable tone**. An invitation, warm and easy. Be curious. And there is a **task tone:** objective, certain, practical. To get better at it, see why something matters to the other person and hold them accountable. Growing up, I swam in the relationship strength of my family. I grew up in a household where my father was a career diplomat. Looking back, one of the biggest observations is that relationship and challenge can and MUST coexist. Nation-building, as I learnt at the dinner table, was never just about being nice to one another; rather, it was about creating relationships that would allow challenge, task, difficult requests, and conversations to coexist.

I'm so lucky that I get to work with people as their coach and support them to fall in love with the future version of themselves. Challenge, task, and holding people accountable was a challenge for me. So that was the work that I did and still do.

Another element of my own practice of exercising the task muscle is the level of honesty (sometimes even brutal honesty) that I practise communicating. What I have learnt is that honesty draws us closer. The message resulting is: I can count on you. I can't challenge you if you don't trust me. And when I challenge, my client must know that I'm on their team and that its never personal.

If you can get the two components of relationship and task in a dance—that is, we are connected AND I'm committed to YOUR success—that will create the possibility for a productive relationship. As a coach, I'm not worried about failure; we will figure it out and move forward. But we can only do that if there is a context/dance and we feel that we have a chance to reach your highest potential.

What makes the unpacking of these tensions so fascinating is not just the healing that occurs between people, but also in the growth that can occur. I see the tremendous amount of courage that people have accessed and the risk they have taken to look at themselves and do things differently.

This has opened up this idea that relationship and being human are organic and never static.

DISTINCTION 4: WE ALL SWIM IN A UNIQUE ECOSYSTEM—WHAT'S YOURS?

I'm going to invite you to take a bird's eye view of your life, your ecosystem, and the relationships that you have built in it. What assessments and decisions were this ecosystem built around?

Here is an example of how an inquiry of what your ecosystem is could go. What kind of people do you gravitate towards? Tough, critical, task-oriented people? Or cosy, warm, 'relationshipy' kind of people? Is there somewhere in between that is your preference? What have you decided about who you connect with and how you connect with them? Is your default to keep a safe distance from people and maintain a formal relationship? Or is your default to be very close and intimate with people? Is there a space in between? What is your sweet spot?

What have you assessed and then chosen that has informed this system that you live in?

You can also take a look at yourself. What have you decided about you and your capacity to impact a relationship. Are these assessments linked to your worth? Are there gaps in your relationships?

This same exploration can be made for all parts of relating. What conversations do you allow yourself to have or not have with people? Are some conversations okay with some people and some not okay with others? Again, what assessments or beliefs are you holding on to that have informed your particular ecosystem?

It is important to have the distinction so you can interrupt, design, or redesign your ecosystem when the need arises. Everyone operates from their own complex ecosystem so it is almost a guarantee that there will be differences between two people. The key is to get into a dance with one another while honouring the differences and recognising that everyone is swimming in their own system.

This understanding allows for compassion, a range of perspectives, appreciation for diverse thoughts, and the capacity to challenge for the sake of growth versus needing to make others wrong.

How can you remedy or expand on this? Firstly, recognise that everyone is swimming in their own ecosystem. Then stand in their shoes. From this new vantage point, what does the world look like through their eyes? Can you see certain things that you couldn't see before?

This inquiry can be made more interesting by simply being curious.

So, what now? I'm going to propose the following…

DISTINCTION 5: I AM 100% RESPONSIBLE FOR THE EFFECTIVENESS AND SUCCESS OF ANY RELATIONSHIP

This is a very challenging point of view and as a practitioner, it is a very powerful point of view.

Another way to hold this thought is: I'm it.
The metaphor is I put my hands on the steering wheel of a car. So, whether I am off-track or on track, as long as MY hands are on the steering wheel, I am in ownership and always have the power to direct.

Power is always in my hands, to directly impact or influence an outcome. Through this lens, I can acknowledge circumstances or other people, but I also need to include myself in the equation and acknowledge my role in the matter.

This statement isn't about assigning fault or blame. Rather, it's an invitation to stand in the world from an attitude of power and with the belief that I can cause something to happen. There is a lot of freedom when the power is back in your hands. That is when you can significantly impact situations and influence them productively.

Here are a few questions to consider:
- What is my role in this situation I am in?
- What is the role of forgiveness? What is it really?
- What are we up to together?
- Have I given myself permission to show up fully?

In a relationship—no matter what kind you want to design—you always have the power to impact it.

I work with a lot of executives and oftentimes, my clients say that they hold back from participating in meetings for fear of messing up and looking stupid. My question is: What's the impact you can have by being in this meeting? What's your contribution even if what you say is incorrect or stupid? Could it serve as the catalyst for a new and better idea that solves the concern being addressed?

So, where can you practise holding yourself 100% responsible for the success of a relationship? What might need to shift for you? What could become possible?

DISTINCTION 6: RELATIONSHIPS ARE CONSTANTLY VIBRATING, NEVER STATIC, AND CONSTANTLY GROWING

Relationships are important, but take note that they are strong because they are constantly changing, as you are also constantly changing. Living with this paradox of strength in change is a key component of relationships.

Have you ever heard of the term 'change is constant'? Well, so are people and so are relationships. Relationships aren't static and people are never static in relationships. There is constant growth, energy, movement, and change.

Everyone has the potential to grow and become someone new. If we were to embrace this idea of constant change in relationship, the possibilities to access ourselves deeply is endless. As human beings, we are always vibrating, in flux, and have the capacity to hold opposing thoughts at the same time. This is what makes the ontological study of ever-changing complexities in relationships so rich and interesting. Playfulness and seriousness can coexist as can joy and grief, sadness and fulfilment.

Esther Perel, a leading expert on relationship, has a popular quote on paradox: "Love rests on two pillars: surrender and autonomy. Our need for togetherness exists alongside our need for separateness."

I AM constantly evolving, YOU ARE evolving as you read this book, and WE ARE growing and shifting as we move through life. Think about it like the vibrations of being human. Relationships are like this too as they consist of people who are on this path of evolution. Change and flux also includes relationships with those who have left us or passed on. What's my new evolved relationship with them and or with the gap that they have left behind?

It is so important for us to be plugged in to the ever-changing nature of being human and the complexity of growth.

ADDITIONAL THOUGHTS TO CONSIDER

A relationship is the capacity for two or more people to connect. Critical elements in relationships are mutual understanding, compassion, emotional connection, and a commitment for the other person to succeed. Relationships show up everywhere, like in friendships, romance, family, professionally—frankly, anywhere that involves another human being.

With this in mind, can you have a good relationship with someone who doesn't share similar views? I would assert that it is indeed possible. What might be the gift of having people who hold opposing views in your ecosystem?

Could opposing views allow for your own growth? Could it allow for you to appreciate a different perspective?

The other thought is to nurture a relationship like tending to a garden. In gardens, there are always flowers, trees, bushes, and weeds. From a context that we can live in contradiction, my question is: Can you discern the flowers from the weeds? Is there value in paying attention to the weeds?

Value could show up in the form of feedback—feedback that might be uncomfortable for you to look at about yourself. Being told that you don't listen might be uncomfortable to hear. But this 'weed' might not so bad to lean into and could be the one ingredient that significantly impacts a particular relationship.

Interestingly, relationships occur between you and yourself as well. A great question to ask is: What is the quality of this relationship? Is it working? Are there places to enhance or improve? Are there places where you can adjust your standards and expectations of yourself?

My standard of relationship with myself today versus 30 years ago has most certainly changed. Thirty years ago, I was driven by what other people thought—my parents, my friends, my colleagues, and bosses. Today, even though some of those elements still exist, I'm more interested in what I think. Did I fulfil my own expectations of a task? Did I leave a stone unturned? Did I hold back? One approach isn't better than the other; just different. Having the awareness of this constant evolution and knowing that you have the capacity to nurture, heal, or inspire a relationship at any time is freedom.

Think about the following questions as you continue on this exploration of self:

- How much permission have you granted yourself and others to exist/succeed/thrive/live fully?
- What's the impact of YOU on US?

CONCLUSION

Let's begin to bring this exploration to a close.

I hope you have taken a glimpse into yourself and seen some areas where you are doing well and areas where you can improve on or expand in.

We are ALL works in progress and could always do with a 'check-up' once in a while. What worked for you many years ago may no longer work now and vice versa.

My dear friend, Angela Cusack, Executive Coach and author of *Discover The Matrix*, said to me recently:

> We, as human beings, are constituted in interpersonal relationships with others. Without relationships, we cannot discover who we are—we can't enter the matrix or the space between and realise our full potential—find our purpose and passion. High integrity, authentic, and confident relationships generate a trust in self and others that far surpasses our imagination.

Awareness and design are lifelong endeavours. So, take a breath and let's dive right back into life.

Tini Fadzillah, MCC, NBC-HWC
TWP Founding Partner and Director
of Coaching

Tini is an executive coach and trainer based in Singapore, with clients throughout Asia. She specialises in coaching C-suite and senior executives in performance, leadership, and change; with a reputation of surfacing and creating sustainable shifts to the underlying conversations needed to unlock a leader's full potential and drive results.

She co-founded TWP in Southeast Asia in 1996 and has worked with thousands of people from diverse cultures on both personal and professional goals. Her passion is working with people to design a compelling future and to translate their goals into reality.

Tini is a passionate advocate for the role of the body in creating a powerful leadership presence. She is certified to use Tension Releasing Exercises™ and Wendy Palmer's Leadership Embodiment curriculum. She also co-designed and delivers the TWP Women & Leadership Presence programme and was an active member of the team that designed the Character Building component of the National Service in Malaysia. Tini is also a certified health coach and embeds wellness within her coaching encounters.

In addition to her own coaching and training, Tini runs the coach development programme for TWP and TCP, and serves on the leadership team, responsible for running the business.

Tini hosts a podcast called TINITALK which unpacks interesting themes around being human.

CHAPTER 4

Becoming a Maestro of Emotional Agility

The Essential Art of Intentional Emotional Shifting

Carol C. Courcy and Amanda Duarte

As long-time coaches and practitioners of ontological learning, we have—in our years of coaching clients and personal practising to embody what we have learnt—found ourselves intrigued and challenged by the idea of emotions as a territory of learning. We, like many people, had assumed our emotions were mostly out of our control, especially those associated with unpleasant emotions like confusion, boredom, anger, frustration, impatience, or fear.

In her 2012 book, *Save Your Inner Tortoise*, Carol created a term for this process of learning in this new territory. She called it Emotional Agility—the ability to ENTER and EXIT emotions—intentionally! Becoming more emotionally agile allows us to add emotions to our repertoire which enables us to make better decisions, resolve issues, and increase our sense of well-being.

Our chapter starts with good news! **We all have EXISTING skills in emotional agility.** Do you ever take a few deep breaths to relieve stress? Go outside to clear your head? Shrug your shoulders to release tension? Call a friend for comfort or fun? Each is an example of emotional agility in action, to intentionally shift from one state to another to increase your sense of well-being!

Emotional Agility Activity #1

Write a brief description of five or more ways you successfully shift from one emotion to another. How do you calm yourself? Motivate or embolden yourself? Find humour? Pick a fight? Feel gratitude? Irritate someone else?

This quote from Aristotle gets to the heart of our challenge of intentionally increasing our well-being via emotional agility:

> Anyone can become angry—that is easy. But
> to be angry with the right person, to the right
> degree, at the right time, for the right purpose,
> and in the right way—this is not easy.

Emotional agility—although doable—is not always easy. Each of us faces situations and old habits we truly want to change for the better and yet, with the skills and smarts we have so far, frustrate or elude us.

Where might you personally benefit from more emotional agility? In this chapter, we pursue the question: How can practising emotional agility help each of us make changes that have been resistant to changing?

We shall focus on three emotional agility skills:
- Becoming a composer of emotions: Emotions are learnable!
- Expanding emotional playlists: Strengthening our capacity to handle difficult situations.
- Becoming a maestro of emotional agility: Daring to step into unknown emotional territories!

BECOMING A COMPOSER OF EMOTIONS

Emotions are learnable!

Good to know as you begin: **You don't have to change everything for everything to change.** No change of our life's circumstances is required to implement emotional agility. You don't have to change jobs, bosses, spouses, significant others, or your past.

In *A General Theory of Love*, authors Thomas Lewis, Fari Amini, and Richard Lannon speak of **emotional reverberation**, where a dominant emotion influences what is seen and not seen; done and not done; said and not said. The impact of their research? We can no longer assume we are free to make choices. Emotional reverberation research shows us that when inside an emotion, we have the choices *that* emotion allows:

- When in the depths of **resignation**, the automatic 'tune' is disappointment—the tone is low, the face, posture and energy are down. Common sense is "Why bother? Nothing's going to change. It is not worth the effort." *When inside resignation, what choices do you have? What decisions do you make?*

- When inside **determination** the music is a steady beat of "I can, and I will … nothing will get in my way. I did …" Eyes and body forward, muscles taut. You have the energy you need for the future you envision. *When inside determination, what choices do you have? What decisions are predictable?*

Emotions are predispositions for action. Each emotion has its emotional tune. When **calm**, we are **prone to** relax physically, eyes closed or partially open, shoulders eased, slow, and even breathing. We are **inclined to** speak in a quiet, calm, and measured voice, without raising it or sounding agitated. We may not say much at all or sigh.

In contrast, when **angry**, we **tend to** be agitated, have a tense posture, clenched fists, furrowed brows, flushed complexion, and intense eye contact. Verbally, we might speak loudly, use harsh or profane language, and have a sharp or aggressive tone. We express frustration, irritation, or resentment towards a specific situation or individual: "I can't believe you did that!", "This is absolutely ridiculous!"

Emotional Agility Activity #2

Look into the emotional tunes you already know. From your own experience, write a short paragraph of how someone in the emotion of RESIGNATION is likely to appear, to say, to do, and behave. Do the same for DETERMINATION. (HINTS: Tend to ... prone to ... inclined to ...)

Have you noticed that the emotion we spend our time in influences how we behave, what we say, do, or don't do? Emotions create our choices. Want more choices and different results? Use emotional agility to learn and practise a different emotion.

How might these human similarities help us with learning emotional agility? Authors Paul Eckman and Richard Davidson offer **activating an emotion**:

> In the course of our research, we found something that surprised us. If you intentionally make a facial expression, you change your physiology. By making the correct expression, you begin to have the changes in your physiology that accompany the emotion. The face is not simply a means of display, but also a means of activating emotion. This is strictly voluntary—but these expressions turn on the involuntary system. In other words, simply putting the face into a smile

drives the brain to activity typical of happiness—
just as a frown does with sadness.

More good news! No waiting to change! Because of our capacity to activate emotions, they are learnable! We don't need to understand any more about why we continue to do what decreases well-being. By designing different emotional patterns, activating and practising them, the emotion becomes available to you. Doing so opens you to different choices, allowing you to take different actions and resolve issues successfully.

Metaphorically, emotional agility is like composing a captivating personal melody. We begin by inventing an 'emotional tune', something to perform. As with a skilled composer, over time we refine the notes, tempo, and words that, with practice, change our tune! In this section, we provide techniques to increase your skills in composing emotional tunes for increased well-being.

Composing an Emotional Tune

How do we compose an emotional tune?

- By being observant, we identify familiar physical attributes of an emotion: a posture, muscle and shoulder tension, breath intensity, facial expression (mouth, eye focus, jaw).
- We create activities to 'activate emotions' by modelling these physical attributes.
- As we practise, the body will enter some degree of that emotion.
- To complete an emotional composition, add what is often said and often done to create a more robust emotional tune!

* * *

Emotional Agility Activity #3

Select an 'emotional tune' to activate:

1. What emotions are missing for you? Satisfaction, curiosity, acceptance, ambition, dignity or something else?
2. Select one. Where in your life would a bit more of that emotion contribute to your well-being? Help you make better decisions? Your why? (List hopes and expectations of how your life would change.)
3. Compose your emotional tune. Head to toe, what is the posture and muscle tension you associate with that emotion? Breath pattern? Facial expression (mouth, eye focus, jaw)? HINT: Mimic a character in a film or video who's 'acting' in your chosen emotion.
4. Exit the emotion by choosing an emotion that is more neutral. (Open, calm, etc.)
5. Re-enter the emotion by repeating your 'emotional tune'. Practise, practise, practise! Initially, you may want to spend 3–5 minutes in your 'emotional tune'. Repeat daily until you feel at ease with ENTERING and EXITING the emotion.
6. Take your emotion into life! Do any familiar task (chores or errands) in that emotion! Once you have a sense of it, practise more challenging tasks: emails, time management, meetings.

Competency comes when you can move into, sustain until new results occur, and exit your chosen emotion intentionally.

* * *

Carol on Learning to Exit Resentment and Enter Satisfaction

I was a pleaser and loved saying yes, mostly to be liked and included. This strategy was smart professionally. Bosses loved me. I was promoted. Without a complementary ability to say no or not yet, however, my workload expanded. Consequence of too much pleasing? Exhaustion. Unbeknownst to me the emotion of resentment grew in me as I blamed others for my unhappiness by 'forcing me' to say yes. My inner voice? "They should know I am overworked. Poor me! They shouldn't ask!" During my coach training programme, I realised I was a classic resentful person: Never ask for help. Say yes when I mean no. Keep my anger mostly private. (Only whine to others who can't help.) Expect others to change—which rarely happened—and that fuelled more resentment. This insight helped me begin to be annoyed with myself.

I finally brought this frustration to my coach. Her observation? "The emotion I never see in you is satisfaction." Could I commit to being satisfied? My typical yes resulted in satisfaction as my first emotional agility 'homework'. Together we designed my 'body of satisfaction': a 'taller' posture with firm backbone for dignity and stability. Every day for a month, I did daily activities in that posture, asking myself: What is enough? Enough for now? (Early on I couldn't say no to others; thought I'd be fired). With a new sense of dignity growing daily, I decided to complete all current promises and posted time needed to fulfil them on my calendar. (I was astounded by how full my calendar was already!) New action? With my stronger backbone, new requests were filtered through my capacity calendar. Also new? All promises had due dates! (I can do by x date or not until x date.) To my surprise, I wasn't fired, and people accepted dates or cancelled their requests. That was decades ago. To this day, satisfaction's 'enough' is an available emotion. Resentment has not disappeared. When it reappears, I am less attracted to the blaming. I prefer ease and satisfaction to righteousness.

* * *

Your journey? Over time, repeating these emotional tunes (activations) build a neural pathway in your brain making that emotion more readily available. With intentional and situational practicing, eventually the emotion becomes a part of your natural emotional playlist.

EXPANDING EMOTIONAL PLAYLISTS

Another way to describe emotional reverberation is to say that, as human beings, we follow habits and patterns. These automatic responses to situations often happen without us realising it. When comfortable, and things are going well, we tend not to notice those patterns. With discomfort, we may notice them but think we have little, if any, control over our emotional responses. For example, always worrying and feeling anxious about what could go wrong; or as Carol shared, never being able to say no and living in perpetual resentment. Imagine your life playing the tunes of resentment or anxiety on repeat in your background playlist!

If you have created a musical playlist, you will be familiar with the idea of grouping songs that will evoke a certain mood or sensation. For example, a gym playlist has tracks to keep our energy high or a meditation playlist has the tracks to tone our energy down. We use an emotional playlist to motivate our actions, just like our brain constructs the emotions that will serve as the predisposition for the actions we are taking.

In *How Emotions are Made,* author Lisa Feldman Barrett offers: "Your brain predicts and constructs your emotions. It doesn't recognise them as emotions until it learns what they mean based on your past experiences."

Each emotion in our playlist is like a unique track, composed of sensory inputs, memories, and interpretations of situations we have lived. When a new situation arises, our brain selects the appropriate track from our current emotional playlist based on its predictions of what is going to happen. This process happens subconsciously in milliseconds, and it shapes our emotional responses, how we make decisions, and ultimately, our well-being.

The not-so-good news is that these emotional responses are transparent and arrive uninvited.

For example, someone has a fear of public speaking. Every time they are asked to speak in front of a group, their brain predicts that it will be a frightening and anxiety-inducing experience based on past situations where they felt nervous and embarrassed. As a result, their body responds with increased heart rate, sweating, and a sense of panic, all of which are associated with the emotion of fear.

Thankfully, we can intentionally create new experiences where we feel safe and supported, such as practising in front of friends or joining a public speaking group with a positive environment. Amanda calls that "practising in a lower stake situation". Over time, our brain learns to construct the emotion of excitement or anticipation instead of fear when faced with similar experiences, strengthening our capacity to deal with difficult situations.

As Barrett reminds us: "When you change the ingredients that your brain uses to make emotions, you change your emotions."

Emotional agility has those ingredients!

What can we do when we recognise a more troubling emotional pattern that jeopardises our well-being? We can expand our emotional playlist!

Emotional Agility Activity #4

Here's how to expand your emotional playlist:

1. Choose a situation where you usually fall into the same pattern, that you regret and would like to change. For example, fear of public speaking, or not speaking up in meetings, or yelling at the kids.
2. To make this pattern visible, briefly describe past experiences that show how you tend to respond to that situation. (What you often do, say, think, and tend to behave.)
3. What emotional playlist is playing in the background of that situation? Name the emotion(s) that typically arise in that situation. (Again, include how your body responds—heart rate, breath pattern, posture, shoulder tension, facial expression, etc.)
4. Say to yourself: To create a different future, how would I behave in the same situation if I were _______________ (excited, calm, confident, etc.)
5. Choose an emotion you prefer to fill in the blank (a thesaurus helps). Describe how your body would respond in that emotion. HINT: If you need ideas, see Activity #3.)
6. What 'low stake situation' could you practise the new behaviours and emotion? What situation would be easy to practise? Where do you feel safe to make mistakes?

As you repeat and practise, notice how the new emotion starts to show up and your results start to change. (Expect mistakes. Adjust as desired.) Soon enough, you will realise that the playlist in the background has new songs. Practising these four emotional agility activities enables you to influence your well-being and strengthen your capacity to handle difficult situations.

BECOMING A MAESTRO OF OUR EMOTIONAL AGILITY

As you walk this learning path, you will inevitably come across uncomfortable or even painful emotions. Author Brené Brown offers: "We cannot selectively numb emotions, when we numb the painful emotions, we also numb the positive emotions."

When we numb painful emotions, we decrease our emotional range and reduce our capability to deal with future challenging situations.

* * *

Amanda on Exploring Unknown Emotional Tunes by Waking Up Anger and Activating Confidence

I grew up in a house where it felt only one person was allowed to feel angry: my father. Seeing so many of his 'careless' actions coming out of anger and frustration, I decided early on that it was not safe to feel angry. I learnt to numb anger. I would push down my anger and put on a silent mask of the 'agreeable and nice person'. That probably served me well while living under the same roof with him, but when I got out in the world on my own, I lacked the ability to stand up for myself and to set boundaries. I would also be frightened to be in front of anyone that was able to stand up for themselves. I felt intimidated by their words and actions. I would push down anger internally, and never say a word in front of the person.

Looking back, I can see now that my father lacked the emotional agility to move beyond his anger. His actions were exactly what the emotions he practised allowed him to do.

Another big lesson came from my daughter. She is capable of a wide range of emotions, and high intensity. In her bursts of anger, I would use the power of a mother's authority and used it to order her to be quiet, and to stop crying!

After my coach training programme, and much exploration around my emotions, I realised that me shutting down my daughter's anger was a sign of my own inability to handle it. (I can tell you, her anger felt so uncomfortable to me in the beginning!) I continued exploring how I could access anger and express it in healthy ways. (Imagine punching a boxing bag or yelling at the top my lungs into a pillow!). This learning allowed me to expand my capacity to access a powerful emotion previously numb inside of me. I learnt to take advantage of the force that anger has to defeat procrastination, exit self-doubt by activating confidence.

I also grew my capacity to notice when I was unintentionally accessing anger. I started to have a choice … Will this anger serve me? I added the capacity to activate confidence to stand up for my ideas and to self-advocate! As I learnt not to be afraid of anger, I also created space for my daughter (and son!) to be seen and heard in their anger. I can now open space for them to express healthy anger, and to take care of what is important: their own space, their boundaries.

* * *

What do we do with more difficult emotions when our emotional playlist is lacking? Lewis, Amini, and Lannon, in *A General Theory of Love*, offers (emphasis by us):

> Gleeful people *automatically* remember happy times, while a depressed person *effortlessly* recalls incidents of loss, desertion, and despair. Anxious people *dwell* on past threats; paranoia instils a retrospective *preoccupation* with situations of persecution.

How do we free ourselves of one of these patterns to make different choices?

- First is the realisation that we had an emotional reaction.
- Second, we have another emotional reaction related to wanting NOT to repeat what we often do.
- Even more good news! We do NOT have to get rid of an emotion we dislike before we can move on!

In this next activity, we take you a step further as you dare to move between contrasting emotions.

Emotional Agility Activity #5

Part 1: Moving Between Opposite Emotional Tunes
Use a dictionary and thesaurus to pinpoint the words and definition for this activity.

1. Pick an emotional tune you want to spend LESS time in (want to be able to exit). Write the name and definition.
   Example: Disappointed—being sad or displeased because someone or something has failed to fulfil my hopes or expectations.

2. Describe that emotional tune physically. (To refresh your memory, see Activity #3.)
    Example: When disappointed, my head, shoulders, and posture slump down. My breathing is shallow. My muscles feel weak (as if tired from effort.) My mouth is turned down as if sad. I feel limp with little energy.
3. Practise! ENTER the emotion by 'mimicking' this emotional tune for 3–5 minutes. Do it long enough to sense the emotion arise in you and 'take hold'. The more you practise the shorter the time it takes for you to ENTER the emotion!
4. Do any low stake task (chores or errands) in that emotion! Once you have a sense of it, practise more challenging or higher stake tasks: emails, time management, meetings. What are the predictable outcomes in this emotion?
5. Exit that emotion by putting yourself into a NEUTRAL emotion (by centering or 'shaking it off' for 1–2 minutes until the original emotional tune is replaced with a neutral emotion.)

NOTE: Our intention for this activity is to build self-trust and confidence that you can enter and exit an emotion. Thankfully, as we practise, we reduce our fear of being 'trapped' or 'taken by' an emotion we don't like.

Part 2: Designing an Opposing Emotional Tune
Choose an opposing emotion to design. HINT: Antonyms in a thesaurus. Compose and practise your opposing emotional tune by repeating steps 1 to 5. What predictable outcomes do you prefer? Head there!

Example: For disappointed, an opposite is some degree of being at ease with, pleased or satisfied, or show pleasure with. In a version of satisfied, I am sitting up straighter, shoulders are more open, head and chin are level (not down). I can breathe more deeply. My face is not tense and I have a bit of a smile (not a grin though). I say to myself, "I am fine. It is okay."

SUMMARY

In this chapter, we have offered two entry points into emotional agility:

1. Selecting and activating an emotion; and
2. Creating lower to higher stake experiences allows us to modify an emotion's intensity or add a totally new emotion.

With practice and embodiment, we can add a variety of emotions to our emotional playlists.

Becoming a maestro comes when you are able to add an emotional tune, return to it as needed for desirable results, and ultimately be more daring in the emotions you wish to experiment with. Being able to ENTER and EXIT any emotion generates trust of this learning process, allowing you 'to try on' unfamiliar or difficult emotions you tend to avoid. As with Carol and Amanda's examples, over time you will notice decisions and behaviours that were unlikely, now become a part of who you can be with greater ease.

We complete our conversation by sharing well-earned wisdom from our exploration of becoming a Maestro of Emotional Agility.

Lessons Learnt

- **Discomfort is a Good Sign that Change is Needed NOT Something to Avoid.**

- **Practise Before You Need It!**
  With habitual patterns of response, we tend to have our 'go to' emotional playlist responses. That is how our brain constructs emotions and is comfortable with the playlist we have. Set aside time to reflect and practise alternatives.

- **Practise in Low Stake Situations.**
  Repetition and success are far more important to our brain's ability to learn than difficulty. As we successfully build new experiences, we are increasing our emotional playlists. When in higher stake situations, the emotions we need will come readily to us.

- **Limbic Resonance: Emotions are Contagious.**
  Ever been around someone or in a crowd and found yourself in 'their' emotion? Another reason for having the agility to change emotions is their contagious nature. We can 'catch' emotions from others. Who are you spending time with and being around? Do you want that influence? If not, find people who resonate with what you want in your life and intentionally 'catch' their emotional energy.

- **Avoid the Temptation to Do Too Much Too Soon!**
  As recovering perfectionists, we have both jumped into important emotional learning situations BEFORE our competence with emotional agility was up to the task. (Carol with a difficult situation with her mother. Amanda with her resistance with some family members.) We each wanted to go from one extreme to the other FAST! We did not succeed. We discovered that emotional agility benefits from understanding the journey between extreme emotions, worked better by travelling through five or six related and less intense emotions in between the extremes. Eventually, that reduced the learning curve, allowing us to successfully go from A to Z. We share some examples of the sequences:

Resentment ⟶ Discontent ⟶ Annoyance ⟶
Satisfaction ⟶ Forgiveness ⟶ Gratitude

Carol: Early on, my exiting resentment took me to discontent. I was sick and tired of being resentful. Its appeal was lessening. What motivated me next was being annoyed with the speed of leaving resentment for a smoother life. My daring step was satisfaction which proved challenging. Initially, I felt nauseated when seeing how far away I was from 'being enough'. I needed and created multiple daily stopping points, telling myself enough for now! A turning point was forgiving myself, knowing that I am only human. That opened me to gratitude on a daily basis.

Overwhelmed $\longrightarrow$ Self-compassion $\longrightarrow$ Self-care $\longrightarrow$ Curiosity $\longrightarrow$ Confidence $\longrightarrow$ Ease

Amanda: Feeling overwhelmed is an old friend of mine. It visits me when I'm not stable enough and it can escalate quickly. The jump from overwhelmed to my wishful state of ease is, at times, too daring. So, I learnt to activate self-compassion: I'm only human and overwhelmed is a common experience. From that space, I can activate self-care. What needs can I take care of to support me in this moment? From that space, curiosity comes easier. How can I approach this in a different way? If I approach it in a different way, what would happen? Confidence comes right in as I trust myself and that, for me, is the doorway to ease.

Enjoy creating your own sequences!

● **You are Creating Art!**

Learning new emotions and breaking ingrained emotional patterns can feel daunting, messy, and full of mistakes. As you compose your emotional tunes and practise your playlists, you are setting the tone of how you want to live your life. It's an art, not a math problem to be solved. We suggest you embrace the artistic process with compassion, grace, and lightness.

We end with gratitude … As Carol often says, "Ontological coaching is a gift that keeps on giving". In writing our chapter together, an unexpected gift is that we nurtured a relationship with Carol as mentor and Amanda as mentee. Our fondest hope is that our writing lessens suffering, increases joy, and allows for fulfilment in the reader's work and personal lives. And finally, our gratitude for being invited to join this talented and thoughtful group of coaches, leaders, and human beings. We thank them for sharing their unique gifts to the world.

Carol C. Courcy
Master Certified Coach (2000–2020),
author of *Save Your Inner Tortoise!*, and
TCP featured speaker

Carol earned her first coaching certification in 1990 after three years of intensive study in ontological coaching. In the decades and coach certifications that followed, she honed her coaching skills by satisfying hundreds of clients as they pursued personal and professional learning initiatives:

2000–2020	ICF Master Certified Coach (MCC)
2012 to present	Featured speaker, guest faculty, and Programme Coach for The Coach Partnership in Singapore
2000–2010	Member of the global International Coach Federation and Newfield Network, USA credentialing teams certifying coaches
2000–2008	Vice President for The Newfield Network, USA; Director of Coach Training for North America and Senior Course Leader
2009 to present	Owner Carol C. Courcy & Associates coaching business

After 6,500+ hours of individual and group coaching, Carol sustains the passion, rigour, and 'lightness of being' to encourage the necessary courage for her clients to make important life changes.

Carol is profoundly grateful for her clients' trust of coaching and emotional learning in particular. Their honesty and commitment to significant changing helped her write her book *Save Your Inner Tortoise!: Learn How to Cross the Finish Line Joyful and Satisfied* (a textbook in selected Coach Partnership programmes.) She introduces the distinction and practices of Emotional Agility—a simple yet powerful emotional learning strategy. She offers the book as a gift in support her favourite audience—the ever striving, exhausted, self-sacrificing overachievers. She is a featured speaker and group facilitator of emotional agility in the United States, Asia, and Europe.

**Amanda Duarte, PCC, NBC-HWC
Executive and Well-being Coach and
Lead Somatic Trainer for TCP Parenting
Coaching Programme**

Amanda's career spans two decades across Latin America, the Middle East, Europe, Asia, and the USA. Her professional journey began in the corporate world before she ventured into entrepreneurship, successfully building and selling her own company. Now, as a Certified Professional Coach (ICF-PCC) and National Board Certified Health and Wellness Coach (NBC-HWC), Amanda specialises in guiding leaders and business professionals through personal and professional transitions with confidence and without overwhelm.

Drawing from her diverse background in various industries and experience coaching individuals from over 26 nationalities, Amanda brings a deep understanding of leadership challenges and the demands of high-performance environments. Her personal triumph over burnout fuels her passionate advocacy for well-being, empowering clients to achieve exceptional results without compromising their health.

Renowned for fostering safe spaces that facilitate profound emotional exploration and the reshaping of self-limiting beliefs, Amanda's approach is both compassionate and transformative. Her expertise lies in enabling individuals to cultivate greater emotional range and resilience, utilising a powerful blend of TRE® (Tension Release Exercises), Somatic Experiencing®, and Ontological Coaching methodologies.

Amanda firmly believes that parenting represents the ultimate leadership role—a conviction that shapes her work as lead somatic trainer on the TPC Parenting Coaching Programme. She guides students through leveraging the role of the body and emotions in parenting. Currently based in the USA with her family, Amanda offers coaching in English, Portuguese, and Spanish. Beyond her private practice, Amanda also serves as Mentor Coach and Programme Manager for the TCP ontological coaching programme, supporting the development of future coaches.

CHAPTER 5

Playing at the Edge

Why 30 Years of Studying Successful Leadership Has Made Me Dead Serious About Play

Chris Balsley

My name is Chris Balsley and all I have ever really wanted to do is to leave behind a more loving world. I have been blessed to have my passion and my profession be one and the same. Since leaving the US Air Force in 1986,[1] I have earned my living by being a massage therapist, a psychologist, and marriage counsellor, a youth-at-risk counsellor, a military trainer, an executive coach, and a facilitator of transformation in large organisations. Helping people succeed has been my career. Certain leaders and companies in my life, both personally and professionally, have been on my radar from day one, because they all seem to succeed, no matter the landscape. To a tee, they all are resilient and can sustain their work tempo indefinitely,

---

1   USAF 1979–1986, Honourable Discharge.

cycling between rest and action. They have a commitment to building/sustaining/repairing deep relationships. They emanate a sense of lightness and curiosity, they take more risks, and they celebrate their failures and victories equally.[2] Which leads me to the last common trait and the subject of this chapter: They all share an inherent culture of play.

> We play only when we feel safe
> Playing instils a sense of safety

To lay a good foundation for the importance and validity of play, I would like to take us back in time a bit. I was born in the early winter of 1959 in Boulder, Colorado. I came into the world premature, weighing just over 4 pounds (about 1.8kg). The obstetrician who delivered me, told my parents that premature babies like me had very poor prognosis. The doctor even counselled them to not name me because I probably wouldn't make it. There was little they knew to do except keep me warm and fed and swaddled up in an incubator. Six days later, against all odds, the doctor said I might survive, so I was christened Christopher Landon Balsley. Sixty-four years later, I am still here, the obstetrician who delivered me is long gone, and any infant weighing over a pound has a greater chance of growing into a productive and healthy human being than at any time in the history of humankind.[3] I share this story to highlight that we live in an age where miracles, such as the decrease in premature infant mortality rate, is commonplace. We are literally

---

2   One pharma sales manager I coached kept a stack of $50 Starbucks cards on hand to pass out to the winner of the week's biggest 'crash and burn'. High performers treasured these cards far more than their $50 face value. When facing their doubts about meeting financial goals, they could say, "I am coming for that Starbucks card" and tensions would be eased.

3   Premature infant survival at 28 weeks' gestation is 69% (63% to 74%) for birth weights of 500g or just under a pound and 92% at 750g or just over a pound and a half.

living longer and healthier lives, with less war,[4] less famine,[5] and less disease[6] than ever in recorded history. Despite that, the markers for feeling unsafe or living in fear—like suicide, addiction, and divorce—are on the rise. The usage of anti-anxiety and antidepressants are making pharmaceutical companies tens of billions of dollars every year. We live in fear, bombarded by images in the news, and on our social media, threads of armed militias storming cities around the planet. Hurricanes are only growing in ferocity, breaking records year after year. Fuelled by climate change, forest fires and floods are impacting millions of lives every year. We are living with the after-effects of two years of mask mandates, virtual schooling, and not being able to go into work and now not wanting to go back to work. Sleep deprivation is a global health crisis according to the Centers for Disease Control and Prevention, striking 1 out every 3 adults.

We have never been this safe,
and yet we live culturally as though the opposite is true.

As an antidote to this, I would like to share with you two things that have changed my life as well as the lives of those around me.

---

4   From the end of World War II (1945) through 2023, battle deaths per hundred thousand people have dropped from 23 to <1%. This reduction in mortality from war is unprecedented and it is known as the long peace, or Pax Americana.

5   One of the greatest human triumphs was the eradication of global famine. In 30 years from the 1990s to 2019, the global rate of malnutrition dropped from 38% to less than 8%. Poverty is rapidly being abolished. We are living longer and have greater wealth than any other generation.

6   Smallpox, polio, guinea, worm disease, measles, and mumps used to kill millions of people a year and now they're almost all a distant memory.

- A distinction known as Above and Below the Line.[7]
- Two relevant 'Play' stories from my career.[8]

> "Play is the highest form of research."
> Albert Einstein

Play isn't respite from work. It is the secret sauce that drives innovation and resiliency. When we play, there is a shift in our blood chemistry that fosters risk-taking and we problem solve much faster. Most importantly, this chemical cocktail turbocharges our imagination, allowing us to dream and to think the impossible, exactly what is needed to create the future we all want, hope for, and deserve.

> "The creation of something new is not accomplished
> by the intellect but by the play instinct."
> Carl Jung

ABOVE AND BELOW THE LINE

Draw an imaginary horizontal line in the space in front of you with your finger from right to left. Let's refer to the space above the line as ATL and the space below the as BTL. As humans, we live either above (ATL) or below this line (BTL). ATL has a quality of lightness and curiosity, while BTL feels heavy and serious. **Being above or below the line is neither good nor bad. It just means we are predisposed to be a certain way and to do certain things.** We may go ATL when we win the lottery, or land that dream job, or maybe all it takes for you is to wake up to a beautiful sunrise.

---

7 "Locating Yourself—A Key to Conscious Leadership." *YouTube*, uploaded by The Conscious Leadership Group, 15 Nov. 2014. www.youtube.com/watch?v=fLqzYDZAqCl.

8 Names, and identifying features have been changed to allow for confidentiality.

Maybe you spend most of your time ATL because you're happy at work, you're happy at home, and you have a great community. BTL, on the other hand, feels serious and heavy. Things that drive us BTL could be getting fired, or global warming, or getting a divorce. It shows up in most people as problems with sleep, diet, and exercise. Look at Fig. 5.1 and ask yourself where you are right now, ATL or BTL?

Fig. 5.1: Characteristics of being Above the Line (ATL) and Below the Line (BTL).

People who are ATL have a certain look and feel to them. They embrace lightness and curiosity above all else. They feel safe and are willing to invest the time necessary to learn. Decades of brain scans have shown the brain structures of an ATL brain looks completely different to the structures of a BTL brain.[9] The safe brain (ATL) shows an increase of blood flow to the executive functioning parts of the brain, the home of the things we associate with being human-like—being creative, analytic, using language, thinking outside the box, and mitigating risk. The scans also show regulation (or balance) in the areas responsible for emotions that allow us to care for one another, to build trust, to grieve, and to celebrate.

Conversely, the unsafe brain (BTL) scans show a marked decrease of blood flow to the executive functioning areas of the brain (decreasing intelligence) and a dysregulation or increase of blood to the limbic and primitive areas of the brain, making us more emotional and more reactive. We are literally hardwired to go below the line when we perceive danger or stress. This happens because the executive brain is remarkably slow in comparison to the emotional and more primitive parts of our brain. If I were to ask you, in the spur of the moment, what the capital of France was, it generally takes about 1.3 seconds to recall the name and to respond, "Paris". If I tossed a dry erase marker to you, and you tried to gauge the trajectory of the incoming marker while correlating it to the wind velocity in the room along with the mass of the pen, it would hit you in the face before you had a chance to even move your hand. The BTL brain is blinding fast by comparison, less than $\frac{1}{10}$ of a second to catch a pen, compared to the relatively slow executive functional response of 1.3 seconds from question to response. Responding fast can lead to a higher survival rate, making the shift into BTL an ingrained survival mechanism. Essentially, we end up not thinking or analysing because it takes too much time. Instead we become predisposed to reactivity, snap

9   Amen, Daniel G. *Change Your Brain, Change Your Life: The Breakthrough Program for Conquering Anxiety, Depression, Obsessiveness, Lack of Focus, Anger, and Memory Problems.* 2nd ed., revised and expanded, New York, NY, Harmony Books, 2015.

decisions, and an over-reliance on old skill sets, particularly those that were successful in the past.[10]

There is nothing wrong with being BTL, in the appropriate environment.

Why is this important? Going BTL in the face of stress is hardwired into us. Coming back to being ATL is hard thing to do; it takes conscious choice and discipline. When you are deep BTL, swimming in judgements, and making snap decisions, choosing ATL is the single most important task a leader has. The intent of this chapter is twofold. First, to show how critical play is to a healthy and sustainable ecosystem. Second, to give leaders, individuals, and teams the tools and mindsets needed to choose between ATL or BTL.

- All mammals, learn by playing;[11]
- Play builds trust;
- Play is a direct indicator of psychological safety; and
- Play is contagious.

Leaders who create a playful culture are bringing out the best in everybody. Playful leaders create curiosity around them, both individually and collectively, knowing full well that whatever you put in front of a curious brain goes straight into long-term memory. This *learning turbocharger* has been deeply ingrained in us over millennia—all mammals, including humans, share a common brain structure allowing for play. By comparison, reptiles have a much simpler brain structure—they can't and don't play.

---

10 For those readers familiar with the term 'amygdala hijack', you will notice it is conspicuously missing here. According to Lisa Barrett Feldman in *How Emotions are Made*, we are never truly hijacked by a lower functioning brain. As humans, we always have a choice in how to respond.

11 Think bear cubs wrestling each other to assert dominance, young monkeys climbing all over their mother in preparation for climbing all over trees, kittens sneaking up on litter mates as they practise hunting skills, young kids practising when they play house, have snowball fights, and tussle with one another. We learn best through play.

Play is also our key to the fountain of youth.

> You don't quit playing because you grow old,
> you grow old because you quit playing.

Play floods our system with a biochemical cocktail, decreasing our pain, allowing us to feel good and driving us to connect deeply with others.[12] When we smile, laugh, and play, we demonstrate the state of psychological safety. When we're playing, our brain is functioning optimally and we're learning, problem-solving, and behaving at our best. A healthy active brain is part of a strong immune system and more connected to others. Research shows ATL organisations have friendlier workspaces with less turnover. Team members are more likely to fulfil their promises, take bigger risks, spend less time on tasks, all while getting more done.[13]

Through habituation and repetition, ATL and BLT become unconscious and invisible to us, just like daily activities such as speaking a language, riding a bike, or driving a car. We do these things and yet we do them for the most part unconsciously. ATL and BTL additionally can be thought of as two distinct moods; and just like moods, they are:

- Contagious;[14]
- Easy to fall into and hard to get out of; and

---

12 Oxytocin is what makes connecting to others feel good, earning its nickname 'the love hormone'. Endorphins are nature's morphine allowing us to feel less pain; babies are highly 'endorphogenic' (feel less pain) because they fall a lot as toddlers. Dopamine is the kick we feel from winning, getting promoted, finding someone special, and from being addicted to anything, including winning. Our serotonin balances out giving us emotional balance and cortisol levels decrease when we feel less stressed.

13 Aghina, Wouter, et al. "The Five Trademarks of Agile Organizations." *McKinsey & Company*, 22 Jan. 2018, www.mckinsey.com/capabilities/people-and-organizational-performance/our-insights/the-five-trademarks-of-agile-organizations.

14 This is best illustrated when we put two happy people together and they get happier, and we put two anxious people together and they get more anxious. Moods are contagious.

- Change with appropriate and intentional input.

I would like to highlight this with a metaphor about taking a shortcut. If you would, imagine walking through an area of dense forest, as you look for a shortcut to the next town. Hacking at branches and clearing away dead trees, you make slow and often unsteady progress, moving forward then backtracking and trying a new way. After a few hard days of travel, you pop out of the forest right near the village, just as you had hoped. You return using the same path, making much better time on the return. You tell a few of your friends about the shortcut. They make better time because they can follow your footprints. In time, more people learn about it, with a few travelling on horseback, and the trail naturally widens. Next, local townsfolk take it upon themselves to cut down a few of the bigger trees and move some big boulders that were blocking the way, allowing oxen to pull carts and people to walk side by side. The trail becomes a known way to the next village. A few years later, the township decides to pave the trail, allowing the newly invented automobile safe and clear passage to the village. Not long later, the trail is widened so cars can travel in both directions. Years after that, the two-lane paved road becomes a multi-highway with tall berms on each side guiding rainwater to the sewer and blocking the traffic noise from nearby communities. Anytime you try to deviate from the multi-lane highway, it becomes very difficult because of the steep berms on each side. This is a great metaphor for navigating ATL/BTL.

In the beginning, we aren't good. We are slow, we make mistakes, and we are clumsy. Just like being the first ones blazing a new trail through the forest, we are clueless and unclear about the direction. This is why we don't want to learn new things. We believe we are not safe, and the last thing we want to do when we believe we aren't safe is to use up precious time and resources to learn something new. BTL relies on old habits, old beliefs, and old mindsets.

The wider the trail gets, the more people end up using it, the more people end up using it, the easier it becomes to navigate. After the trail gets paved over, travel becomes even easier and faster and very few people get lost. Once it becomes a multi-lane highway with high berms running along both sides, traffic can travel at ridiculous speeds, and nothing short of intentional focus and conscious effort can get you travelling in a different direction. When we spend time in any mood, be it ATL or BTL, or anxiety, joy or sadness or … it becomes easy to do and hard to get out of.

Next, I would like to share two stories to ground these ideas and principles.

MAJOR HAPPY

I was facilitating a multiple year resiliency and trauma training for front-line combat soldiers. It was some of the hardest facilitation I have ever done as most attendees came in BTL because successful Army combat teams are usually sceptical, wary of outsiders, and always on high alert. I am a third-generation Air Force veteran, a branch of the military that didn't garner much street cred from boots on the ground because we were usually supporting combat missions from a safe distance away, while the Army took the casualties. Most of the 7,000 brigade members were between 19–35 years old. They all had either Iraq OIF (Operation Iraqi Freedom) or Afghanistan OEF (Operation Enduring Freedom) battle experience and many were on their third, fourth, or fifth combat tour. Frequently, I was confronted with: "With all due respect sir, why should I listen to you? You're 50 years old and from the Air Force and you have never seen combat." Even though it made people laugh, the challenge was also a relevant point. Respect and attention were never freely given, which was why the mood in the room was always serious (remember when I said that BTL doesn't want to learn?). Participants usually came in looking the same—arms folded, shoulders rounded forward, and not moving much. There are good and valid reasons for this. First was the desire to be the smallest target possible. Second, the posture reflects the miles of heavy rucking,[15] and lastly, hunkering down in a Humvee or other transport vehicle, sliding down below the windows so you were protected by the armour plates in the doors. Being in with so many contracted, traumatised, and often angry participants made the work exhausting. Until one day…

…we were told that that day, we would be working with a unique platoon. A highly decorated platoon that inflicted severe damage to the enemy, while having the lowest casualty and injury rate in the 3,500-person brigade, and the highest reported morale. When this platoon entered the training room, the effect was palpable. They were light and jovial, even laughing a bit. There were some injured soldiers (men and women) in the room and even they seemed to be smiling and alert. The commander, an Army Captain, entered the room to "Atten Hut! Officer in the room!" The 65 men and women quickly snapped to attention, moving as one, executing flawless skill and precision, honed by months of drills on the parade grounds, learning to move, breathe, and think like one living breathing organism. "Circle up and take a knee." Silently and smoothly, the platoon reformed around him and dropped to one knee, all eyes locking on him. "Listen up, I know you might have heard this training is a joke. Some called it a Lamaze class." A murmur of a chuckle travelled through a sea of camouflage. "The people who share those rumours have not been through this training. I know these gentlemen and the quality of their training. I want you to put aside everything you've heard, and I want you to really pay attention. Can we do that?" Heads nodded sincerely. "Can I get a Hooah[16]?" With one voice, the room responded with Hooah! "Okay, let's

---

15 Marching with heavy packs and rifles usually in harsh terrain.

16 In the Army culture, 'Hooah' is a war cry whose roots go back generations and it's a code word to be 'in' or in agreement.

take our seats." Silently they stood up, filling the seats in the room, every face looking to the front, eyes bright with curiosity.

When I opened my part of the training—the Neuroscience of Stress—I made a sweeping statement: "Everybody has some amount of stress." Immediately, several hands shot up all over the room. I pointed to a young corporal in the front row. He politely said, "I disagree with you, sir." I smiled, in perhaps a slightly condescending way. He kept on, "I understand you are saying that everyone in this room has some amount of stress and I agree, except for Major Happy." There were cries of "Hooah" and "Major Happy! Major Happy!" All hands were pointing to the back of the room where a man in desert camouflage fatigues stood up to impromptu applause. He was smiling broadly and looking around at the members of his platoon. He was in his early thirties, an easy six foot tall, dark-skinned with muscles that rippled like a cat, and comfortable being in the centre. I could see a half dozen grey hairs at his temple, and a small gold cross inlay on his front tooth that flashed when he smiled, which was most of the time. His voice was deeply resonant with a strong friendly southern twang. He stood relaxed and in command. Every eye in the room was on him, clearly, he was a respected leader within the team. I asked, "Is that true?" He said, in a very down-to-earth way, "Yes sir, that's true." There was such a look of genuine calm in his unwavering eyes that I put the training on hold to ask him a couple of questions.[17]

"What is your role on the team?" I asked. He replied, "12-Bravo[18], sir" I continued, "I must ask the obvious. I see you are a Sergeant 1st class,

---

17 Our five-man team's broad directive was to increase resiliency and morale amongst front-line combat platoons and he was the poster child of a self-regulated human being. I needed to know how he was able to achieve such a remarkable outlook.

18 12-Bravo is a Combat Engineer, the one responsible for engineering the safety of his troops as they travel into a theatre zone, as they engage the enemy and as they return home. A soldier became a 12-Bravo not by rank but by respect of those around them.

yet people call you Major Happy?" He laughed, genuinely, saying: "I pretty much don't like it. I tried to shut it down cos it feels like I'm impersonating an officer. But once our Captain started calling me Major Happy, I knew there wasn't too much I could do about it." Everyone in the room hooah-ed and laughed, shouting that he would always be known as Major Happy! I kept on: "How can you say you don't have stress as a combat engineer?" He said calmly, "I guess the good Lord ain't ready for me yet. I've had to write 42 incident reports[19] both in OEF and OIF. Too many times, good men to my immediate right and left have been killed while I came out with nothing worse than cuts and bruises. In OEF, I woke up to a six-foot long, unexploded Katyusha rocket with four pounds of high explosives, buried half in and out of the ground so close to my barracks door that I had to walk around it to get to the mess hall. The Lord has had many opportunities to take me. I am at peace. I know I am here for a reason. Everybody in this room knows how precious and uncertain life can be. I aim to enjoy life as much as possible. The more people who follow me the better." Applause rippled across the training room. Another soldier spoke up, "Even when bullets are slapping the walls around us, Major Happy would be whistling and joking with us, making us feel safe." Another soldier said, "When we are inside the wire[20], everything becomes a game. Major Happy always has us doing something—platoon barbeques and volleyball tournaments, where the loser must do KP[21] for a week. If it's not that, it's the weekly music and talent show where the winners get a day of R&R in Dubai." The room was filled with a chorus of enthusiastic Hooahs because their compound was dry and there was plenty of booze

---

19 Incident reports are filled out after each enemy engagement.

20 A term meaning the guarded and fortified perimeter of a compound or combat unit within a battle theatre. A safer area to recuperate, shower, send emails home, and stay a bit connected to the outside world.

21 Short for kitchen patrol. Anyone on this duty would be involved in kitchen and dining hall tasks which ranged from cooking, cleaning, preparing the dining areas and even serving food.

in Dubai. He continued, "Oh, and by the way, did I mention soooo much volleyball?" At this the whole room clapped, laughed, hooah-ed, and pretended to be annoyed by rolling their eyes and groaning.[22] We really needed to resume the training so I thanked Major Happy and asked if, before he sat down, he would answer one more question. The gold cross in his tooth flashed and he said, "Yes, sir, of course." So, I asked, "Why so much play?" He thought for a moment, "As a psychologist, you probably know this inside and out. When we all play as a team, when we all laugh together, when I can see my people smiling, we make better choices. I believe in my heart this is why we take fewer casualties and how we recover faster after we take a hit. I make *playing at the edge* my mission because it is critical to our thriving in such a demanding place." Applause and Hooahs of confirmation resounded in the room as he took his seat.

Insight Discussion

- A group that shares smiles, laughs, and plays is living in psychological safety. Where do you see that here?
- Group movement creates entrainment, this is why militaries have always marched. Breathing together also creates entrainment, which is why militaries also call cadence as they march. It's an intentional way to move and sound and breathe in unison. Where does this entrainment show up in the story?
- What are your thoughts on the relationship of play to fewer casualties/faster recoveries?

---

22 Barrett, Lisa Feldman. *How Emotions are Made: The Secret Life of the Brain.* Boston, MA, Mariner Books, 2018. According, the field of collective neuroscience, a group laughing at the same time shows limbic resonance and neural entrainment.

THREE TIMES

At 27 years old, my next client is the youngest director of leadership development (LD) in this company's 120-year history. Alexi is a rising star, Iranian by birth, with long black hair and a model's poise. She was hired right out of college, and this was her first job. In only six short years, she found herself leading several senior teams. Because of her rapid ascent and knowledge of the company, she was selected to facilitate a two-day meeting between her company and a smaller company that had a patent they were interested in. My job was to train her to facilitate difficult conversations in the moment. The patent in question was essentially 3D printing of living tissue, and Alexi's company was exploring DNA and RNA technology that made cancer easier to target and kill. They were exploring a possible merger with a focus on, first, modifying the 3D printed tissue, making it tastier to cancer cells than the human host tissue. And second, they wanted to see if they could use 3D printed tissue as a delivery mechanism for their DNA/RNA technology, thereby making the cancer cells that eat it, easier to kill. The opening of day one of negotiations wasn't going well; everyone was BTL. The smaller company didn't want to open their patent to scrutiny and the possible parent company wasn't convinced how close they were to market.

At the end of the first morning break, it was evident things weren't going well. There were people not participating in activities or the focus groups. Looking around the circle, it was easy to see most everybody had their arms folded, heads were looking down at their feet, or they were on their phones. They seemed suspicious and uncomfortable. No one wanted to go first.

After sending the group to break, Alexi and I huddled in the back talking about options. She said, "What do we do now? This isn't going well at all."

I said, "I know how to fix this but it's going to take a lot of courage." She said, "I'm interested." I said, "When they come in from break, as soon as they have sat down and are comfortable, ask them to get up and move to another chair." She said, "That's going to get the energy changing a little bit." I agreed. "The next one's a little bit harder," I told her. "After they sit down for the second time, once they are comfortable, coffee is down on the ground, laptops put away, ask them to gather their things and find another seat." Alexi said slowly, almost uncertainly, "Okay, that is not too complicated." I said, "The next one's going to take a lot of courage and you need to stand your ground. Once they've sat down and gotten comfortable, pause for effect, and then ask them to get up for the third time and find another seat." Alexi looked at me wide-eyed and said, "They're going to think I'm crazy!" I said, "That's the point. You've got to break the mood in the room. Better that they think you a bit wacky than be thinking the next two days are going to be a waste of time." I could see a bit of worry creep in. After all, almost everyone in the room was: (a) male and (b) twice her age. Slowly, she started to smile, "I guess we don't have anything to lose. And I love it when things get edgy. Let's do it!"

Alexi called them in from break and asked them to take a seat. It was clear the mood hadn't changed a bit. People were not speaking to each other, busy on their phones, and not engaged in any meaningful way. As most people sat down, you could hear a heavy sigh. As soon as they were comfortable, she stood in the centre of the room and said, "Thank you. Now, everybody, please get up and find another chair." People looked around a little bit to make sure they had heard her right. Slowly they mumbled and grumbled and resentfully got out of their chairs, walked over, got another chair, and sat down, although this time with fewer sighs. As soon as the coffees were on the ground and laptops were safely put away, she stood quietly, taking in a deep breath. Everybody was looking expectantly at her. She said, "Thank you. Now, will everybody standing and please find another seat?" This time, people looked at her and said, "What? Really?" They weren't sure what to think and eyebrows were going up a little bit, and I think I saw a hint of a smile at more than one spot in our circle. As people got up and walked across the room, this time, the buzz in the room was completely different. People were laughing and asking each other if this was really happening, trying to confirm the sanity of this young female facilitator. It took a couple of polite requests from her before people sat down.

Standing at the centre of a lot of attention, she was relaxed. Her confidence was amazing to witness, and I could see now why she was so well regarded. The pause felt like an eternity to me; in reality, it may only have been 8 or 10 seconds, before she said, "Okay, now everybody, get up and find another seat." The room burst into genuine ATL laughter. A voice on the far side, cried, "Mutiny!" The room stood up facing a common enemy, shouting and laughing like pirates, calling for her to walk the plank! God as my witness, Alexi jumped up on a chair so she was the tallest object in the room and got the room to be quiet, which wasn't easy. And then she shouted in her best pirate voice, "I will walk the plank just as soon as you scurvy dogs take your new seats." The room cheered, releasing so much pent-up energy. I saw people laughing to the point of crying. Standing tall and proud on her chair, Alexi turned and flashed me a happy thumbs up!

By the time people sat down, which took a full 10 minutes, everyone was smiling and paying attention, and not one phone was out. Everybody was curious for what was next. Alexi asked the room, "Is it okay if we pick up where we left off before break?" As one, the group spoke a clear yes, their engagement evident by the depth of the conversations that followed. So much progress was made that by lunchtime, it was clear they weren't really competitors, and a merger was not the most mutually beneficial plan. Committed to keep exploring options, the group pitched in and sourced other ideas and options. In a very few short hours, they reached a mutually beneficial agreement. The smaller company would open the patent to print living tissue unconditionally to the larger company. And the larger company would loan two bio engineers, to start up using their RNA and DNA technologies. We ended a day early. Everybody was happy, the mood was bright, and the group dinner was full of laughter and joy. Alexi was honoured at the next all-hands meeting for successfully guiding a positive outcome from a tenuous situation.

Insight Discussion

- What was the importance of everyone seeing Alexi as a (friendly) enemy?
- Why was changing seats three times so important?
- How did everyone speaking and shouting like pirates, get the group ATL?

TOOLS/IDEAS TO MOVE ATL

One way to move ATL is to change your body shape into something that is not contracted and tense (BTL).

- Stretch your arms up over your head. Breathe deep, breathe slow, lift your eyebrows up and smile. Try being angry with your hands up in the air and a smile on your face. It's next to impossible.
- Alternatively, drop your shoulders, turn your head slowly from side to side. Keep your breath in sync, one breath with each rotation. Breathe in and out solely through your nostrils. Repeat for 7 to 10 breaths.

Another way is to surround yourself with people who are ATL. Moods are contagious and ATL and BTL are both moods:
- Go to a comedy club;
- Pick up pickle ball;
- Go ballroom dancing;
- Walk in nature;
- Listen to radically happy music; and/or
- Spend time with children playing.

> "Time spent playing with children is never time wasted."
> Don Lantero

Finally, remember that going BTL is a stress response where we believe there is a ninja, tiger, or armed combatant nearby and all predators eyes track movement. Moving as little as possible, we breath shallow and move less, we tend to scrunch into a contracted state to attract less attention. To reverse this and go ATL, we must remember two things:
- Breath facilitates movement.
- Movement is the antidote to fear.

If you are BTL and you don't want to be, try on one of these ideas:
- Breathe deeply, slowly and repeat often.
- Set an alarm to go off every 15 minutes, 30 minutes, or hour. Stretch your arms up over your head and smile each time the alarm goes off.
- Get up and walk around the building (or block), breathing on purpose the whole time.
- Go do something different.

Chris Balsley, MA, LPC, PCC
Author of *Stop Controlling, Start Leading*
and Lead Somatic Trainer with TCP

As a US Air Force veteran, corporate trainer and leadership expert, Chris has learnt that accountability, focusing on cost-based analysis, and driving outcomes are crucial to success in any venture. As a psychologist, coach, mentor, and parent, he also sees the other side of the coin where he witnesses first-hand, the unreasonable power that mindfulness, a focus on personal health, and a commitment to ritual has on nurturing great leaders. He is deeply grateful for the healing and success he has experienced in multinational organisations, high performing teams, bold leaders, and within his own family.

Besides being a senior trainer with the global Newfield Asia family, Chris is an external consultant with Mckinsey & Company/Aberkyn (2019–present). He holds certifications in: Leadership Circle 360° Profile (LCP), iEQ9 Enneagram Assessment, Agile program management, Gestalt coaching ,and Aberkyn's Lotus flagship leadership offering.

He is also the author of *Stop Controlling, Start Leading: 27 Secrets for Leadership at Work, Home and Play*.

Chris is in Boulder, Colorado where he lives with his wife of 30 years and their two lovely daughters. He loves practising yoga with his whole family, trampoline wall-running, playing Afro-Cuban music, and making the occasional piece of furniture.

CHAPTER 6

The Interplay of Body and Emotions in Ontological Coaching

Movement and Dance in Ontological Exploration

Beatriz Garcia

INTRODUCTION

Rafael Echeverría defines ontological coaching as an exploration of 'the way of being of individuals and social entities', emphasising how our embodied experiences shape our actions and interactions.[1] This holistic approach enables coaches and clients to uncover and transform underlying patterns of behaviour and perception.

---

[1] Echeverría, Rafael. *Ontología del lenguaje [Ontology of Language]*. Santiago, Chile, Dolmen Ediciones, 1994, p. 22.

I am Beatriz Garcia Madrigal. At 23 years old, I got my first managerial position and for 20 years, I worked in a corporate environment in different areas and various companies, which allowed me to learn many aspects of the corporate world. On the other hand, I learnt dancing practically since I was born and throughout my life, dancing has been one of my main passions. At the age of six, I studied ballet for a couple of years, and I remember myself enjoying, with lots of passion, any kind of dancing at home and also how much I loved to perform in my school festivals. I have invested time to learn different styles of dancing from Mexican folklore to Latin rhythms, tango, and a little bit of hip-hop.

In 2008, when I started to study in the ontological coaching programme at the Newfield Network with Julio Olalla in Colombia, the first thing that I noticed was that the programme was going to integrate the body and emotions, like everything else previously in my life. I was willing to learn for my own practice but also, I wanted to share this with other people.

I met Mark Hemstedt in 2011 in Boulder, Colorado and a few months after meeting him, he invited me to participate in the sales process of the programme in Singapore for eight weeks. I was having a call with Joylynn Seetoh to coordinate my trip when she had a fantastic idea. "Let's have a workshop for the Hong Kong alumni," she said. After accepting this proposal, we agreed that it would be interesting to do the same workshop for the alumni of Jakarta and those of Singapore.

I was excited to do these workshops and it was a wonderful experience. I never imagined that this moment was going to be the starting point to participate as a somatic trainer in the ontological coaching programme with The Coach Partnership that is offered every year and that has students not only from Singapore but from all over Asia, Europe, Australia, and America.

Ontological coaching, in addition to exploring linguistic distinctions, explores how our bodily sensations and emotional states profoundly impact our personal and professional lives. This chapter will delve into foundational theories, practical applications, and personal experiences, highlighting the integration of body awareness and emotional intelligence in ontological coaching, enriched by insights from corporate and dance backgrounds.

THE ROLE OF EMOTIONS

Emotions play a crucial role in leadership effectiveness and organisational dynamics. Daniel Goleman's concept of emotional intelligence highlights the importance of self-awareness and emotional regulation for effective leadership and personal growth.[2] In ontological coaching, understanding emotions involves integrating bodily awareness to enhance decision-making, communication, and team dynamics.

Throughout my corporate career, I had observed how leaders' emotional states influence team morale and performance. Drawing from my experience in dance, I have guided executives and students to explore how their physical presence and movement patterns reflect their emotional states. By integrating dance-inspired exercises into coaching sessions, coachees gain insights into their embodied responses to stress and learn strategies to foster resilience and empathy with others.

In the ontological approach, emotions are regarded as integral components of our human experience that profoundly influence how we perceive, interact with, and respond to the world around us, particularly within family and corporate settings. Developed by thinkers like Rafael

---

2 Goleman, Daniel. *Working with Emotional Intelligence*. New York, NY, Bantam, 1998.

Echeverría, this approach posits that our 'way of being' includes emotional dimensions that significantly shape our behaviours, relationships, and overall effectiveness in personal, family and organisational contexts.

Ontology emphasises the importance of emotional awareness—understanding and acknowledging our own emotions as well as those of others. In corporate environments, leaders who are emotionally aware can better manage interpersonal dynamics and cultivate a culture of authenticity. This fosters trust and transparency among team members, leading to more effective communication and collaboration.

On the other hand, emotions play a crucial role in decision-making processes and leadership effectiveness. Leaders who are in tune with their emotions can make more informed decisions, considering not only rational factors but also emotional implications. For instance, a leader who recognises the fear or uncertainty within a team during times of change can address these emotions constructively, thereby enhancing team morale and productivity.

Furthermore, ontological principles emphasise the development of emotional regulation skills—the ability to manage and modulate one's emotions effectively. This is vital in high-pressure corporate environments where stress and uncertainty are commonplace. Professionals who can regulate their emotions are better equipped to maintain composure, think clearly, and adapt to changing circumstances, thereby contributing to organisational resilience.

I would like to share some examples I have experienced regarding emotions:

- **Leadership Development**

Integrating emotional intelligence training into leadership programmes helps executives cultivate self-awareness and empathy. Practical exercises might include learning and practising the breathing pattern of each basic emotion to be able to recognise their collaborators' emotions all the time, role-playing scenarios where leaders practise empathetic listening or delivering feedback with sensitivity. Such skills enhance leadership effectiveness by fostering a supportive and inclusive work environment.

During leadership workshops and our coaching programme in Singapore, integrating dance techniques like body awareness exercises or improvisation drills can help participants enhance their emotional intelligence and leadership skills. For example, practising non-verbal communication through movement can improve one's ability to convey empathy and understanding in one's interactions with classmates, family members, and colleagues at the workplace.

- **Conflict Resolution**

Emotionally intelligent approaches to conflict resolution focus on understanding the emotional dynamics at play. Techniques such as active listening, perspective-taking, and mediation help to de-escalate tensions and promote mutual understanding among conflicting parties. This fosters a culture of cooperation and problem-solving within teams.

- **Team Building**

Activities that encourage emotional expression and connection can strengthen team cohesion. For example, workshops incorporating creative arts, mindfulness practices, or team-building exercises like trust falls to promote open communication and trust among team members. Incorporating dance-inspired team-building activities, like group choreography sessions, has proven effective in fostering collaboration and boosting team morale. These activities encourage creativity, improve communication, strengthen interpersonal relationships among team members, collaboration, and collective problem-solving abilities.

By integrating ontological principles into corporate practices, organisations can create environments that nurture emotional intelligence and resilience. This holistic approach acknowledges the importance of emotional well-being and its impact on individual and organisational performance. Leaders who embody ontological principles are not only better equipped to manage their own emotions but also better able to inspire and support their teams through periods of change and challenge.

As a passionate practitioner in dance and movement who navigates the ontological coaching and corporate world, I have experienced first-hand how the ontological approach to body and emotions can profoundly impact both personal development and professional interactions.

From my personal experience integrating dance and movement in corporate life, I have noticed the following:

- In my role as somatic trainer and coach, I have utilised my background in dance to enhance emotional expression among students and team members. For instance, during team meetings, classes, or workshops, I have incorporated movement exercises inspired by dance techniques to break the ice, encourage creativity, and foster a more relaxed and open atmosphere. These sessions not only helped team members feel more comfortable expressing their ideas but also promoted a sense of camaraderie and collaboration; and as I have mentioned to our students, what does not pass through the body, does not pass.

- In a situation where team dynamics were strained due to conflicting priorities, I applied principles from my dance training to facilitate conflict resolution. By guiding team members through improvisation exercises that required them to mirror each other's movements and emotions, I helped foster empathy and understanding. This approach enabled team members to recognise the underlying emotions driving their disagreements and find common ground more effectively.

- As a leader, maintaining a strong presence and emotional regulation are essential. Drawing on my experience in dance, where control over movement and expression is key, I have developed practices to manage stress and maintain composure during high-stakes presentations or negotiations. Techniques such as breathing exercises and mindful movement have been instrumental in enhancing my ability to lead with confidence and clarity.

- Personally, my journey as a dancer has taught me the value of self-awareness and authenticity. By embracing my unique movement style and incorporating it into my professional identity, I have been able to cultivate a leadership presence that is grounded in authenticity and emotional resonance.

EMBODIMENT AND EMOTIONAL AWARENESS

Embodiment theory, as discussed by George Lakoff and Mark Johnson, asserts that our bodily experiences profoundly shape our cognitive processes and emotional responses.[3] In different environments, cultivating emotional awareness through embodied practices such as dance and

---

3   Lakoff, George, and Mark Johnson. *Philosophy in the Flesh: The Embodied Mind and Its Challenge to Western Thought.* New York, NY, Basic Books, 1999.

movement enhances people's ability to access deeper insights and facilitate meaningful personal and professional transformation.

My background in dance from a young age has been instrumental in my coaching practice. Dance taught me to listen to my body's cues and express emotions through movement. This foundation allows me to offer clients and students alternative ways to explore their bodies and emotions authentically. Whether guiding a team through team-building exercises, coaching an individual executive, or an ontological coaching programme student, I leverage dance-inspired techniques to facilitate self-discovery and enhance emotional intelligence.

Embodiment and emotional awareness play pivotal roles in shaping our daily lives, both personally and professionally. These concepts highlight the interconnectedness between our physical experiences and emotional states, influencing how we perceive, react to, and navigate through the world.

In personal contexts, embodiment refers to being fully present in our physical bodies and aware of our sensations, emotions, and inner experiences. This awareness allows us to better understand ourselves, manage stress, and cultivate resilience. For example, practising mindfulness or yoga can enhance embodiment by encouraging us to pay attention to bodily sensations and emotions, leading to improved self-regulation and overall well-being.

In the workplace, embodiment and emotional awareness contribute significantly to leadership effectiveness, team dynamics, and organisational culture. Leaders who are attuned to their own emotions and those of others can inspire trust, foster collaboration, and navigate challenges with empathy and clarity. This emotional intelligence is crucial for making informed decisions, managing conflicts constructively, and promoting a positive work environment where employees feel valued and understood.

In my role as an ontological coach and somatic trainer, I have facilitated processes that enhance embodiment and emotional awareness, drawing from my own experiences and practices:

- I incorporate mindfulness techniques into coaching sessions to help clients develop greater awareness of their bodily sensations and emotional responses. For instance, guiding coachees through meditations or mindful breathing exercises can increase their ability to stay present and regulate their emotions during stressful situations at work or in personal life. From the ontological approach we called this 'centering'.

- Utilising somatic experiencing techniques helps coachees or students explore how their emotions are stored and expressed in their bodies. Through gentle movement or body-awareness exercises, for body dispositions, they can release tension, process past experiences, and develop a deeper understanding of their emotional patterns.

- During coaching sessions, I use role-playing and visualisation exercises to help coachees explore different perspectives and emotional responses. For example, simulating a challenging conversation with a colleague allows clients to practise empathetic listening and assertive communication while being aware of their own emotional triggers and responses.

Personally, integrating embodiment and emotional awareness has transformed how I approach challenges and interactions. By developing a stronger connection between my physical sensations and emotional states, I have become more attuned to my needs, more resilient in facing adversity, and more effective in managing relationships both at home and at work.

TECHNIQUES AND PRACTICES

Practical techniques in ontological coaching leverage body awareness to foster emotional resilience and authenticity. Richard Strozzi-Heckler's work on embodied leadership emphasises somatic practices to cultivate presence and adaptive capacity in leadership roles.[4]

In a corporate coaching engagement, I integrated dance-based exercises to help a leadership team improve collaboration and communication. Through rhythmic movements and partner exercises, team members explored trust-building and emotional expression in a non-verbal context. This embodied approach enabled the team to deepen connections and enhance cohesion, leading to improved productivity and innovation. I also use these body and awareness exercises, emotional regulation and somatic coaching techniques and practices in our ontological coaching programme classes and in one-to-one sessions like:

- Guide students and coachees through a body scan meditation to help them become aware of bodily sensations and tensions. This practice encourages mindfulness and fosters a deeper connection between mind and body.

- Incorporate movement exercises inspired by dance techniques. Encourage students and coachees to explore different movements and notice how each movement affects their mood and energy levels. This helps in enhancing body awareness and emotional expression.

---

4   Strozzi-Heckler, Richard. *The Leadership Dojo: Build Your Foundation as an Exemplary Leader*. Berkeley, CA, Frog Books, 2007.

- Teach coachees and students various breathing techniques (for example, diaphragmatic breathing, box breathing) to help them to regulate emotions and reduce stress. Breathing exercises can be integrated into coaching sessions to help them ground themselves and manage emotional responses effectively.

- Guide coachees and students through progressive muscle relaxation techniques to release physical tension and promote relaxation. This practice supports emotional regulation by allowing them to notice and release bodily stress that may be linked to emotional states.

- Utilise somatic experiencing techniques to explore how past experiences are stored in the body and impact current emotions and behaviours. Help coachees and students release trauma or tension held in their body through gentle movements or guided visualisations.

- Integrate expressive arts such as dance, drawing, or writing into coaching sessions to facilitate emotional expression and exploration. These creative methods provide alternative ways for clients to process emotions and gain insights into their inner experiences.

- Use role-playing exercises to help coachees gain different perspectives on challenging situations. Encourage them to embody different roles or personas to understand varying emotional responses and potential outcomes.

- Draw on corporate client experience as an executive to provide practical insights and examples related to leadership challenges, decision-making under pressure, and team dynamics. Use body and emotional awareness techniques to enhance leadership presence and effectiveness.

- Incorporate movement-based practices and techniques derived from dance to help coachees and students embody confidence, express emotions authentically, and improve non-verbal communication skills.

- Leverage my life coaching expertise to create a supportive environment where coachees feel safe to explore and express their emotions. Help them to be in their centre to tailor techniques which can accomplish their individual needs and goals.

CASE STUDIES AND EXAMPLES

These following case studies illustrate how ontological coaching principles translate into tangible outcomes for some clients (coachees) who are leaders in different organisations.

Case Study 1
Leadership Development and Emotional Intelligence

Scenario
A senior executive, struggling with managing a diverse team and navigating organisational change, seeks coaching to enhance leadership effectiveness.

Proposal
- Body Awareness
  Through body scan meditations and movement exercises, the executive learns to recognise the physical manifestations of stress and emotional triggers.
- Emotional Regulation
  Techniques like breathwork and progressive relaxation help the executive to stay grounded, be centred during challenging situations, and regulate emotions effectively.

Result
The executive develops a stronger leadership presence, improves decision-making under pressure, and fosters a more inclusive team environment by demonstrating empathy and emotional intelligence.

Case Study 2
Conflict Resolution and Team Dynamics

Scenario

A project team experiences recurring conflicts due to miscommunication and differing priorities, affecting project timelines and team morale.

Proposal
- Body-Centred Techniques
  Using somatic experiencing and role-playing exercises, team members explore how their emotions and bodily responses contribute to conflict dynamics.
- Emotional Expression
  Expressive arts therapy sessions, including movement and creative expression, encourage team members to communicate feelings and perspectives non-verbally.

Result

Team members develop greater empathy, communication skills, and trust. They learn to recognise and address emotions constructively, leading to improved collaboration, problem-solving, and project outcomes.

Case Study 3
Personal Development and Well-Being

Scenario
An individual seeks life coaching to enhance personal well-being and overcome limiting beliefs that hinder career advancement.

Proposal
- Body-Mind Connection
  Integrating dance-inspired movement and mindfulness practices into coaching sessions helps the client reconnect with their body and inner emotional landscape.
- Exploration of Inner Dialogue
  Using different techniques, the client explores and resolves internal conflicts and self-limiting beliefs.

Result
The client experiences increased self-awareness, emotional resilience, and clarity in goal setting. They develop strategies to manage stress, enhance self-confidence, and make empowered decisions in their personal and professional life.

Case Study 4
Team Building and Collaboration

Scenario
A newly formed cross-functional team in a technology company struggles with communication barriers and lacks cohesion, affecting project progress.

Proposal
- Embodied Leadership
  The team leader introduces movement-based team-building activities inspired by dance and improvisation. Team members engage in exercises that promote trust, cooperation, and non-verbal communication.
- Emotional Expression
  Expressive arts therapy sessions allow team members to express emotions and share personal stories through movement and creative expression.

Result
Team members develop a deeper understanding of each other's strengths and communication styles. They improve collaboration, problem-solving, and collective decision-making, leading to enhanced project outcomes and a more cohesive team dynamic.

Case Study 5
Stress Management and Wellness Programme

Scenario

A corporate wellness initiative aims to reduce employee stress levels and improve overall well-being.

Proposal

- Mind-Body Integration
  The wellness programme incorporates mindfulness practices, yoga sessions, and breathwork exercises to help employees manage stress and enhance emotional resilience.
- Somatic Coaching
  Individual coaching sessions include somatic experiencing techniques to release tension and trauma stored in the body, promoting emotional healing and well-being.

Result

Employees report reduced stress levels, improved focus, and increased job satisfaction. The company observes higher productivity, lower absenteeism, and a positive shift in workplace culture towards greater support and empathy among colleagues.

Case Study 6
Career Transition and Self-Discovery

Scenario

An executive undergoes a career transition and seeks coaching to explore new opportunities and align personal values with career goals.

Proposal

- Body-Mind Connection
  Coaching sessions integrate reflective practices, journaling, and body-awareness exercises to help the executive reconnect with personal values and aspirations.
- Role Play
  Role-playing and visualisation exercises were used to explore different career paths and potential challenges, encouraging the executive to embody different roles and perspectives.

Result

The executive gains clarity on career priorities, discovers new interests, and develops a proactive action plan. They navigate the career transition with confidence, leveraging emotional intelligence and self-awareness to make informed decisions and pursue fulfilling professional opportunities.

Case Study 7
Leadership Presence and Authentic Communication

Scenario

A senior manager seeks coaching to enhance leadership presence and improve communication skills in cross-cultural settings.

Proposal

- Presence Practices

  Coaching sessions focus on embodied presence techniques, including posture, breath awareness, and vocal modulation exercises, to enhance leadership presence and charisma.

- Cultural Sensitivity

  Role-playing scenarios and cross-cultural communication workshops help the manager develop empathy and adaptability in diverse workplace environments.

Result

The manager improves their ability to connect authentically with team members and stakeholders from different cultural backgrounds. They demonstrate enhanced emotional intelligence, build trust, and effectively lead initiatives that promote inclusivity and collaboration across the organisation.

From my perspective, these case studies illustrate that integrating body and emotions in personal and professional contexts offers numerous benefits like:

- Individuals become self-aware, more attuned to their own emotions, bodily sensations, and thought patterns, enabling them to make wiser decisions and manage challenges effectively.

- Team dynamics are improved by improving communication, collaboration, and cohesion among team members.

- Individuals build stronger connections, improve communication in their relationships, foster empathy, and resolve conflicts more constructively in interpersonal interactions by understanding and expressing emotions authentically.

- Clarity in career goals, enhanced decision-making, and successful transitions.

- Techniques like mindfulness, breathwork, and movement help individuals regulate stress, maintain composure under pressure, and sustain high performance over time. Better stress management, increased resilience, and improved overall health and wellness

By focusing on the interplay between body and emotions, individuals can cultivate greater self-awareness, emotional intelligence, and resilience, leading to enhanced personal growth and professional success.

CHALLENGES AND CONSIDERATIONS

Challenges in integrating body-emotion awareness in corporate coaching include cultural differences in communication styles and scepticism towards somatic approaches. Drawing from personal and professional experiences, coaches adept in ontological principles tackle these challenges by creating inclusive coaching environments that honour diverse perspectives and foster trust and psychological safety.

Incorporating body and emotions in coaching and business contexts presents both challenges and considerations that are important to navigate effectively.

Challenges

- In corporate environments focused heavily on rationality and tangible outcomes, there may be scepticism or resistance towards integrating practices that involve the body and emotions. Some executives—and sometimes, some of our programme students—may view these approaches as unconventional or unrelated to their personal or professional goals.

- Coachees and some of our students often operate under tight schedules and demanding workloads. Finding time for activities like mindfulness, movement exercises, or expressive arts therapy may be perceived as a challenge due to competing priorities.

- Not everyone may be comfortable with or have experience in practices that involve emotional expression or physical movement. Overcoming initial discomfort or scepticism requires sensitivity and effective communication about the benefits of these practices.

- Quantifying the impact of body and emotions integration on organisational outcomes such as productivity, teamwork, and employee well-being can be challenging. Demonstrating return on investment (ROI) and tangible benefits to stakeholders may require thoughtful evaluation and metrics that align with business objectives.

Considerations

- Recognise that each individual and organisation is unique. Tailor body and emotion integration practices to align with organisational culture, individual preferences, and specific goals. Flexibility in approach ensures relevance and acceptance.

- Educate coachees and students about the benefits of body and emotion integration through evidence-based research, case studies, and pilot programmes. Building a compelling narrative around how these practices contribute to their development, can foster buy-in.

- Ensure that practices involving emotional exploration and physical movement are conducted in a safe and respectful manner. Respect boundaries and individual comfort levels and provide clear guidelines on confidentiality and consent.

- Embed body and emotion integration into existing programmes, wellness initiatives, and team-building activities. Create a supportive environment where these practices are normalised and encouraged as part of ongoing professional programmes.

- As a somatic trainer, leverage my personal experience to demonstrate the benefits of body and emotion integration. Sharing personal anecdotes and success stories to inspire others and showcase the practical relevance of these practices in enhancing leadership effectiveness and personal well-being. I recommend, if possible, to integrate this practice.

RECOMMENDATIONS

Integrating awareness of body and emotions into daily life and professional settings can significantly enhance well-being, personal growth, and professional effectiveness. Based on my insights from ontological coaching, here are practical recommendations for individuals to cultivate this integration:

- Incorporate daily mindfulness practices such as meditation, deep breathing exercises, or body scan techniques to become more aware of bodily sensations and emotional states. Start with short sessions and gradually increase duration to build consistency.

- Engage in regular physical activity that connects you with your body, whether through dance, yoga, walking, swimming, jogging, or any form of exercise you enjoy. Movement helps release tension, improve mood, and enhances body awareness.

- Keep a journal to reflect on your emotions, experiences, and the physical sensations associated with them. Writing can help clarify thoughts, identify patterns, and track personal growth over time.

- Explore creative outlets such as art, music, dance, or writing to express emotions non-verbally. Creative activities foster emotional release, self-expression, and provide insights into inner experiences.

- Develop self-care rituals that prioritise your physical and emotional well-being, such as a bedtime routine, healthy eating habits, or regular relaxation practices. Consistent self-care supports overall resilience and enhances emotional regulation.

- Incorporate regular emotional check-ins throughout your working day. Take brief moments to pause, identify your current emotional state, and consider how it may influence your decisions and interactions with others.

- Practise techniques to enhance your leadership presence, such as maintaining mindful posture, using intentional breathing before important meetings, and actively listening to colleagues' non-verbal cues.

- Integrate body and emotions-aware activities into team-building exercises or workshops. Consider activities that encourage movement, expressive arts, or mindfulness to foster team cohesion, trust, and creativity.

- When faced with personal or professional conflicts or challenging conversations, practise active listening and empathetic communication. Pay attention to both verbal and non-verbal cues and consider how emotions and body language impact the exchange.

- Seek out professional development opportunities that include aspects of emotional intelligence, body awareness, and ontological coaching. Attend workshops, seminars, or coaching sessions that focus on these skills to continually grow and adapt in your career.

Be intentional about integrating awareness of body and emotions into your daily routines and professional practices. Set specific goals or intentions related to emotional well-being and body awareness, and revisit them regularly.

Stay curious and open to learning more about emotional intelligence, somatic practices, and their impact on personal and professional growth. Explore new techniques and approaches that resonate with your interests and goals.

As you cultivate greater awareness of body and emotions, be a role model for others in your personal and professional circles. Share your experiences, insights, and the benefits you have observed to inspire and encourage others to embark on their own journeys of integration.

By implementing these recommendations, individuals can enhance their self-awareness, emotional and interpersonal effectiveness both in their daily lives and within professional contexts. This holistic approach not only promotes personal well-being but also contributes to creating more empathetic, supportive, and productive environments in workplaces and communities.

CONCLUSION

Ontological coaching offers a transformative pathway for personal and professional growth by integrating body awareness with emotional intelligence. From my perspective, through dance and movement practices, individuals cultivate resilience, authenticity, and adaptive capacity, pursuing sustainable success and fulfilment in their careers and personal lives, navigating challenges more easily.

The ontological approach to emotions in the corporate world emphasises its significance in shaping organisational culture, leadership effectiveness, and interpersonal dynamics. By fostering emotional awareness, regulation, and authenticity, companies can create environments where employees feel valued, understood, and empowered to contribute meaningfully. This approach not only enhances individual well-being but also drives organisational success by fostering a culture of emotional intelligence and collaborative excellence.

Combining my dance expertise into my coaching role has not only enriched my professional practices but also empowered me to contribute uniquely, on the one hand, to our ontological coaching programme students and coachees who are really committed to deeply learn more about themselves; and on the other hand, to corporations and their organisational dynamics. By applying ontological principles to embrace emotions, foster empathy, and enhance communication through movement, I have seen first-hand how this approach can transform persons and corporate cultures and elevate leadership effectiveness. I facilitate processes that empower coachees and students to deepen in their self-awareness, enhance their emotional intelligence, and cultivate meaningful connections with themselves and others. Ultimately, leveraging dance as a tool for emotional expression and interpersonal connection has been instrumental in creating a more inclusive, collaborative, emotionally intelligent, personal, and familiar workplace environment.

From my perspective, this holistic approach not only enhances personal well-being but also fosters a more empathetic and inclusive organisational culture where individuals can thrive and achieve their fullest potential.

Integrating body and emotions in coaching and business environments requires navigating challenges related to perception, time constraints, skill levels, and measurement of impact. By considering these challenges thoughtfully, however, and addressing them with tailored approaches, ethical considerations, and a focus on building trust and buy-in, organisations can effectively leverage these practices to enhance leadership capabilities, foster teamwork, and promote holistic well-being among employees. As a coach and business executive with a dance background, my unique perspective and experiences can play a pivotal role in advocating for and implementing these integrative approaches to drive positive outcomes.

***

All my gratitude to The Coach Partnership—Marcus, Sari, Tini, Chris, Terrie, Kat, Carol, Chalmers, Amanda, Clémence, Rina, Nabil, Eya, and Mark—for creating this space where each of us can share their experience and perspective on the ontological coaching approach to serve all our students, coachees, and clients in a much more comprehensive way.

Beatriz Garcia, PCC
Lead Somatic Trainer with TCP

Beatriz is a passionate people-driven professional with the ability to develop strong professional worldwide relationships. She specialises in Somatic, Personal, Teams, Executive, and Conscious Business Coaching by leveraging on people's talents and abilities to produce meaningful work and a balanced life while inspiring them to turn their visions into reality.

Beatriz started her coaching practice in 2009. She has more than 30 years of diverse experience spanning from strategic business planning to sales management, organisational development, leadership development, change management, multicultural team effectiveness, as well as executive, personal, and somatic coaching for individuals, national, and international companies in Mexico, South America, Europe, and Asia. She works with her clients to identify strategies to promote leadership and organisational efficiency and to design actions and practices to achieve their goals.

She holds a degree in Business Administration from the Autonomous University of Baja California, Mexico. She has a Certificate in Business and Management Administration from Harvard University, and an MBA in Business Administration with a major in Leadership from DUXX in Monterrey, Mexico.

CHAPTER 7

Mind Over Body or Body Over Mind

Unleashing the Ultimate Gift that Lies Within Us

Rina Ho

INTRODUCTION

Mind over body. Most of you may be familiar with this saying—the ability to muster mental strength and willpower to overcome the body's limitations, enduring challenges, hardships, failures, and breakthroughs. I grew up with this all my life.

"Ouch! Daddy, don't use that needle to dig out the splinters in my hand!" I was 12, already messing around at my grandpa's timber factory where my dad had worked nearly all his life. He would say, "Oh, it's nothing.

See?" He plunged the needle straight into his hand, thick with callouses. "Doesn't hurt at all. It's all in your head."

Whenever I had a fall or bumped my head, my dad would tease, "See, you made a hole in the ground (or the wall)." I would stop sobbing and giggle.

Pain became subjective. I think I became addicted to the idea of 'no pain, no gain'. Familiar, right?

I trained hard in sports—from track and field to cross-country running, winning biathlons and triathlons. Each time, crossing the finish line and collapsing was a sign that I had given it my all; that is, 100%.

Similarly, at work, everything had to be 100% perfect—whether it was a business strategy, a report, or a presentation. This mindset was further entrenched in a micromanaging organisation that thrived on flawless details and hard work, often quoting 'blood, sweat, and tears' as the path to rewards.

Even when I received feedback about having a high pain tolerance, I took it as a compliment, unaware that my body was protesting until it started burning inside my stomach, unexpectedly crippling me. For once, I felt my mind was no longer in control of my body. There was no warning; the pain would come suddenly—a sip of orange juice, a gin and tonic, a spicy snack, or right in the middle of a competitive race—triggering excruciating pain that sent me to the emergency room each time. I remember one instance at the Hong Kong airport, being rolled like luggage across the departure hall to the emergency clinic. I was perplexed. Had my mind finally succumbed to my body?

This chapter shares my journey of discovering the mind-body connection and finding the right balance in life, work, and coaching.

MIND OVER BODY

When I was racing competitively, I often visualised the route to winning. As a triathlete, I would repeatedly envision my transitions and see myself overcoming fatigue by focusing on the competitors ahead and overtaking them one by one. The thrill of overtaking and progressing to the front excited me and generated adrenaline, like a burst of endorphins propelling me forward towards the finish.

Neuroscience shows that when you visualise performing an action, your brain activates neural networks similar to those used when you actually perform the action. This reinforcement of pathways makes the action more familiar and automatic. Several athletes, including Tiger Woods, Michael Phelps, Serena Williams, and Muhammad Ali, practise visualisation by mentally rehearsing and visualising positive outcomes. This technique helps them prepare, remain calm, and achieve remarkable success. Translating this to personal life, Oprah Winfrey spoke about the power of visualisation and intention setting in her life to overcome her challenging upbringing and achieve her goals. Inventors like Albert Einstein and Nikola Tesla were known to visualise their inventions entirely in their minds from start to finish before building them.

On the other hand, visualisation of failures can prepare one to identify potential pitfalls and obstacles, develop strategies to avoid them, and rehearse how to address them. Most importantly, it helps one stay calm if and when they occur. The first thing they teach you in inline skating is to always wear your guards and learn how to fall—lean forward, drop the knees, then your palms, and stretch out like a prostrate move to the ground. This is practised repeatedly until it becomes an automatic response when you fall.

In the corporate world, the goals of a company, department, and team guide the journey and motivate employees. When goals are set too low, there is no challenge, no stretch, no learning, and no motivation. Conversely, when goals are set too high, they feel out of reach, leading to a sense of helplessness and a tendency to give up or just do whatever the boss says. It is crucial for leaders to help employees visualise how the end point looks and feels. Leaders can guide their teams to visualise not only the successful achievement of their goals but also the potential obstacles they might encounter along the way and prepare contingency plans.

Connecting to a larger purpose serves as a powerful motivator in both corporate and coaching settings, enhancing the effectiveness of visualisation practices. When individuals can see how their daily tasks and long-term goals contribute to a broader mission, their engagement and commitment increase. For instance, in a corporate setting, aligning personal and team objectives with a company's mission—like adidas's mission of 'Through sports, we have the power to change lives'—can ignite passion and drive. Similarly, in coaching, helping clients visualise how their efforts and personal growth align with their deeper values and aspirations can foster a profound sense of purpose. This connection to purpose not only motivates individuals to overcome challenges but also instils a sense of fulfilment and meaning in their journey. When encountering setbacks or resignations, reminding them of their compelling desire and strong sense of purpose through visualisation can pull them back on track, reigniting their determination and focus on achieving their ultimate goals. Leaders and coaches can then coach them to shift their perspective of the issue at hand and explore new possibilities.

A powerful metaphor I experienced and use in my coaching is this '50-cent coin'. Let me explain.

I had just graduated and was going for an interview, but in a very bad state as my parents had had a huge fight the night before. Unfortunately (or fortunately), the interviewer sensed it, paused the interview, and asked, "Are you alright?" I burst into tears, feeling embarrassed and helpless, and apologised.

He said, "You see that 50-cent coin on the table? Close one eye and hold it up against the other open eye. What do you see?"

"Huh?" I said, sobbing and bewildered. "I see only the coin."

"Okay, now extend your arm. What do you see?" he asked.

"Well, I see a small coin, the office, lights, and you," I paused, drowning in realisation. The size of the issue (coin) can be big or small, depending on how we perceive it. Seeing it so big had blocked my vision from my purpose that day (interview)..

I didn't get the job, but it was a necessary intervention and a lifelong learning moment. I remind myself of it often and share this with my friends and coaches as an intervention.

You might have heard of the placebo effect. The story behind the term is said to have come from Henry Beecher, a medical doctor who graduated from Harvard Medical School in the early 1930s, who faced a critical situation during World War II. A wounded soldier needed surgery, but Beecher had run out of morphine. In a remarkable improvisation, he injected the soldier with a saline solution (salt and water) to match the body's fluids. Surprisingly, the soldier relaxed, and Beecher carried out the operation without anaesthesia. This moment made Beecher realise the power of the mind over the body, and he dedicated his career to studying the placebo response.

Whether this story is fact or myth, one cannot deny the power of our mind.

BODY OVER MIND

While body over mind is less commonly said, I came to realise its importance the hard way. What was my excruciating stomach pain, described in the introduction, trying to tell me?

I was finally hospitalised for seven days, suspected of having Crohn's disease. After numerous tests—X-rays, endoscopy, CT scans, barium tests, etc.—they found nothing. The doctor who grew to know me concluded it was irritable bowel syndrome, a gastrointestinal disorder. During my discharge, she pulled me aside and said, "Girl, my observation is that you work too hard, you exercise too hard, you play too hard … everything you do is too hard. You are not listening to your body. Your gut is telling you to stop, slow down, and take a break!"

That's when I stopped racing, sadly, to avoid the trigger. Then I came to realise that the body has a voice—my inner voice.

Ever heard of "I've got a gut feeling?" The gut has its own nervous system known as the enteric nervous system—often referred to as a 'second brain'—with a system of neurons that can operate independently of the brain. The bidirectional communication system between the gut and the brain called the gut-brain axis, involves various pathways, including the vagus nerve, which transmits information from the gut to the brain. This connection can influence emotions, decision-making, and overall mental health. Gut feelings are closely related to intuition, which involves the brain's ability to synthesise vast amounts of information rapidly. Intuition draws on both conscious and unconscious knowledge, allowing individuals to make quick assessments and decisions.

How does listening to your body's gut feeling or intuition play a significant role in leadership and coaching?

- **Relationship Building and Psychological Safety**
  Reading social cues and sensing the emotional states of coachees, team members, peers, stakeholders, and bosses can enhance the ability to provide support, resolve conflicts, build rapport, and create a safe and trusting environment to facilitate open communication and deeper conversations. Intuitive leaders often inspire trust, credibility, and confidence.

- **Deepened Insight and Risk Management**
  Sensing underlying issues that are not explicitly expressed helps to address root causes rather than symptoms. In rapidly changing environments and situations, gut feelings enable adaptive leadership and coaching to pivot strategies, navigate uncertainty and emotions, and be more effective when combined with data and noticing patterns for well-rounded decisions.

- **Facilitating Growth**
  Sensing when to ask open questions or challenge current assumptions can encourage new perspectives. Intuition provides a sense of when to push staff or coachees out of their comfort zone and when to simply listen, providing support and encouragement

It might seem that some people have stronger intuition than others. In my case, I suppressed my gut feelings until a breakdown occurred. Why?

Cultural factors play a significant role. Societal norms often prioritise intellectual and cognitive achievements over physical awareness. The relentless pursuit of the next medal, A-grade, promotion, compliment, or branded outfit is a familiar narrative for many. Work cultures that glorify long hours and high productivity further diminish the importance of listening to the body's signals, reinforcing the mind's dominance over physical well-being. Growing up, discussing feelings about success or failure was uncommon for me, as vulnerability was seen as a weakness. Different cultures respond uniquely to a simple 'How are you?', revealing varying levels of openness and emotional expression.

Past incidents and trauma can also lead to a disconnection from bodily sensations. Growing up with fighting parents, I built an emotional wall to protect myself from being hurt, which may have prevented me from loving fully in my relationships, out of fear of further pain and disappointments. Additionally, limiting beliefs about not being good enough drove me to relentlessly pursue success while suppressing my inner voice. For some, a negative body image leads to avoiding drawing attention to their physical selves, using this as a defence mechanism to cope with feelings of inadequacy or discomfort.

Education systems, particularly in Asia, often place a strong emphasis on scholastic achievements through tests and exams, often at the expense of physical education, music, outdoor play, and body awareness. There is a lack of awareness on how engaging in these activities fosters self-awareness, understanding, a deeper connection with the environment and oneself, and the development of social and emotional skills, stress coping mechanisms, and overall mental well-being.

Technological advancements in the digital age have heightened our focus on mental tasks while decreasing physical activity. Desk jobs, screen time, and sedentary lifestyles make it easy to ignore the body's needs and signals, as we are constantly mentally stimulated. This shift has led to a further disconnect between mind and body, underscoring why we often ignore our body and gut feelings.

But all these factors are real and exist in our lives, influenced by our upbringing, environment, school systems, work culture, etc. We cannot just ignore them. Embracing and accepting them is necessary, and the first step is awareness. So how can we activate this awareness, of feelings, emotions and what is present around us?

The most powerful tool exists within us—our breath. It's the first thing we take when we enter this world and the last we give when we leave this life. We often underestimate the profound power of breathing to control and influence our moods, emotions, and actions. By controlling our breath—breathing faster or slower—we can influence our heart rate and, consequently, our mental state in any circumstances.

Before an important presentation to a large audience or sprinting off the blocks in a race, my heart pounds so loudly I can hear it. My breath becomes short and quick, and my body stiffens. This is an automatic fight, flight, or freeze reaction. Bodily feedback profoundly affects mental states, with 80% of vagus nerve fibres transmitting messages from the body to the brain. Taking deep, intentional breaths can rapidly influence brain regions that regulate behaviour, thought, and emotion. Combining this with somatic movements—such as adopting an open body posture and placing my palm over my heart—slows and calms me down. This leads to a noticeable lowered vocal tone and helps regulate nervousness before a presentation, allowing me to focus on the message and the audience. Athletes use similar techniques, shaking up their bodies and jumping up and down to loosen up before a race, helping them focus on optimal performance and be in The Zone—a supreme focus state, seeing nothing but the sprint to the finish line.

In yoga, meditation, psychotherapy, or hypnosis sessions, breathwork is the starting point to slow down and feel, initiating mindfulness. Being present and attuning to my inner voice helps me understand what it is telling me and provides valuable information and choices.

In coaching, I find that centering myself through breathwork and adopting an open body position enhances my ability to listen and be attuned to my body sensations, making me 100% present for the client. Similarly, as a leader, whether coaching a team or working with peers, this approach elicits better engagement and buy-in, builds relationships, and creates followership.

It is, however, an ongoing conscious effort. If you tend to sit forward at the edge of the chair like I do, consciously push back until your back touches the chair and tilt your pelvis inward to avoid arching forward. To open up the chest, first relax your shoulders and feel your shoulder blades squeezing together, pulling your shoulders backward. Feel both feet on the ground, take deep breaths, and open your palms. I often invite my coachees to try this, and it's amazing to hear their feedback on how it changes conversations and mood.

I started volunteering for the Red Cross Home for the Disabled where I was told that most patients cannot speak and hearing constant shouting and screaming is normal as their way of expression. I was surprised to find a hospital-like setting rather than a home and many patients were strapped to their beds to prevent falls or self-harm. The loud screams were initially shocking and I felt a mix of helplessness and sympathy, as well as gratitude for my own blessed circumstances. With no other volunteers to consult and busy nurses, I took a few deep breaths, set my intention to be curious, and began colouring with a patient who struggled to hold the colour pencils due to her deformed fingers. As I helped her finish her masterpiece, we both chuckled, and I felt a connection forming. My feelings of sympathy evolved into empathy and eventually into a genuine connection.

In the next bed, a fully-strapped young girl with completely disabled hands stared at us. Her big eyes showed fear initially and she looked away when I caught her eye. I took a deep breath, softened my eyes to express my feelings without a word. She could not smile but her eyes softened as if they smiled. It was a long silent gaze. That moment felt timeless, and my body, possibly through activated mirror neurons, experienced an incredible warmth and love. We communicated with our eyes and the energy we shared.

In Amanda Blake's *Your Body is Your Brain*, she emphasises the significance of tuning into our bodily sensations to access valuable insights and wisdom. She discusses how we sense with our entire bodies, through functions, such as mirror neurons, which allow us to sense and empathise with others' emotions and states.

I felt the power of tuning into my body to sense, feel, and set an intention. This experience highlighted the profound influence of the body over the mind, showing how our physical presence and embodied awareness can transcend verbal communication and create deep connections. Ontologically, it reinforced the understanding that our bodies are not just vessels for our minds but active participants in our interactions, shaping our experiences and relationships in powerful ways

WHAT NOW? MIND OVER BODY OR BODY OVER MIND?

This journey into embodied awareness has been a significant discovery for me. I started practising breathwork, mindful meditations, and yoga, tuning into myself first to be centred or grounded before leading or coaching others. Just as in life-saving, if you cannot save or protect yourself first, you cannot save others. But what about the qualities of mind over body, which have their merits and purpose? How do I balance this?

It's about pausing and practising new habits to create awareness, leveraging the power of both mind and body, understanding how both connect and work together, to make wise, informed choices.

Covid days led me to take stock of my life, prompting a call to return home after 17 years working abroad to be closer to my ageing parents. After 20 years of loyal service and delivering results, I was devastated when no roles were available for a transfer home, forcing me to resign with a 'mediocre' package. Did I make the right choice? Why do I feel conflicted and distressed? I sought help from a psychotherapist who introduced me to Internal Family Systems (IFS), a psychotherapeutic approach developed by Dr Richard C. Schwartz in the 1980s. IFS is based on the concept that the mind comprises multiple sub-personalities or 'parts', each with its own perspectives, feelings, memories, and roles. The goal of IFS therapy is to help individuals access their core Self and harmonise these internal parts, leading to healing and personal growth.

The three parts in IFS are:

- **Exiles**

  Parts that carry painful emotions and memories, often resulting from past trauma or negative experiences. They are typically hidden or suppressed to protect the individual from psychological pain.

- **Managers**

  Proactive parts that seek to control and protect the individual by managing day-to-day activities and avoiding situations that might trigger the exiles. They strive to maintain order and prevent distress.

- **Firefighters**

  Reactive parts that try to extinguish emotional pain by engaging in impulsive or destructive behaviours, such as substance abuse or self-harm, to provide immediate relief.

The Self is considered the true core of an individual, characterised by qualities such as compassion, curiosity, calmness, clarity, confidence, creativity, courage, and connectedness (the 8Cs). The Self is seen as the natural leader capable of healing and integrating the parts.

I learnt about how external factors and internal imbalances has stressed my system. I had been suppressing my Exile—the childhood experiences that led to a belief that I am not good enough. And my Manager worked hard to protect my perfectionist image, always striving for achievements to prove my worth, while my Firefighter overdid sports to release the tension. All this suppression led to burnout, sports injuries and ultimately, my irritable bowel syndrome. The therapist guided me to breathe, slow down, and to understand and acknowledge the different parts of me without any judgement. Self-compassion was key to embracing myself and with this awareness, I have more control and choices.

You might have watched the movie *Inside Out*, which is based on the IFS model, that provided a clever perspective on how different parts of our mind work together to make us unique. The film emphasises allowing various emotions to play equal roles in our lives. As coaches, we are not therapists, but a fundamental knowledge of psychology provides valuable insights in helping clients embrace who they are and move toward creating their future. Enhancing self-awareness of the various internal parts, recognising different voices, emotions, and motivations within them—each playing different roles—is crucial.

Similarly, ontological coaching focuses on exploring and transforming one's being—how we perceive, interpret, and interact with the world. As Marcus Marsden states in his book, *Start With Who*: "A map is useless until you know where you are now". While having a vision is essential, understanding who we are now is the starting point. By fostering a deeper connection with ourselves and cultivating calmness and curiosity, ontological coaching helps clients align with their authentic selves. This awareness is the first step toward self-leadership, regulating internal conflicts, and achieving personal and professional goals.

I had a client from China who constantly called me a teacher instead of a coach. He hesitated to speak up, considering it disrespectful to speak before his boss, and related goals to hard work and long hours, which led to burnout and severe neck pain, necessitating in a two-month medical break. Despite evoking this awareness, the comfort zone of doing what he was used to was too overpowering. It was heartbreaking to see him wearing a neck brace during our coaching sessions. The manager in me wanted to tell him to wake up and stop, but I centred myself, took a deep breath, and listened with empathy, sensing with my gut.

I had him try breathwork followed by a body scan. As I led him through the scan from head to toe, I allowed myself to feel and sense my heart contract. I then invited him to place his right palm on his heart. His tears began to roll, and I paused, holding the silence and space for him to immerse in his emotions. This led to a powerful breakthrough in transparency for him. He looked up, sharing that he finally understood how he had been focusing on others and protecting his perfect image through pleasing others, neglecting self-care and his own needs.

In our following session, I could tell that his being had evolved. He had been working on expanding his body and pausing to reflect before speaking. He even changed his daily outfit from suits, which created a contracted feeling for him, to smart casual shirts. His transformation felt like his once-filled cup had been emptied, allowing space for new perspectives and learnings.

Going back to my narration, it changed after these experiences. It felt as if my body had connected to my mind, signalling me to slow down and focus on what matters most to me—health, family, and a bigger purpose: to love and give. I made a conscious choice to resign, come home, spend quality time with family, fall in love, travel, indulge in learning and new experiences, and feel the joy of giving, especially through coaching. This does not mean 'happily ever after' as it takes a conscious practice to pause, feel, and have healthy conversations within myself to connect my mind to my body.

In summary, the mind-body connection is complex, and finding the right balance is key. While the mind can drive us to achieve great things, it is equally important to listen to our bodies and understand their signals. Intuition and gut feelings play a significant role in leadership and coaching, helping us build relationships, gain insights, manage risks, and facilitate growth. By integrating physical awareness into our daily lives and professional practices, we can achieve a more holistic approach to success and well-being.

Rina Ho

Executive Coach, Chief Evangelist

In her extensive 25-year career as a business and marketing professional, Rina is as passionate about meeting consumer needs as she is in coaching executives, especially women, to unleash their potential and build a purpose-led career.

Having shattered barriers, Rina crafted her professional journey with stints at Sony, Reebok, and adidas. Eventually, she assumed leadership of the largest business unit overseeing the Asia Pacific and Greater China markets, with proven track records of elevating revenue, market share, and brand equity.

Recognised as a positive catalyst, Rina excelled in steering diverse, multicultural, and multigenerational teams. Her leadership involved coaching and nurturing these teams into capable leaders, while supporting women to embrace strength from within.

Rina experienced a transformative breakthrough during her Newfield ontological coaching training—to integrate her drive and compassionate nature into a broader mission—*spreading lightness and purpose to others*. This transformation has led her clients to gain heightened self-awareness and confidence, fostering a sense of lightness and positivity in both their personal lives and professional journeys. She coaches clients from non-profit and multinational companies such as adidas, Siemens, Porsche, PETRONAS, and Dyson.

Having lived in Singapore, Hong Kong, and Shanghai, and with a penchant for globetrotting, Rina's passion for sports is evident. She finds joy in road and mountain biking, yoga, hiking, and dancing with an unwavering eagerness for new adventures.

Parenting Coaching

Nurturing Growth and Fostering Connection

Dr Katrina Gisbert Tay

Our journey as parents is not just about guiding our children but also growing together as fellow travellers on a shared path toward awakening and consciousness.

Parenting is a beautiful and challenging journey that touches the deepest parts of our hearts and souls. Raising little humans isn't for the faint of heart—it stretches our patience, resilience, and sometimes even our sense of self. Those who say it's easy may not fully grasp the weight of this role, or perhaps they've had the blessing of extra hands to lighten the load. As a medical doctor, executive and well-being coach, wife and mother of three—one young adult and two teenagers—I've survived the long days and felt how quickly the years pass. Few experiences bring you to the brink of exhaustion while filling your heart so profoundly.

Would I walk this path again? In a heartbeat.

Would I do some things differently? Absolutely.

Not out of regret but because I've learnt just how important it is to nurture my own growth, alongside my children's. Looking back, I wish I had found the emotional support I needed—spaces where I could reflect, process my feelings without judgement, and become more self aware. Raising my awareness and consciousness as a human being, not just as a parent, would have allowed me to be the parent my children truly needed rather than trying to mould them or fit them into the vision I held in my mind.

Parenting isn't just about raising our children; it's about evolving ourselves. I remember becoming so consumed by the role of 'Mother' that I lost sight of who I was. At the time, I thought sacrificing myself was the right thing to do, but now I see how that affected me and my family. In losing myself, I wasn't showing up as the best version of myself for them, either.

Embracing the parenting experience with a mindset of mutual growth and connection is essential. Our journey as parents is not just about guiding our children but also about growing together as fellow travellers on a shared path toward awakening and consciousness. Together, we grow, learn, and become our best selves, creating a nurturing and loving environment for our children to thrive.

The Coach Partnership ontological coach training programme greatly impacted my life and how I parent, so much so that we have pioneered a new coach training programme with experts in developmental psychology, neuroscience, and ontology. I will dive into ontological parenting and parent coaching as a supportive space for parents' personal growth and development. First, it's essential to discuss the history and evolution of parenting.

PARENTING IN THE MODERN AGE: EVOLUTION AND CHALLENGES

Parenting has evolved significantly over millennia, adapting to changes in societal structures, economic demands, and cultural expectations. In ancient civilisations, parenting was often a communal effort, deeply rooted in extended family systems and tight-knit communities. Children were raised in the proverbial village, with the help of extended family and neighbours, creating a network that shared responsibilities. Needs and wants were more straightforward, and life expectancy was a third of what it is now. The primary goal of parenting was to ensure that children survived in order to continue the family line and be an extra pair of hands to share the workload.

With the Industrial Revolution came unprecedented changes in how people lived and worked. The shift from agricultural lifestyles to urban environments introduced new stressors, including the demands of factory work, the fragmentation of extended families, and the relentless pace of life. The focus on survival and economic contribution meant that work and home life became distinct and separate spheres. This separation significantly altered the interaction between parents and children, as time and energy were often consumed by the need to provide financially. This is also when the traditional form of education came into existence, structured such that it allowed parents to work in factories and farms most of the day.

In contemporary society, advances in education and psychology have transformed parenting attitudes and mindsets. Parenting has evolved to become more holistic and child-centred, emphasising the child's emotional and developmental needs alongside their physical well-being. The rise of mass media and digital technology has provided unparalleled access to information, enabling parents to educate themselves on various parenting philosophies and practices. Additionally, the ease of communication and connectivity allows for the sharing of experiences and support among parents globally.

Despite these advancements, the expectation to achieve more with less has only intensified. Modern parents juggle multiple roles—partner, parent, income earner, caregiver to elderly parents, friend, housekeeper—while striving to provide the best for their children. This pressure can lead to heightened stress and a constant search for 'balance'. The challenges of the 21st century require parents to adapt continuously, often seeking new strategies and support systems to navigate the complexities of modern parenting. The integration of work and home life, facilitated by technology, has blurred boundaries, making it even more crucial for parents to find ways to manage their time and maintain a healthy family dynamic.

The pervasive belief that more is always better—more work, more achievements, more material possessions—has permeated every aspect of our lives. This mindset has also infiltrated parenting, leading to a relentless pursuit of perfection and an unending cycle of comparison and competition, reinforced by the constant presence of social media. Parents feel immense pressure to provide the best for their children while excelling in their careers and personal lives, leaving them feeling inadequate and exhausted. The result is widespread physical, mental, and emotional fatigue among parents. Burnout is on the rise, affecting even stay-at-home parents. The cumulative impact on our children and future generations is profound. Understanding these challenges is crucial in fostering empathy and support for parents.

Over the past several decades, family structures and values have also undergone significant transformation, reflecting broader social, economic, and cultural shifts. One of the most notable changes has been the increasing diversity in family forms such as single-parent households, blended families, same-sex parent families, and multigenerational households. Additionally, the role of women in society has transformed dramatically, with more women pursuing higher education and careers and dual-income households becoming the norm. This shift has necessitated a more equitable distribution of domestic responsibilities and parenting roles between partners. Mothers/mother figures, however, still bear most of the mental and emotional workload of the family.[1]

Family values have also evolved significantly. Today, there is a greater emphasis on individual fulfilment and personal growth within the family context. Parenting styles have shifted from authoritarian to more authoritative, democratic, and child-centred approaches, emphasising open communication, emotional support, natural consequences, and fostering independence in children. Additionally, there is a growing recognition of the importance of mental health and well-being for parents and children. The World Health Organization estimates that "1 in 4 people around the world suffer from a mental health condition, with a treatment gap of up to 90% in some countries".[2] These changes underscore the need for a broader societal push towards inclusivity, equality, and prioritising quality of life over rigid adherence to traditional roles and expectations.

---

1   Hogenboom, Melissa. "The Hidden Load: How Thinking of Everything Holds Mums Back." *BBC Worklife*, 18 May 2021, www.bbc.com/worklife/article/20210518-the-hidden-load-how-thinking-of-everything-holds-mums-back.

2   Kestel, Dévora. "The State of Mental Health Globally in the Wake of the COVID-19 Pandemic and Progress on the WHO Special Initiative for Mental Health (2019-2023)." *UN Chronicle*, 10 Oct. 2022, www.un.org/en/un-chronicle/state-mental-health-globally-wake-covid-19-pandemic-and-progress-who-special-initiative.

DISCONNECTION AND THE LOSS OF THE 'VILLAGE'

We live in an age where we are more connected than ever through digital means, yet increasingly disconnected in our physical and emotional lives. The proverb, 'It takes a village to raise a child', has lost relevance in many modern contexts. Individualisation and the breakdown of communal living have left many parents feeling isolated and unsupported. In the past, the extended family and community played a crucial role in child-rearing. Today, parents are often left to navigate the complexities of parenting on their own without the support of a close-knit community. Parents may be a child's primary caregivers, but a family does not exist in a vacuum.[3]

The belief that parenting should come naturally and instinctively only adds to the pressure. Some people think that parents should automatically know how to raise their children without seeking outside help. The truth, however, is that many parents struggle with the complexities and demands of modern parenting. This struggle often leads to increased stress, higher divorce rates, and mental health issues for both parents and children. The pressure to meet societal expectations without enough resources or support systems can worsen feelings of inadequacy and isolation, showing the need for more accessible and comprehensive parenting resources and community support. Understanding that seeking guidance and building a supportive network are important parts of effective parenting can help reduce these challenges and promote healthier family dynamics.

From my nearly decade-long experience coaching hundreds of individuals, I've seen first-hand that personalised and individualised parental

---

3   Reupert, Andrea, et al. "It Takes a Village to Raise a Child: Understanding and Expanding the Concept of the "Village"." *Frontiers in Public Health*, vol. 10, art. 756066, March 2022, doi.org/10.3389/fpubh.2022.756066.

support is often lacking. Despite the plethora of parenting books, blogs, and forums available, the advice offered tends to be solution-focused and prescriptive. While this can be beneficial in specific situations, it often acts as a temporary fix rather than addressing the core issues. This approach emphasises correction over connection and fails to address the fundamental need for parents' increased self-awareness and personal development, which are key to sustainable change.

SOLUTION-FOCUSED PARENTING AND PARENT DEVELOPMENT

Solution-focused parenting is often appealing because it promises quick and tangible results. Techniques such as time-outs, reward charts, and structured discipline strategies can offer immediate relief in challenging parenting moments. These methods, however, can be superficial, addressing symptoms rather than underlying issues. When parents rely solely on these techniques, they may find themselves in a cycle of constant correction without understanding the deeper dynamics at play. This approach can feel like a band-aid solution, providing temporary fixes but failing to foster long-term, meaningful change in the child's behaviour and the parent-child relationship.

In contrast, focusing simultaneously on parent development as much as solutions emphasises a more holistic, introspective, and reflective approach. It encourages parents to dive into their emotional landscapes, examining how their past experiences, beliefs, and current stressors influence their parenting. Much like the advice to put on your own oxygen mask first before assisting others, this approach promotes self-awareness and emotional intelligence, helping parents manage their children's behaviour while modelling healthy emotional regulation and resilience. Parents can break generational patterns by investing in their personal growth, healing their inner child, and cultivating a nurturing environment. This approach fosters a more profound connection, empathy, and understanding within the family.

THE CONTEXT OF THE PARENT

'Context' refers to the circumstances in which something exists or occurs, while 'content' refers to the issue or situation at hand. In his book, *Start With Who*, author Marcus Marsden asserts that "content is meaningless until the context is visible".[4] Understanding the situation (content) requires an appreciation of the underlying circumstances (context) that give it meaning and relevance.

In parenting, the context encompasses the parent's history, experiences, and conscious or unconscious beliefs that have shaped who they are today. This includes their upbringing, past relationships, cultural background, and personal traumas or triumphs. These elements form a complex tapestry influencing their parenting style, decisions, and reactions to various situations.

Without acknowledging this context, any advice or strategies provided to parents may fail to resonate or be effective. For instance, a parent who experienced a highly authoritarian upbringing may unconsciously replicate those patterns, even if they consciously wish to adopt a more authoritative and democratic parenting style. Similarly, a parent dealing with unresolved trauma might struggle with patience or emotional regulation, affecting their interactions with their child. By bringing the context to light, parents

---

4   Marden, Marcus. *Start With Who: Reveal the Hidden Power of Identity to Create a Purposeful Life.* Singapore: Candid Creation Publishing LLP, 2022.

can better understand their actions and behaviours, allowing them to make more informed and compassionate choices that align with their values and goals. This holistic approach enhances the effectiveness of parenting strategies and fosters personal growth and healing for the parents.

THE PAST IN THE PRESENT: THE INNER CHILD, TRAUMA, AND SHADOW SELF

**The act of parenting unfolds in the present,
yet it is deeply rooted in the past.**

The journey inward, towards understanding one's own childhood, is a foundational step in the quest to become a better parent. It demands courage, honesty, and vulnerability to confront and learn from the past. Ultimately, the greatest gift we can give our children is not perfection but presence—being fully aware, empathetic, and engaged parents, guided by a deep understanding of ourselves and the profound impact our own childhoods have on the way we parent. Diving into the parent's context involves exploring their inner child, trauma, and shadow self.

The Inner Child is a psychological concept that might be useful here. Experts say it's part of our subconscious that was shaped during our formative years. It wants to be nurtured and loved and yearns for acceptance and recognition. When neglected, it can make one feel disconnected and wounded. This part of the psyche holds the innocence, wonder, and creativity of our younger years but also the unresolved emotions and unmet needs. In the context of parenting, the Inner Child may show up as emotional reactions that seem disproportionate to the current situation, driven by past experiences. For example, a parent's frustration with a child's behaviour may stem from their own unmet needs for attention and validation during childhood. Our relationship with our Inner Child significantly affects how we interact with and relate to our children. How many of us have neglected that Inner Child, only to have it show up in rage or tears when we least expect it?

Our experience of trauma also impacts how we parent. Dr Gabor Maté, world-renowned expert on trauma, addiction, stress, and childhood development, states that "trauma is an invisible force that shapes our lives. It shapes the way we live, the way we love, and the way we make sense of the world."[5] Trauma refers to distressing or disturbing experiences that can have long-lasting psychological effects.

Some experts refer to the major life-threatening events that result in significant psychological distress as big 'T' Trauma, while smaller, more common events that are less intense but still do cause substantial emotional and psychological distress as little 't' trauma. These experiences can range from overt incidents like violence, abuse, or neglect to more subtle forms of emotional harm, such as persistent criticism or lack of affection. Trauma often leaves imprints on the subconscious mind, leading to patterns of behaviour and emotional responses that persist into adulthood. In the parenting context, unresolved trauma can manifest as overprotectiveness, anxiety, perfectionist behaviour, or difficulty in establishing healthy boundaries with children.

The Shadow Self is a concept introduced by Carl Jung, which refers to the parts of ourselves that we reject or do not acknowledge.[6] These aspects are often deemed unacceptable or undesirable by societal or personal

---

5   Maté, Gabor. "Trauma." *Dr. Gabor Maté*. drgabormate.com/trauma/.

6   Perry, Christopher. "The Shadow." *The Society of Analytical Psychology*, 12 Aug. 2015, www.thesap.org.uk/articles-on-jungian-psychology-2/about-analysis-and-therapy/the-shadow/.

standards, and as a result, they are pushed into the subconscious mind. The Shadow Self can include traits like anger, jealousy, and fear. When unaddressed, the Shadow Self can influence a parent's actions and reactions, sometimes projecting these hidden traits onto their children. For instance, a parent might criticise a child for being lazy, reflecting their suppressed feelings of inadequacy.

When parents explore these distinctions, they can gain insights into why they parent the way they do. Their history deeply influences the narrative they create. By accepting that the past is showing up in their present behaviours and mindsets, they can begin to heal past wounds, allowing them to respond to their children with greater empathy and patience. Acknowledging and addressing these can help parents break free from destructive patterns and create a more supportive environment for their children. This integration involves embracing all parts of oneself, leading to more authentic and conscious parenting.

Ultimately, by examining and integrating the inner child, trauma, and shadow self, parents can transform their past experiences into powerful tools for personal growth and positive change. This self-awareness and healing process benefits the parent and fosters a healthier, more nurturing relationship with their children.

THE ONTOLOGICAL APPROACH TO PARENTING COACHING

The main distinction of ontological parenting coaching is that it shifts the focus from merely addressing the child's behaviour to understanding and transforming the parent's inner world—increasing their awareness of their observer and the co-creation in their narrative. This approach emphasises the importance of the parent's context, as we all carry unresolved traumas and unmet needs from childhood, which influences how we are currently 'being' in the world. Ontological parenting coaching helps parents gain awareness and empowerment, allowing them to parent from a place of wholeness and presence rather than reactivity. This empowerment stems from living a life by design rather than by default, fostering intentional and mindful parenting.

Ontology raises questions about what it means to BE, how individuals perceive and construct their reality, and how these perceptions and constructions influence their interactions. When applied to parenting, these considerations encourage parents to reflect on their own and their child's existence in a deeply connected and purposeful way. It prompts an awareness of how a parent's understanding of being and relatedness affects their parenting style, the environment they create for their child, and the values they impart. It aims for connection rather than correction.

Consider a parent, Sarah, who often finds herself getting frustrated and angry when her pre-teen child, Alex, refuses to do his chores. Traditional parenting approaches might suggest techniques like setting strict rules or creating reward systems. By being more aware of her perspective and the way she sees the world, Sarah explores her reactions and emotional triggers. She realises that her frustration is not just about Alex but is deeply rooted in her own childhood experiences. Sarah remembers her own anxiety and punishment when she did not abide by her parents' strict rules. This led to her self-limiting belief that she is 'not enough', and that perfection and obedience is key. This unresolved trauma causes her to react strongly to Alex's resistance, as it unconsciously brings back feelings of her own inadequacy and neglect.

With this new awareness, Sarah starts to transform her parenting approach. She acknowledges her own emotional needs and begins to heal from her past traumas. Instead of reacting with frustration, she practises self-regulation techniques and approaches Alex with empathy and understanding. Sarah starts conversations with Alex and listens to his concerns without judgement. She also shares some of her own childhood experiences, creating a deeper connection and understanding between them.

As a result, Alex feels more supported and understood, leading to improved cooperation with chores and a stronger emotional bond with his mother. Sarah's shift from reactivity to presence allows her to parent from a place of wholeness and intentionality.

Ontology-based parenting coaching stands out among various parenting coaching philosophies due to its comprehensive and deeply reflective approach. The following are distinct in ontological parenting coaching:

- **A Focus on Being Rather than Doing**
  While many parenting philosophies concentrate on actions, outcomes, and behaviours—the 'doing' aspects of parenting, such as discipline techniques, educational strategies, and daily routines—ontological parenting coaching places a significant emphasis on the 'being'. This way of being shows up as the dynamic relationship between three areas of human existence—body, emotions, and language. Shifts in this way of being creates new perspectives and possibilities, creating transformative change.

- **Emphasis on Awareness and Self-Reflection**
  In the journey of parenthood, individuals are often confronted with the echoes of their own childhoods. The way parents react to the challenges of parenting, their methods of discipline, their capacities for patience and understanding, and even how they express love, are

all deeply influenced by their past experiences. Yet, their experience of the world is not the way the world is; it is just the way *they* see the world. We all see the world from our specific and unique point of view. Deep introspection helps parents understand how they can break cycles of ineffective behaviour to create a healthier environment for their children. This level of self-reflection is less explicitly emphasised in many other parenting philosophies.

● **Dynamic and Adaptive Approach**
Rather than prescribing a one-size-fits-all set of rules or guidelines, ontological parenting coaching is inherently dynamic and adaptive. It recognises that as individuals grow and change, their needs, relationships, and contexts also evolve. This approach allows for flexibility and change in parenting strategies, always addressing the deepest needs of both parent and child.

● **Fostering Connection Over Correction**
Ontological parenting coaching emphasises building strong, empathetic connections between parents and children rather than focusing solely on correcting behaviours. It encourages parents to understand their child's perspective and emotions, promoting a nurturing and supportive environment. This connection fosters trust and open communication, which is essential for healthy relationships and effective parenting.

● **Integration of Somatic and Emotional Awareness**
Integrating somatic and emotional awareness in ontological parenting coaching highlights the importance of the connection between how we show up in our bodies and the emotions that shape our narratives. This aspect is key to shifting one's Being, enabling access to more dispositions and empowering narratives that align with one's values and vision.

Embracing the Concept of the Legitimate Other

This acknowledges that each individual is a unique observer of the world, with their own perspectives, experiences, and ways of being that are inherently valid and legitimate. In the context of parenting, this principle encourages parents to recognise and honour the distinct individuality of their children, rather than seeing them as extensions or reflections of themselves. From an ontological perspective, the Legitimate Other is rooted in the belief that every person perceives and interprets the world differently. These differences are shaped by a myriad of factors, including personal history, culture, emotions, and beliefs. When parents fully embrace this concept, they acknowledge that their children are not simply mini-mes, but rather independent beings with their own unique ways of seeing and interacting with the world.

Systems Perspective

Ontological parenting coaching recognises that neither parent nor child exists in isolation but is part of a broader, interconnected web of relationships and influences created within a matrix of internal and external villages. From the close personal dynamics within the family to the larger societal and cultural contexts, every individual is shaped by their environment. This approach encourages parents to understand not just their own role in their child's life but also how their child's development is impacted by everything around them—their relationships, communities, and even societal norms and expectations.

This understanding aligns with Bronfenbrenner's Bioecological Theory, which states that various overlapping layers of experience influence human development.[7] For example, a parent's relationship

---

7   Tudge, Jonathan R.H., et al. "Uses and Misuses of Bronfenbrenner's Bioecological
     Theory of Human Development." *Journal of Family Theory & Review*, vol, 1, no. 4, Dec.
     2009, pp. 198–210.

with their child is directly influenced by their own upbringing, culture, and current social environment. Likewise, children are shaped not only by their parents but also by their schools, peers, community values, and the larger societal structures they grow up in.

This emphasises that parents must be aware of the broader systems affecting their family to raise well-adjusted and emotionally resilient children. This includes being mindful of how personal values, social norms, cultural expectations, and external influences—such as media or the modern village and community—can impact parenting choices and a child's development. By embracing this broader perspective, parents are empowered to make conscious, intentional decisions that support their child's growth within this interconnected system.

Ontological parenting coaching encourages a more holistic understanding of the parent-child relationship, reminding parents that their journey is not isolated but part of a much larger tapestry of influences that affect both who they are and who their children are becoming.

ONTOLOGICAL DISTINCTIONS

Ontology is the study of what it means to be human. The ontological model of Observer–Action–Result is a second-order model that focuses on the Observer's role in creating transformational change. Let's discuss what this looks like in the context of parenting.

Observer

In ontological coaching, the 'observer' refers to our awareness of how we perceive and interpret the world around us. Our narratives, the stories we tell ourselves, are crafted from our assessments of our experiences. In parenting, our observer encompasses our context, past, history, and experiences, shaping how we understand and interact with our children, partners, and caregivers.

As parents, our observer is influenced by our upbringing, cultural background, personal experiences, and the lessons we've learnt along the way. These elements form the lens through which we view ourselves, our children's behaviour, our partner's actions, and our family dynamics. Recognising that our own unique history shapes our perspective is crucial. It helps us understand that our reactions and decisions often reflect our internal narrative rather than an objective reality.

Equally important is recognising the observer in our children and spouse or partner. Each family member has their own context, unique experiences, and background that influence how they see the world. Our children's perceptions are shaped by their developmental stage, interactions with peers, and evolving understanding of their environment. Our partners bring their own histories, expectations, and emotional landscapes into the family dynamic. Awareness of these different contexts allows us to empathise and communicate more effectively.

The ability to access the 'balcony view' and the 'dance floor' is critical in ontological coaching and particularly relevant in parenting. The balcony view represents a reflective perspective, where we can observe our thoughts, emotions, and actions without immediate judgement. This view allows us to see the bigger picture, understand patterns, and gain insights into our behaviours and those of our family members. It's a space of observation and reflection, where we can pause and consider our responses before reacting.

On the other hand, the dance floor represents our active engagement in the moment-to-moment experiences of life. It's where we interact, respond, and participate in the dynamics of our family life. Balancing these two perspectives—stepping back and reflecting from the balcony, and then re-engaging with intention on the dance floor—is crucial for effective parenting.

We become more mindful and intentional when we apply this dual perspective in our daily interactions. For example, when a child throws a tantrum, the immediate reaction from the dance floor might be frustration or anger. Stepping back to the balcony view, however, allows us to see the tantrum in the context of the child's developmental stage, emotional state, or unmet needs. This broader perspective enables us to respond with greater empathy and understanding, addressing the root cause rather than just the behaviour.

Similarly, in our relationships with our partners, accessing the balcony view helps us recognise the underlying issues in conflicts or misunderstandings. We can see beyond the immediate argument to understand the emotional triggers and past experiences that might influence our partner's reactions. This awareness fosters more compassionate and constructive communication, strengthening the relationship.

Awareness of the observer and the observer's context for ourselves and our family members enriches our understanding and enhances our ability to connect and grow together. It encourages us to embrace a holistic approach to parenting, where we are not just reacting to situations but thoughtfully engaging with them, guided by a deeper awareness of our own and others' internal narratives.

Action

The expansion of the observer opens up a world of possibilities for action. In ontological parenting coaching, this expanded awareness allows parents to explore a broader range of actions rooted in sound scientific principles from developmental psychology and neuroscience. Parents can make more informed and effective decisions by understanding their own and their children's perspectives. They can see beyond immediate reactions and consider long-term impacts. For example, instead of reacting with frustration to a child's tantrum, an expanded observer might recognise it as an opportunity to teach emotional regulation. The expanded possibilities for action consider the developmental needs of their children, their own emotional states, and the specific context and content of the situation. This comprehensive view enables parents to choose actions that are not only effective but also nurturing and supportive.

Results

Here, results encompass more than just tangible goals. It is about aligning these goals with the parent and family's vision and values. It is about the experience that parents want to create with their children and their families.

For instance, instead of merely focusing on a child's academic success, a parent might identify a vision of nurturing a lifelong love for learning and curiosity. This shift in perspective emphasises creating a home environment that encourages exploration, celebrates questions, and values the learning process over grades. As a result, the child not only achieves academic milestones but also develops a passion for knowledge and a growth mindset.

Another example could be shifting from a goal of ensuring compliance and good behaviour to fostering a deep, respectful relationship based on mutual understanding and trust. Here, the desired result transcends obedience and creates a relationship where the child feels heard, valued, and respected. This approach nurtures emotional intelligence and strengthens the parent-child bond.

What Does This Look Like in Real Life?

Consider a scenario where a parent, Angela, finds herself constantly clashing with her teenage daughter, Mia, over homework. Angela's observer, shaped by her own strict upbringing, views academic success as paramount and interprets Mia's reluctance as defiance. Stepping back to reflect, Angela realises that her frustration stems from her own childhood pressures and fear of failure.

Angela shifts to the balcony view. From this vantage point, she sees Mia's struggle not as defiance but perhaps as a sign of being overwhelmed. With her expanded observer, Angela decides to take a different approach. Instead of reacting with frustration, she sits down with Mia and listens to her concerns. Angela learns that Mia feels pressured by the sheer volume of assignments and fears not meeting expectations.

Angela then collaborates with Mia to develop a structured yet flexible homework plan that includes breaks and stress-relief activities. She also shares her own experiences and reassures Mia that it's okay to feel overwhelmed and ask for help. This action not only addresses the immediate issue but also teaches Mia valuable skills in time management and emotional regulation. Instead of merely focusing on Mia completing her homework, Angela shifts her goal to nurturing a love for learning and building resilience. She creates an environment that encourages exploration and values the process over the outcome.

The results are transformative. Mia starts to approach her homework with less anxiety and more curiosity. She feels supported and understood, which strengthens her confidence and willingness to tackle challenges. The parent-child relationship improves as Mia feels more connected and valued.

By applying these ontological distinctions—observer, action, and results—Angela not only helps Mia manage her homework, but also fosters a supportive and nurturing home environment. This holistic approach enhances their relationship, promotes mutual growth, and aligns with the family's vision of learning and resilience.

CONCLUSION

The journey of parenting is complex and ever-changing. As we navigate the complexities of modern parenting, it's clear that supporting parents is essential for the integrity of society. As of this writing, the US Surgeon General has just issued a warning that "parental stress is an urgent public health issue". Studies have found that parents are facing more stress than at any other time in recent history.[8]

Ontological parenting coaching offers a valuable space for parents to cultivate self-awareness, resilience, and deeper connections, fostering a more fulfilling family life. By understanding our own narratives and by growing *with* our children, we can parent with more love and intention. This process is not about achieving perfection but about being truly present, authentic, and curious.

---

8   Office of the U.S. Surgeon General. *Parents Under Pressure: The U.S. Surgeon General's Advisory on the Mental Health & Well-Being of Parents*. Washington, D.C., U.S. Department of Health and Human Services, 2024. www.hhs.gov/sites/default/files/parents-under-pressure.pdf

The true gift we can give our children is our wholehearted presence—willing to learn and grow alongside them.

In embracing our own transformation, we set the stage for our children's growth. We break generational patterns, heal from past traumas, and create a nurturing environment where love and understanding flourish. This commitment to self-awareness and personal development ripples out, impacting our children and creating a legacy that will resonate through generations.

It is my hope that by applying these ontological distinctions to parenting, deeper relationships and connections can be fostered within family systems, as it has in mine.

**Dr Katrina Gisbert-Tay, PCC, NBC-HWC
TWP Partner, Executive and Well-being
Coach; Director of Health and Well-being
Coaching and Parenting Coaching**

'Dr Kat' is a medical doctor trained in Functional Medicine, an executive coach, integrative health coach, parenting coach, and coach supervisor with extensive experience in coaching executives and developing wellness programmes for multinational corporations across Asia. With a passion for human behaviour and development, she holds an honours degree in psychology and later pursued her medical degree. She then pursued her first coaching certification with Newfield Asia followed by a diploma in coaching supervision with Coach Supervision Academy and went on to become a Certified Integrative Health Coach with Duke Integrative Medicine in North Carolina.

As a National Board Certified Health and Wellness Coach—the first in Asia—Dr Kat created the Health Coach Certification Programme for TCP. She combines her background in coaching, psychology, and healthcare through integrative health coaching, working with clients to support their health and wellness goals. She envisions a shift in the dynamics of healthcare to be patient-driven and patient-centred, creating more effective and sustainable results. Dr Kat also advocates for coach training within universities and healthcare systems, aiming to empower individuals to take ownership of their wellness journey for lasting change.

Dr Kat leads the Parenting Coach Certification Program with a purpose and passion to reinvent parenting support worldwide. Her most important and challenging role started at 22 years old, when she became a parent whilst completing her medical education and training. She has been studying and applying different parenting approaches and methodologies for the past 22 years as well as supporting her coaching clients to become more conscious, self-aware, and intentional in their parenting. She advocates for a focus on connection rather than correction, with an unwavering belief in the potential of every parent to nurture, inspire, and lead with heart.

A Quest for Passion

What Are You Willing to Struggle For?

Sari Marsden

I love the French-Algerian philosopher Albert Camus's take on passion: "There is scarcely any passion without struggle."

The quotation holds a double meaning. It speaks of the deep connection between passion and struggle; that true passion often involves facing and overcoming challenges. On the one hand, it can be interpreted as a reminder to endure hardships and persevere in the pursuit of something meaningful. But on the other hand, it also suggests that passion can bring about suffering and pain. Perhaps this is why passion is not easily attainable—it requires both desire and determination to push through difficulties and confront obstacles. In essence, it is a constant battle between intense desire and the willingness to endure struggles for what we are truly passionate about.

As I have worked with many individuals and organisations, both in the context of corporate or personal growth, a recurring pattern has emerged. A sense of dullness and lack of fulfilment in their lives, coupled with the belief that finding their passion will bring them a newfound sense of vitality, they often declare, "I need to find my passion." This perspective suggests two assumptions:

- A passion exists somewhere external, waiting to be found.
- Finding this passion will automatically bring a sense of liveliness.

Is this, however, always the case? What if the truth is more complex?

This chapter explores the concept of 'passion' and its connection to struggle and compassion. What exactly is passion? Does it have a specific appearance or form? Is it something that can be discovered or ignited? Is it something that must be created or found? I will share my personal reflections on how coaching has helped me connect with true passion in my life, along with a case study of coaching for genuine passion and optimism. In this chapter, I also invite you to consider an alternative approach to understanding passion, an ontological approach that involves language, emotion, and the body. Ultimately, it is up to you to determine how you want to interpret and give meaning to passion.

At the end of this chapter, as with any classic coaching conversation, we may not find definitive answers, but perhaps we will uncover even more questions—and that's perfectly acceptable.

WHAT IS PASSION?

So, let's talk about passion. The word 'passion' comes from the Latin word *passio*, which means 'suffering' or 'enduring'. The Latin verb *pati* means 'to suffer' or 'to endure'. Originally, passion was all about enduring suffering. Over time, it evolved to mean any strong, intense emotion or feeling, not just suffering. Today, passion is all about a powerful enthusiasm or love for something, a deep, compelling drive. But despite this evolution, the idea of enduring strong emotions is still at the heart of what passion means.

The evolution of the word 'passion' can also be seen in other languages. For instance:

- In French, *passion* retains similar meanings as in English, encompassing both strong emotions and enthusiasm.
- In Spanish, *pasión* also mirrors the English usage, with emphasis on intense emotions and dedication.
- In German, the word for 'passion' is *Leidenschaft*. This term is a combination of *leiden* (to suffer) and *schaft* (a suffix that turns verbs into nouns). In German, the suffix *–schaft* is used to form nouns that denote a state, quality, or collective group associated with the root word. It is similar to the English suffix *–ship*, which is used in words like 'friendship' or 'leadership'. The suffix *–schaft* helps in creating abstract nouns that often describe relationships, qualities, or collective entities. *Leidenschaft* captures the deep, often intense emotional commitment to an activity, interest, or cause.
- In Bahasa Indonesia, the word for 'passion' is *gairah*. This term encompasses strong emotions, enthusiasm, and intense interest in an activity or pursuit. It conveys a sense of fervour and eagerness that drives individuals to engage deeply with what they love.

I am curious, what is 'passion' in your own language?

I am Indonesian, and I was born into the Javanese ethnic group. In Javanese, the word for passion is *karep*, which means will—a conscious power to manage and execute behaviour driven by inner strengths. *Karep* encompasses the acts of desiring, yearning, wishing, and planning. One of the most important aspects of *karep* is the will to live or survive. Every human action, from the simplest to the most complex, derives from one's *karep* to preserve one's existence. Thus, one's actions are influenced by one's will, which is considered the core meaning of life.[1]

The etymology of 'passion' intrigues me, as it traces a path from its origins in pain and perseverance to its current connotations of zeal and intense feeling.

The Common Views of Passion

Passion is often described as a powerful emotion or drive that compels us towards particular activities, goals, or people. Common theories of passion, such as the Dualistic Model by Robert Vallerand, categorise it into two types: Harmonious Passion and Obsessive Passion. Harmonious Passion arises from an intrinsic love for an activity, promoting balance and well-being. Obsessive Passion, on the other hand, stems from external pressures or insecurities, often leading to conflict and stress. Understanding these distinctions helps us recognise the healthy and unhealthy manifestations of our passions.[2]

How do we know if our passion is genuine? How do we differentiate between fleeting interests and true conviction? Because let's face it—when

---

1   Muhni, Djuhertati Imam. "The Pursuit of Happiness in American Mind and in Javanese Thought." *Humaniora*, vol. 14, no. 1, February 2002, pp. 27–33.

2   Vallerand, Robert J., and Virginie Paquette. "On the Role of Passion in Optimal Functioning: A Multidimensional Perspective." *Handbook on the State of the Art in Applied Psychology*, edited by Peter Graf and David JA Dozois. Hoboken, NJ, John Wiley & Sons Inc, 2021, pp. 111–137).

things get tough, when there are risks involved, when we face rejection and ridicule, most people would give up on their so-called passions. So, what sets apart those who are truly passionate from others?

Could it be that our true passions are the things we stick with, even when they become excruciatingly difficult? The pursuits we continue despite the risks? The endeavours that resonate deep within us, far beyond mere enjoyment or satisfaction?

COACHING: A GROWING PASSION

Becoming a coach was not an immediate passion for me, not by any means.

When I was six years old, I remember watching a poised news anchor on TV and turning to my father to declare, "When I am big, I want to be just like her." That was all I knew—I wanted to follow in that TV lady's footsteps.

I could vividly imagine myself behind the news desk, delivering the headlines with confidence. The thought alone made my heart race, my eyes light up, and a grin spread across my face. I felt flushed! It was like love at first sight for me to consider being a news anchor! But, of course, what did I know about love at six years old?

I was well on my way to achieving my dream, or at least close to it. I was a radio DJ and had even made my debut as a television presenter. But then, life took an unexpected turn when I met a man who captured my heart without me realising it. Being with him meant starting a new chapter in my life: saying goodbye to my job, leaving behind everything familiar, and moving to a foreign country. It was nerve-wracking; but it also filled me with excitement for the adventure ahead.

So, as a six-year-old, if you had told me I would not become a TV presenter but instead pursue a career as a personal development and leadership coach, I wouldn't have believed you. In fact, I might have even argued with you (my mother can attest to this). And to top it off, I never could have imagined that I would also become a gold medal-winning fitness athlete and spend a decade working as a Nike SEA trainer in the fitness industry.

It's funny how passions can sneak up on you. Some light up your personal world from the start, and others? Well, they surprise you by opening up entirely new worlds. Take me, for example—I thought my passion was in front of the microphone and camera, but it turns out it's actually in the world behind them. The people. Who knew?

At the start of my coaching journey, my biggest challenge was realising that everything happens in relationship. I came into coaching as a private person, totally fine being a solo player, always getting results on my own. Then I learnt from The Works Partnership (TWP) and The Coach Partnership (TCP) that "coaching is relationship". Unfamiliar territory for me, to say the least. Building relationships felt like work. I was driven by this need to be 'right' (about pretty much everything), to stay in control, and to hold onto the superwoman cape I'd stitched together over the years. Letting that go and allowing myself to be vulnerable? Nope, not part of the original plan! The ontological approach wasn't just about techniques—it was about redesigning myself, approaching conversations like a dance rather than a one-sided performance.

In those early days, I often questioned my approach, bumping up against resistance. Every time I thought I had it figured out, reality would remind me that relationships—especially in coaching—don't follow any set script. They need trust, responsiveness, and an openness to the unscripted. The real work? Letting go of control, dropping the need to always be right, and embracing the unpredictability of human connection. Over time, I found my rhythm as a coach, learning how to navigate relationships while staying true to myself and bringing something meaningful to the table. This whole coaching dance has taught me how to connect deeply, all while staying grounded in who I am.

Then came the lesson I didn't see coming: I've actually learnt to love listening. Not the 'check the box' kind of listening, but the type that grows with practice and repetition. It's about listening from both sides—not just as a skill but as a genuine willingness to hear the 'who' and all the unspoken layers. It's not about getting the job done; it's about the art of it. As I continue practising, I've grown to love this thing called 'coaching'.

Just like the Javanese proverb says, *Witing tresno jalaran soko kulino*. It means love can grow out of habit. It conveys the idea that love can develop over time through repeated interaction or familiarity. I believe passion works the same way. Coaching, for me, is both a job and a passion. It's a way of living that opens up a whole new version of the world—a world rich with human dynamics. And here's the kicker: I find myself falling back in love with people. Honestly, it's been the best kind of surprise.

For Your Reflection

Let's reflect to this quote: "What you're willing to struggle for can reveal your true passion."

The quote has often been attributed to Mark Manson, a popular self-help author and blogger. In his book, *The Subtle Art of Not Giving a F*ck*, Manson discusses the idea that the things we are willing to endure and struggle for can provide insights into our true passions and values. He suggests that in our quest for passion and fulfilment in life, maybe we've been asking the wrong question and perhaps it would be better to confront ourselves with this question instead: What are you willing to struggle for?

THE EMBODIMENT OF PASSION

I first encountered the concept of somatics early in my coaching career, back when I was still primarily working as a personal trainer. My interest in fitness had been growing steadily, and in 2017, my husband Marcus Marsden and I co-authored *Fit To Lead*, a book that focuses on integrating physical, mental, and emotional states to achieve peak performance.

In *Fit To Lead*, we explore how the body plays a critical role in leadership. It's not just about the physical benefits—how we hold and move our bodies deeply influences the decisions we make and the actions we take. Our beliefs can be reflected in the way we carry ourselves, too. This realisation truly hit home during a memorable session with a client, deepening my interest in ontological coaching.

I used to be a personal trainer at a popular gym chain with a small workout area. I can still recall having to compete for space every time I had a client during peak hours. One busy afternoon, I managed to find a tiny spot in front of a mirror for my client to do lunges.

I gently gestured for her to lift her chin and hold her head high, encouraging good posture. But her eyes remained fixed on the ground, avoiding any glimpse of her reflection. When I inquired about this behaviour, she confessed that she disliked seeing herself in the mirror. With my curiosity piqued, I moved her to a spot without mirrors, but still she kept her gaze downcast. It puzzled me—what was the underlying reason for this avoidance? She seemed unaware that it had become an automatic pattern, in the mind and physical body.

I really got into how body posture affects our confidence—a big thing in ontological coaching. Basically, it looks at how our way of being—what we say, feel, and do—shapes our lives. That's when I connected the dots for my client. Her slumped posture was like a mirror for her self-doubt and discomfort with herself.

I was so inspired by this discovery that I decided to challenge myself and compete in bodybuilding! I declared this goal when I was in the Newfield Coach Certification Program. Gulp.

Polarity of Passion: Grit and Grace

Bodybuilding. At first, I smirked at the thought—how hard could it be? I mean, I didn't need to be a tennis pro or a sprinting champ. All I had to do was look good on stage for a minute of posing. Easy peasy, right? Boy, was I wrong.

It turned out to be one of the toughest challenges of my adult life. Sure, the physical work was gruelling and definitely pushed my limits, but the real test? Stepping out in front of that judging crowd. Words were useless; my body had to do all the talking. Suddenly, all those hours of perfecting poses and sculpting muscles felt like a drop in the ocean. You know those moments when you think: Why on earth did I sign up for this?

Under those bright lights (the same ones I used to love in my previous job, mind you!), I wanted nothing more than to disappear into the shadows. In that moment, it hit me like a ton of bricks—I had been dimming my own light out of fear of criticism. The harshest critic? Yep, my own voice. It reminded me of my client who struggled with lunges; I was holding myself back, just like her. As I looked down at my shaky legs, I couldn't help but see myself in her shoes, facing the same inner battle.

But something inside me pushed me upward and forward. With shaky legs and trembling fingers, I took a deep breath, stood up straight, and as

I exhaled, I directed my energy downward, grounding myself so I could stand like a queen, with my arms open. I paused. I expanded my body (and self). I felt exposed. *Wait a minute, something else is happening inside of me.*

It's interesting how, when I planted my feet firmly on the ground, that sense of certainty was no longer an illusion. With that certainty came a surprising gentleness in my chest and face. Under the spotlight, I softly said to myself, "I am here," defying all the inner doubts and insecurities. I welcomed grace in.

For once, I gave up the war within myself and allowed grace to take its place. It co-existed with the gritty side of me. In doing so, I discovered that passion truly resides in our bodies—in the energy of motion that is both tender and bold, gritty and graceful. Two interdependent forces that exist on a spectrum, complementing each other, like the push and pull of a magnet. When provoked by a cause bigger than yourself, these two forces form a remarkable alliance, driving you forward with power and purpose.

My journey on the bodybuilding stage epitomises the embodiment of passion. The intense dedication, rigorous training, and unwavering focus required in bodybuilding mirror the essence of passion—grit and grace. Grit is evident in the perseverance through physically and mentally challenging regimes. Grace is displayed in the poise and confidence exuded on stage. This experience taught me that passion is not just about the outcome but the process—the relentless pursuit of excellence and the graceful acceptance of the highs and lows.

A master coach once shared a powerful message with me: "As a coach, you will coach with your wounds, the things you struggle with—they are part of you. It's the very thing that makes you a unique observer." I take her message personally, and it has profoundly supported leaders in navigating their lives and creating the results they want. This insight has helped me understand that our struggles shape our perspective and enhance our ability to connect with and work with my coaching clients.

CASE STUDY: COACHING FOR GENUINE PASSION AND OPTIMISM

Client Profile

- Name: Emily (pseudonym)
- Role: Team Leader in a Marketing Department
- Traits: Highly optimistic, energetic, and passionate about her work. Known for her relentless positivity and enthusiasm

Emily, often described as the 'foster child of joy, passion, and optimism', was confident that her infectious energy was a key driver of her team's success. She believed there was no room for negativity in the workplace, thinking that maintaining a positive atmosphere was crucial for productivity and morale. Her somatic experience was dominated by expanding upward and forward, taking up space, and moving at a fast speed.

The Challenge

Despite her upbeat demeanour, Emily received a surprisingly low score on her engagement at work. Confused and hurt by the feedback, she embarked on a journey of deep reflection and was open to understanding the underlying issues. Through discussions and feedback from her team, Emily discovered a startling reality: her boundless positivity was perceived as inauthentic and disconnected. Her team felt pressured to match her energy, leaving no space for expressing fears, doubts, or frustrations.

Coaching Approach

Initial Reactions

- Emily initially struggled to accept this feedback. She felt misunderstood and hurt, as she genuinely believed her positivity was beneficial.
- With compassionate and honest coaching, Emily was guided to explore her emotions and the impact of her behaviour on her team.

Key Insights

- Emily's positivity was not perceived as genuine. Instead, it was seen as forced and dismissive of the team's real challenges.
- Her insistence on maintaining a positive façade prevented her team from feeling safe to express their true feelings and struggles.

Deeper Reflection

- Through coaching, Emily uncovered a significant blind spot: Her projection of positivity stemmed from her own insecurities. She feared being perceived as weak and thus overcompensated with excessive optimism.
- This realisation was pivotal. Emily saw that the judgement of her team's need to 'look strong' was a projection of her resistance to acknowledging her own vulnerabilities.

Transformation

Shifting the Perspective

- Emily learnt to reshape her version of optimism with compassion and passion. She began creating space for her team to express their fears, doubts, and frustrations without judgement.
- She embraced her vulnerability, understanding that authentic leadership involves acknowledging and addressing emotional honesty without assessing whether it's negative or positive. She looked at the purpose of every emotion and, instead of managing, navigated her

team's mood and emotions, while simultaneously mastering self-acceptance and expanding her range of emotions and moods.

Practical Steps

- Emily practised listening, showing up with openness, and allowing her team members to voice their concerns without immediately trying to 'fix' the situation with 'positivity' (read: everyone must follow her way with the same level of energy). She was able to meet her team where they were and let go of her façade.
- She initiated regular check-ins focused on understanding her team's challenges and providing support tailored to their needs.
- She allowed herself to access a different kind of somatic experience—softening her face and the front part of her body, while keeping her spine upright and expanded into openness, and practising a slower pace kind of dance.

Outcome

- Over time, Emily's team felt more connected and trusted her leadership. They appreciated her willingness to listen and her genuine interest in their well-being.
- Emily's engagement scores improved significantly, reflecting a healthier, authentic team dynamic.

In my view as her coach, Emily's journey underscores the importance of infusing passion and optimism with authenticity and compassion. Struggles are part of the journey. Instead of being dismissive about them, struggles become a catalyst for change, and compassion was her ally. Her transformation from projecting forced positivity to fostering a genuinely supportive environment highlights the power of coaching in uncovering and addressing deep-seated insecurities. By embracing her vulnerabilities, Emily not only improved her leadership effectiveness but also strengthened her team's trust. The joy and electrifying passion are always there within her, and now she has more gears, more range. Sounds easy, but it was not—a journey that everyone must have with their coach by their side!

CATEGORY OF PASSION

Based on my personal and professional experience, I have come to see that passion can fall into two categories: initial passion that brings us joy and energy in our personal spaces, and developing passion that opens up new worlds for us.

This categorisation helps clarify how passions can evolve and how they impact our professional and personal lives differently.

- **Skill-Based Passion (Mastery-Oriented)**
  Focus: The pursuit of personal excellence, developing skills, and achieving high levels of proficiency.
  Example: An artist honing their craft, driven by the desire to perfect their skills.

- **Value-Based Passion (Purpose-Driven)**
  Focus: Making a meaningful impact, aligning actions with broader values and purpose.
  Example: A social worker striving to improve the lives of underprivileged communities, driven by a sense of purpose.

How is your relationship with your passion? Is it healthy or unhealthy? What makes you say so?

THE KEYS TO CREATING A HEALTHY RELATIONSHIP WITH PASSION

Pursuing your passion—the one you are willing to struggle for—requires both sides of you: your toughness and tenderness. It demands the willingness to challenge your limitations with curiosity and ask: What is enough? Recognise that you have done more than enough, or consider the possibility that it might not be. Then, have the guts to declare when enough is enough, from a place of caring for your vision. Understand that this has nothing to do with your self-worth; whether you are good, smart, or strong enough. It has everything to do with the filter you are wearing—how you see yourself and the world.

Say yes to both self-acceptance and a healthy, fulfilling relationship with your passions and pursuits. It's possible! Healthy warning: The path is not always filled with unicorns and rainbows. But the journey itself is a fundamental part of ontological coaching for me: to challenge and expand the observer that we are!

THE SWEET SPOT: THE INTERSECTION OF PASSION AND PURPOSE

In my world, there is no one who embodies passion and purpose quite like my husband, Marcus. His very presence exudes a sense of commitment and inspires growth in those around him. Like his favourite animal, the giraffe, Marcus stands tall and proud, fearlessly sticking his neck out for what he believes in. His dedication to his values and work is remarkable, creating a space where others can flourish and discover their own passions and purposes. His unwavering determination and integrity serve as a constant reminder for me to pursue my own passions with the same level of conviction and at the same time being at ease in my own skin!

The intersection of skill-based and value-based passions can be described as a 'sweet spot' where personal fulfilment and professional contribution align. This is where you enjoy the work you do as well as feel that you are making a meaningful impact. In this space, you are not only utilising and honing your skills but also providing significant value to your job. This intersection represents a harmonious blend where personal joy and professional purpose meet, leading to a deeply fulfilling career and life. Here's an elaboration on this concept.

Characteristics of the Sweet Spot of Passion

- **Engagement**

  You are highly engaged and motivated in your work because it aligns with both your personal interests and professional goals.

- **Growth**

  There is continuous growth as you develop new skills and competencies while also contributing your unique value to the job.

- **Impact**

  Your work has a meaningful impact on others, whether it's within your organisation, industry, or broader community.

- **Satisfaction**

  You experience a deep sense of satisfaction and fulfilment because your work resonates with your core values and passions. *(No one sent me a memo that this rewarding feeling comes with tears! Tears of joy!)*

- **Sustainability**

  This sweet spot creates a sustainable career path, preventing burnout and fostering long-term dedication and enthusiasm.

EXPLORING DIFFERENT APPROACHES TO PASSION

Many of us don't know what our passion is or how to ignite it. So, here are alternative approaches or to living life passionately, at work and at home.

Stop 'Finding Your Passion' and Start Creating It

One myth is that passion is like a pot of gold at the end of the rainbow—you either find it or you don't. This belief can turn us into job-hoppers, looking for that role that makes us jump out of bed with joy. But surprise! Passion often needs time to brew, like a fine wine. It involves developing skills, confidence, and relationships.

Focus on What You Care About

If passion is simply what makes you happy, you'll quit doing it when it gets tough, when it becomes too risky, when you're ignored and mocked. Your true passion is what you're driven to create, even if it pushes you to your limits. It's what you stick with even when it's excruciating or risky. It's about the things you do because you believe they will make a profound difference. These things simmer in the deepest parts of your soul—far beyond what's fun or what feels good. It's about what you stand for.

Struggle: The Catalyst for Passion

Struggle often gets a bad rap, but it actually can be the gateway to connecting with your true passion! Think of passion as a flame ignited by heat. Passion is born when personal struggle is met with persistence. This magical combo transforms raw talent into excellence, seriousness into fun, commitment into pleasure, and makes time fly. And the secret sauce? Struggle—it paves the way to discovering your passion.

The key ingredient is recognising the struggle and committing to overcoming it. Without recognition, you're just courting disaster. But once you acknowledge the struggle, the flame of passion is ignited. So, embrace the struggle—it might just lead you to your true passion!

Move Your Body, Move Your Life

Physical activity can be a game changer in sparking passion. Moving your body not only boosts your physical health but also supercharges your mental well-being. Exercise releases endorphins, lifting your mood and energy levels, making it easier to pursue your passions. Plus, movement brings new experiences and perspectives, potentially uncovering new passions or reigniting old ones. Whether it's a morning jog, a dance class, or a yoga session, adding movement to your daily routine can be a step towards a passionate life.

Exercise might be optional, but movement is fundamental. My fellow somatic trainers, Beatriz and Chris, and I just love to move our bodies. Beatriz inspires me with her presence and dance, and Chris with his wisdom and playfulness. For me, passion lives in the body—an energy in motion. So, get moving and see how it can transform your life!

Start With Who, Start With You

Your passion is never just about you. It's about the impact you have on others and the world around you. Starting with an internal focus helps you connect deeply with your values and motivations. Reflect on your life experiences, values, and what truly matters to you. Understanding your internal drivers can guide you towards activities and pursuits that align with your true self, creating an authentic and sustainable passion.

In *Start With Who*, Marcus argues that, while conventional thinking encourages us to focus on setting 'SMART goals' and 'starting with why', there's a deeper level that needs to be addressed first. Only by identifying and working with your underlying beliefs—about who you are today and who you can become—will you truly unlock your full potential. One of my favourite quotes from the book is: "Ultimately, authenticity is a creative force."

If you want to create passion in life, start by choosing yourself to be a passionate person!

MY ALLY: COMPASSION

Let's shine a light on this thing called Compassion, and you can decide for yourself why it matters in the quest for Passion.

Linguistically, compassion comes from the Latin word *compati*, which means 'to suffer with'. It's a blend of *com–* meaning 'with, together' and *pati* meaning 'to suffer'. So, compassion literally means to suffer together or to feel another's pain and suffering as if it were your own. This concept involves both an emotional element—empathy for another's suffering—and a motivational drive—the desire to alleviate that suffering.

Think of compassion as your trusty sidekick that bridges the gap between struggle and passion. It's the gentle force that helps us navigate challenges and fuels our drive to pursue our passions with kindness and understanding. Self-compassion allows us to be open and resilient, recognising that the path to our passions isn't always smooth. Compassion for others nurtures connection and support, creating a community where passions can thrive. As we navigate the ups and downs of our passions, compassion keeps us grounded, empathetic, and genuinely engaged.

One thing I've learnt over time is the profound impact of compassion, especially in high performers. It's fascinating to realise that this powerful force isn't some magic pill, workout programme, or special diet. Nope, it's just good old-fashioned compassion that allows us to truly thrive as human beings.

In my experience, when people tap into self-compassion, their performance and fulfilment go through the roof. Some can easily access it by recalling a moment they felt compassion for others and turning it inward. But for many, especially those raised in environments where compassion wasn't exactly on the menu, the concept feels foreign or even 'too soft'.

True compassion isn't about letting people off the hook. It's about seeing and acknowledging the struggle without ignoring boundaries. It's honest, real, and incredibly powerful. Without it, thriving isn't really an option.

In my journey toward personal development as a coach and trainer, especially over the last two years working with my mentor Ken Ito, a senior trainer at The Works Partnership, I came face-to-face with how much I resisted the idea of compassion—particularly self-compassion (because, let's face it, my ego insisted I wasn't weak!). But once I finally allowed myself to experience it, I unlocked new capacities within and developed a deeper ability to truly listen to others. It's wildly counterintuitive, yet it works!

Around the same time, I crossed paths with Dr Krista Scott-Dixon, then Director of Curriculum at Precision Nutrition, who has been a huge influence on my work ever since. Now a Product Director at Simple App, Krista introduced me to a practice I still use today—**Self-Critic Day** and **Self-Compassion Day**. I apply it not only to myself but also to my high-self-critic, high-performer clients. This practice has become a powerful tool in helping them pursue excellence without overlooking the power of compassion.

Self-Critic Day and Self-Compassion Day

How It Works
On your toughest day, designate it as your Self-Critic Day—go all out and criticise yourself 100%, holding nothing back. Then, the next day, flip the script entirely. Make it your Self-Compassion Day—acknowledge and celebrate everything you did well, 100%, without any reservations.

IGNITING YOUR PASSION

As you read this chapter, what's surfacing for you? How do you want to make meaning of passion? What might it mean to live a passionate life? When do you feel most passionately alive? At home? At work? What do you notice about your body when you experience passion? What are some things you're passionate about or have been passionate about? Were you passionate about them right from the start, or did the passion grow over time? If it developed over time, what do you think sparked that growing passion? When you choose to be passionate, how did it impact people around you? What's life worth living for you? How do you want to be remembered?

Like Kelly Poulos—co-author of *Secrets to Winning* and an all-around passionate and awesome coach—often asks me and the next generation of leaders: What is life compelling you to create? What's your compelling desire?

As I dig deeper into the meaning of passion, I can't help but think that passion is not just about suffering for the sake of suffering; it must be pure and willing. But is it enough to simply suffer for something we love? Is that the true definition of passion? Or is it about being willing to endure any amount of suffering for a cause we believe in?

Society often romanticises passion as an intense form of love, but perhaps the real meaning goes beyond that. It's about discovering what we are truly willing to sacrifice for and, in doing so, connecting to our life's purpose, our essence in this world.

In the quest for passion, let me close this chapter with one of my all-time favourite questions, a gift from my dad: "*Apa panggilan ing atimu sing mung kowe wae sing bisa njawab?*"

In English, it means: What is the calling of your own heart that is only yours to answer?

He asked me this when I was just six years old, watching a lady TV news anchor. This question has taken me far, deep, and always brings me back to love. My hope is that it resonates with you in the same way.

**Sari Marsden, PCC, NASM-FNS, CES, PES
Co-author of *Fit To Lead*, Leadership and
Somatic Trainer, Executive Coach with TCP
and TWP**

Sari is a leadership development trainer with over 15 years of dedication to coaching. She specialises in working through the medium of the body to facilitate personal growth and development. Throughout her career, Sari has worked with people from a wide range of backgrounds and cultures throughout Asia, in both corporate and personal contexts.

Sari is a former NASM-certified personal trainer with extensive experience in corrective exercise, sports performance, and fitness nutrition. Her passion for fitness led her to become an elite trainer for the Nike Training Club in Southeast Asia, where she spent 10 years sharing her expertise with the community. She has also won gold medals for Team Singapore in Southeast Asian fitness physique competitions. In 2018, Sari was honoured with the CMO Asia Indonesian Women Leaders Award and has been recognised for her role as a champion of women in the Women Who Lead With Purpose initiative, a collaborative project by Women In Asia, TEDxSingapore, and the National Library Board of Singapore.

Sari's vision is 'to facilitate empowerment and excellence through powerful conversation and purposeful movement'. Having worked with athletes and corporate leaders, she uses a wide range of training techniques that combine the person's physical, mental, and emotional states.

In addition to improved performance, her clients report a shift in the way they see the world and the way they hold their body, often resulting in increased 'executive presence', authenticity and performance excellence. Her approach is purpose-driven, holistic, and dynamic. Sari also contributes to her community via volunteering to work with foreign domestic workers in Singapore.

Sari translates as 'essence' in Indonesian. She believes that for anybody to speak with conviction and to be heard, their 'essence narrative' must resonate with them emotionally and live in their body. Sari was born in Indonesia, is married to Marcus Marsden, and currently resides in Singapore.

CHAPTER 10

Happiness

Harnessing the Power of Coaching for a Happier Life

Clémence Blondel

Bonjour! I am Clémence Blondel, originally from France and living in Asia for the past 20 years. Currently based in Singapore with my husband and three children, I work as an executive coach at The Works Partnership and as programme manager for the team coaching certification programme at The Coach Partnership. I am passionate about helping others to boost their personal effectiveness while also taking care of their well-being and happiness.

Despite an incredible diversity of definitions for happiness, I aim to bring you closer to your own, reflect on what it means for you, and how you can nurture it. Let us explore how coaching can serve as a powerful tool to bring happiness to our lives and to others. This is truly at the core of my coaching and my life overall.

WHY TALK ABOUT HAPPINESS?

Do all human beings, in one way or another, seek happiness? Do you know anyone who wakes up in the morning hoping to suffer or have a really bad day, month, year, or life? Whatever we do or dream, it somehow revolves around happiness and well-being.

Happiness is one of the primary emotions that we experience as human beings, together with fear, anger, disgust, sadness, tenderness, joy/gratitude, and it is essential to examine it and learn how to cultivate it in our lives. Emotions are not inherently 'positive' or 'negative' but rather, they guide us and indicate what is important for us. In the ontological approach, emotions serve as 'pre-dispositions for action' and all emotions come and go in the moment. Happiness is the emotion that allows you to pause, reflect on your current state, and appreciate the things that matter to you. What is fascinating is how happiness manifests in different ways over time:

- in your past: happiness can come from gratitude, mercy, forgiveness;
- in your present: happiness appears with joy, satisfaction, contentment, wholeheartedness;
- in your future: happiness shows up in ambition and optimism.

In our society, we are taught to prioritise efficiency and speed, leading many people (including myself) to struggle with taking a pause in their lives and setting aside worries.

The ontological approach of emotions offers a helpful way to pause and notice our happiness. It assists in identifying the stories linked with that emotion, looking at them and determining future actions. Let me elaborate with the following examples:

- I assert that X did or did not happen = *the fact*
  A simple example for me could be: I assert that I live in a house with a garden and my three children go to school, practise sports and other activities on a weekly basis.
- I assess X as Y = *my opinion on the fact*
  Based on the above example: I assess this situation as wonderful for me and my family.
- I declare that I will (or will not) do Z = *my action in the future*
  Thus: I declare my desire to be grateful for life, to invite my friends over to my house more often, and be happy when I bring my three children to their activities.

There is also a strong push to the pursuit of happiness with a myriad of self-help books on that topic, the rise of the positive psychology, and the culture of being a master of our destiny. It seems that it boils down to simple questions that come to mind:

- How often do you notice that you are happy in the present moment?
- Do you even know what makes you happy?
- How do you know and how do you measure that you are happy?
- What do you feel physically and mentally when you are happy?

THE PARADOX

I used to believe that happiness was being optimistic and never experiencing sadness, frustration, anger, or any form of 'negative emotions'. After going through my Newfield coach training programme and engaging in personal development work, I realised that:

- it is perfectly normal to feel angry, frustrated, stressed, ungrateful, sad, and unkind;

- these are not 'wrong emotions' and unlike the idea of 'positive thinking' that makes you 'wrong' if you have such thoughts that are not 'positive'—such as resentfulness, hatred, jealousy—they are totally normal feelings that every human being experiences. Moreover, I have learnt that suppressing these emotions over time only causes them to resurface in a more twisted and exaggerated way;

- to fully experience happiness, I now let these so-called 'negative' emotions play their part and live within me, embracing life wholeheartedly. That means, for example, accepting when I feel sad and reflecting on what I have lost, what I am currently losing, or what I fear to lose in the near future.

LET US TRY TO DEFINE HAPPINESS

The etymology of the word happiness comes from 'hap' meaning luck or chance in old English and the word *bonheur* in French comes from *bon* which means favourable and *heur* meaning sign.

French philosopher André Comte-Sponville defines happiness as the possibility of experiencing happiness at any moment in our lives. It does not mean that every day, you wake up feeling happy; but you know it is possible during the day.[1]

---

1   Rebeihi, Ali, host. "How to Define Happiness in These Anxious Times? [*Comment définir le bonheur en ces temps anxiogènes?]" Good For You! [Grand bien vous fasse*], 18 Aug. 2024. *France Inter*, https://www.radiofrance.fr/franceinter/podcasts/grand-bien-vous-fasse.

In this chapter, I will not talk about happiness as:

- Felicity: a constant high state of happiness;
- Plenitude: when everything is always great;
- Pleasure: when all our needs and desires are constantly fulfilled; or
- Satisfaction: when we feel we have a cognitive assessment of whether our needs, desires, or goals have been met.

Instead, I will explore happiness as the predisposition or capability inherent in every human being to be serene, joyful, content, or even ecstatic. Happiness is a state of being, whereas other emotions like joy are a momentary feeling triggered by a particular event. Happiness, when practised, can become a foundational mood for your life. Ultimately, the sensation of happiness transcends ordinary experience, making you feel expanded, and revealing that there is more within you than what you realise.

Both external and internal factors influence happiness, and we have all heard some stories of people in painful situations who were able to experience happiness, and others in privileged situations who were not happy at all.

Happiness is related to your wellness and here are some factors that play a part in you being physically and mentally well, adapted from Margaret Swarbrick[2]:

- Physical: recognising the need for physical activity, diet, sleep and nutrition;
- Intellectual: expanding knowledge and skills, practising creative abilities;
- Financial: satisfaction with current and future financial situation;

---

2 Swarbrick, Margaret. "A Wellness Approach." *Psychiatric Rehabilitation Journal*, vol. 29, no. 4, April 2006, pp. 311–314.

- Environmental: pleasant and stimulating environments (home, workplace, etc.), access to healthcare;
- Social: sense of connection, social belonging, being part of an inclusive and welcoming community;
- Spiritual/existential: expanding your sense of purpose and meaning in life and satisfaction at work, being of service, spiritual life; and
- Emotional: recognising, expressing, sharing emotions appropriately, satisfying relationships, and support system.

Matthieu Ricard, a French Buddhist monk, author and photographer, and translator to the Dalai Lama, defines happiness as well-being. According to the Buddhist view, well-being is a deep sense of serenity and fulfilment that underlies all our emotional states, even sorrow. It is a state of being you can always reach, and it is ultimately an inner freedom and an inner strength.[3]

How often do you notice the physical sensations that you experience while being happy? It can be a warm sensation in your chest, a burst of energy, a simple smile, or a feeling of being more alive, or even a general sense of comfort with reduced muscle tension. Paying attention to these sensations can help you pause and notice your happiness.

Sometimes I still feel guilty to be happy in a world with a lot of suffering. How can I be happy while so many dreadful wars are happening, while we are facing a climate crisis, and while social inequalities are increasing? I believe empathy and happiness coexist and we, human beings, can experience a wide range of emotions simultaneously and hold paradoxes. We can also individually and collectively involve ourselves in actions that impact the world around us.

---

3   Ricard, Matthieu. "The Habits of Happiness." *TED*. February 2004, https://www.ted.com/talks/matthieu_ricard_the_habits_of_happiness.

CAN COACHING BRING HAPPINESS?

Matthieu Ricard shares again that:

> Our control of the outer conditions is an illusion but there are some enablers to our inner conditions to happiness. Certain states of our mind such as anger, jealousy, obsessive desire can be detrimental to our well-being and the more they invade our mind, the more we will feel tormented.

He also claims that with brain plasticity, you can change your way of being, traits, and moods. You can literally train in patience, openness, love, and kindness—the same way you train in a sport, a musical instrument, or in any other skill.

What I love to explore as a coach, for myself, and for others, is my core belief around happiness:

- Are you happy? (Such a simple yet powerful question indeed!)
- When was the last time you experienced joy?
- What if there was more joy in your life, what would be different? What possibilities could surface?
- Do I deserve to be happy?

According to Dr Tony Grant, Director of the Coaching Psychology Unit at Sydney University: "There is a correlation between coaching and increased well-being" like a "causal domino effect"[4]:

---

4   Clark, James. "Does Coaching Bring Lead to Happiness ...?" *LinkedIn*, 22 Nov. 2017, www.linkedin.com/pulse/does-coaching-lead-happiness-james-clark.

- The self-reflection which takes place in coaching leads to self-insight or increased self-awareness;
- Greater self-awareness leads to better self-regulation; and
- Better self-regulation leads to higher goal attainment and 'self-efficacy' which, in turn, makes you happy!

In the corporate world, it is now widely accepted that a happy employee is a win-win:

- For employees: finding meaning and fulfilment at work is much more engaging.
- For organisations: happy employees are more motivated, potentially more performant, promote the company, attract talents, and create a great work environment.

This applies to any organisation, community, or team working towards a shared goal.

There are even 'happiness coaches' now! Tal Shahar from the Happiness Studies Academy (USA) describes the role of a 'happiness coach' as increasing their client's well-being in five domains: spiritual, physical, intellectual, relational, emotional.

THE UTMOST IMPORTANCE OF RELATIONSHIPS

I strongly relate to the TED talk 'What Makes a Good Life: Lessons from the Longest Study on Happiness' where Robert Waldinger shares that, after 75 years of research, our happiness is strongly linked with the quality of relationships in our life.[5]

Happiness happens with others through friendship, love, and connection. It involves connecting with individuals and groups, such as a community that shares the same values and purpose. A coach will support you in how you show up with others and how that impacts all your relationships. This could mean moving from a dysfunctional to a functional relationship, from a not working to a working one, from a good to a great one, from a great to an amazing one. I believe this journey never stops.

Last year, I coached a senior leader during an intense crisis. Two of his plants had simultaneous breakdowns, which had not happened in 30 years. He had to work non-stop for two months, handling upper management pressure while keeping his ground teams motivated to solve the problems instead of playing the blame game. Throughout our conversations, he shifted his perspective and saw the situation as an opportunity to work together, gain more exposure with his CEO, and learn from this unusual and challenging situation. He was not happy about being overloaded with work, but he integrated his life around it by having his children visit his plants, celebrating small wins with his team over dinners, and maintaining the ability to experience happy moments during tough times.

---

5   Waldinger, Robert. "What Makes a Good Life? Lessons from the Longest Study on Happiness." *TED*, November 2015, www.ted.com/talks/robert_waldinger_what_makes_a_good_life_lessons_from_the_longest_study_on_happiness?language=en&delay=2m&subtitle=en.

EMBRACE ACCEPTANCE AND HARNESS THE POWER OF CHOICE

A great tool I gained from all the coaching I experienced—and am still experiencing—is the ability to look at any current situation and be aware of 'what is' and 'what could be', then decide if I want to change it or not. This gives me a sense of ownership. A coach can help you move from feeling resigned or defeatist in a particular situation to clarifying why you are making a certain choice and opening different possibilities. A powerful example is your relationships with parents. There is a high chance that their character or behaviours will not change, and as they age, they may show less openness or flexibility. Pausing to understand them, identify their love language, and choose how you interact with them brings you all closer. For example, I know that offering my parents some gifts will not mean much to them, but if I fly from Singapore to France for a few days to celebrate an important family event with them, it will make a difference.

A few years ago, I coached an airline hostess during Covid times. She felt exhausted and powerless as she was about to get fired by the airline that she had worked for over the past 20 years, while also going through a divorce. One of the most important takeaways she got from our coaching was to consciously pause and deeply breathe during her day, becoming aware of her current situation and her possible choices. Our conversations did not change the course of her being fired, but it allowed her to regain some energy, be present with her peers, and look at her future with possibilities in other domains where she could find a job.

Bringing back choice and meaning in your career is crucial. One of my coachees felt stuck after a burnout, and coaching helped her to regain energy to choose another career path and explore new possibilities.

Provided that your basic needs are met, personal agency fosters a sense of control, autonomy, purpose, resilience, and intrinsic motivation, all of which contribute significantly to happiness and overall well-being.

GOING BACK TO PLAY!

One of the ways to instil joy in life is to bring more play into it, and a coach can help you to let go and lose grip of the 'shoulds' and the omnipresent to-do lists so you can embrace play.

Play can happen anywhere with anyone. At home, my 10-year-old daughter constantly reminds me to play and not overthink things. At bedtime, she pretends to be a cat, and I must convince her to jump into bed ready to sleep (as a cat, of course)! She also pretends she is dead in a weird position, and my mission is to put her body back into a proper position to sleep. Countless times, she hides in her bedroom before I come to kiss her good night, and she loves this game repeatedly.

Humour can help you bring play and joy into your life, and journaling daily three funny things that happened to you during the day is a great practice.[6]

Reflecting on how I integrate play into my life and into my work with my colleagues, my clients, or stakeholders proves very useful. I love meeting old people who are playful and incorporate play into their lives. I remember a grand-uncle who always joked around at family reunions, his energy and liveliness are a model for me. It also brings me joy to see a picture of my mentor, Chris Balsley, who is 65+, jumping on a trampoline

---

6   Keltner, Dacher, host. "The Science of Happiness." *Spotify*, 2024–, open.spotify.com/
     show/4dq0wmiZlk58Eu0NcqgWei.

in his colourful tie-dye t-shirt! Nothing is cast in stone in the way you show up in life.

EMBRACE SELF-CARE AND SIMPLICITY

How can you create enough 'space' in your busy life to keep some 'pockets of happiness' or 'sparkles of joy' without rushing through life and never stopping?

A way to start creating that space is through self-care. I worked with a senior leader who experienced burnout from working across two time zones (Malaysia and Argentina) and not sleeping enough. One practice that supported his well-being was setting up boundaries for his work hours and saying no to early or late meetings during the night. As my colleague and friend, Katrina Gisbert Tay, often reminds us: "Sleep is the mother of health". Other self-care practices could be to go for a short walk with your partner or take a bath at the end of your day. For me, it is making sure I go for my weekly run and yoga class and see friends during the weekend.

You can find millions of simple ways to create these sparkles of joy. Two simple examples for me are walking in nature and riding a bike, even if only for 10 minutes. Both keep me present, help me observe the sky, the clouds, and the beauty around me, even when life hurts. When I feel stressed or anxious, riding a bike becomes a 'promenade': I feel my legs moving, experience the wind's resistance, and appreciate the effort of riding uphill and the gliding downhill—like life's ups and downs. I also actively contribute to preserving the planet. And you, what are the things that create joy in your life?

Another powerful way to create that space is to be open to embrace the unexpected and treat it like an adventure. A delayed flight or cancelled train might initially seem like a hassle or disrupt your well-oiled schedule (and it can be!), but it also can be a call for adventure. Who knows whom you might meet or what you might do during those 'lost hours'? I know someone who wrote an entire book while stuck alone for two weeks in a hotel for his Covid quarantine!

BRINGING HAPPINESS TO THE COLLECTIVE

I often wonder how we, as coaches or leaders, can bring happiness to teams and organisations, and create a working environment with less suffering and more fun!

We can bring happiness to a team by focusing on these elements:
- Building a sense of belonging for all team members, regardless of their motivations;
- Supporting each other to manifest our individual purpose and having each other's backs;
- Learning, growing, and having fun while delivering great results;
- Having open and honest conversations to succeed and grow; and
- Celebrating wins together.

This year, a team of three co-founders of a social enterprise start-up realised, during our coaching sessions, that each of them had a different motivation for the business to succeed. Despite this, they were all committed to doing whatever it takes for their success. This commitment led them to have open and honest conversations about what was not working in their collaboration and how to shift some of their ways of working.

A senior leader I coached was losing faith in his company's ability to invest in his market (a country in Africa, whereas the headquarters were in India). He realised that his top priority was to sustain his entire team so no one would lose their jobs, as they were the breadwinners for their families. This connection with his team strengthened his motivation to stay in this organisation and grow the business with the current circumstances.

Feeling useful to someone or a group is also part of being happy. When you focus your attention on others or a larger cause, you experience a sense of fulfilment.

I sense that newer generations, such as Millennials and Generation Zs, are more attuned to seeking happiness and meaning at work. They actively request support for their 'work-life integration', their learning opportunities, and their alignment with their purpose.

Practices to Foster Happiness

I use various practices to nurture happiness for both my clients and myself, and here are a few examples.

Practice #1
Bringing Awareness with a '100 Things List'

One way to bring happiness and joy into our lives is to pay attention. I took this idea from my mentor and friend, Jim Smith (The Executive Happiness Coach) who pulled the practice from Positive Psychology. Also called a Joy List, the idea is to capture, on a page, 100 things that bring you joy. Pull from everywhere: your felt sensations, your environment, your relationships, the beauty/calm of nature, intellectual challenges, etc. The list may include big items like family vacations or tiny moments like watching a baby sleep. Often the first 30 emerge easily, the next 30 require more thought, and the last items require deeper reflection. Once complete, set the list aside and pull out for review whenever you need a mood boost. And keep adding as you go—100 is a start!

Practice #2
Feeling Aligned with Your Choices

To align with your choices, the starting point is to become aware of where you stand with your current decisions. I find that using the few questions below help me to reflect on my choices, as it clarifies what I want and why.

You will feel more congruent when you understand why you are making your current choices, such as staying or leaving your organisation—once you have decided to stay in your organisation and you know why, you feel much more in the driver's seat than in the passenger's seat.

Reflecting on your current choices, ask yourself:
- How does staying the same serve me?
- What benefits could come from making improvements or change?
- What price am I paying by remaining the same?

Here is what it looks like for me when it comes to alcohol, for example:
- It serves me by helping me to unwind from stress at work; it brings me closer to my friends; it disinhibits me to express my feelings
- Benefits to stop drinking alcohol: I will be healthier, I will have less risk for chronic diseases; I could live longer
- The price I am paying by staying the same: it is harder to maintain a healthy weight; it worries me that I may be increasing the risk of cancer recurrence

For now, I decided to reduce my consumption of alcohol, and I do not feel guilty every time I say yes to a glass of wine.

**Practice #3
Strengthening Your Happiness in the Past, Present, and Future**

In the Past
Studies show that gratitude improves well-being. Take a pause during your day (at a time that works best for you) and write down three things that happened that day for which you feel grateful.

In the Present
Smiling can boost your mood and increase positivity. When you face these so-called 'negative emotions', have a light-hearted conversation with a friend or seek out humorous content to help you cope. Consider taking a break to listen to a funny podcast or watch your favourite stand-up comedian on YouTube.

In the Future
Nurture your satisfaction with what you have accomplished, focus on the feeling of 'that is enough for now' and 'I am enough', and give yourself permission to dream.

**Practice #4
Bring Play!**

We need to take time out to recharge, even if they are short and tiny. Every day, make time for play or do something unplanned with total freedom: sing a karaoke song, practise parkour in your living room, chase your children around the house, or perfect your gym move in a park. Whatever you choose, play and laugh!

Find more examples in *The Science of Happiness* podcast on Spotify.[7]

---

7   Keltner, Dacher, host. "The Science of Happiness." *Spotify*, 2024–, open.spotify.com/show/4dq0wmiZlk58EuONcqgWei.

**Practice #5
Daily Connection With Others**

Most leaders I coach excel at solving problems, but they often forget to connect with others at work in their effort to be efficient.

A manager of a large team in Malaysia who I coached a few years ago felt disconnected from his team members. Through our conversations, he decided to greet people in the office every morning. At first, it felt forced and awkward but over time, this small, consistent change helped him to start his days differently and create the missing connection with the people around him. It made a big difference in his mood going to work.

Another way to connect with others is to focus out and practise curiosity: ask one open-ended question before the start of each meeting to encourage conversation.

Whatever method you choose to connect with people, build relationships!

Practice #6
Creating a Body of Happiness: Smile!

In the ontological approach, our emotions and moods can shift with our body. For example, change of facial expression and posture appear to induce emotional states.

Practise this simple exercise anywhere in just a few minutes:
1. Stand grounded on both feet, shoulder-width apart, and stand as tall as possible. Notice how your shoulders drop and your chest opens. Release any tension in your shoulders, arms, neck.
2. Breathe regularly and deeply from your belly instead of your chest.
3. Smile for 2 minutes. You can hold a pen horizontally between your teeth and keep your lips apart so that they do not touch the pen to create that smile; your brain cannot tell the difference between a fake and a real smile, so it will release dopamine, the happiness hormone. You can also lift your both hands over your head while you smile.
4. When you no longer smile, bring it back on your face and let yourself feel the energy of a genuine smile.

Repeat this exercise several times throughout your day.

Refer to Carol Courcy's book *Save Your Inner Tortoise!* for more practices to smile, bring gratefulness into your life, and expand your range of emotions.

PRACTISE YOUR HAPPINESS MOOD AND LET IT SHINE!

I see coaching not as a promise of constant happiness, which is utopian, but as a support for our well-being for a period of weeks, months, or even years.

In life, things happen, and we can choose our response. Here are some guidelines I find useful for improving my well-being as well as that of others:

- **Find Your Fire and Act On It**

  Reflect on what you want and what truly matters to you. Identify the areas where you feel inspired and take action.

- **Be of Service to Others**

  Focus out: offer your help and support to those around you.

- **Wish Happiness for Everyone**

  Support others in overcoming anger, arrogance, and hatred, and work towards positive conditions in society.

- **Manage Worry**

  If a solution exists, take action. If you cannot do anything about it, let go of worry, change your perspective, and focus on other activities.

- **Train in Attention, Love, Kindness, Compassion**

  There is no magic—these qualities require effort and time to develop.

- **Build the Best Relationships You Can**

  Cultivate meaningful connections with your family (parents, siblings, partners, children, etc.), friends (who may have become your chosen family), work relationships (colleagues, peers, bosses, clients, stakeholders, etc.) and yourself.

On this life journey of practising happiness, I am grateful for the amazing people I work with, my friends, and my family, who all support my growth. I am committed to creating happiness in the world, one person at a time.

Clémence Blondel, PCC
TWP Coach and Corporate Training Director

Clémence began her career with 15 years in Marketing, Communication, and Sales. She achieved success in these roles because of her deep understanding of buyer behaviour.

It was this love for human psychology, linked to decision-making and behaviours, that attracted her to the field of Education, Learning and Development, and Coaching.

She now partners with clients throughout the APAC region to design and deliver leadership development and executive coaching initiatives.

Clémence is an ontologically Newfield-certified Executive Coach with a passion for helping leaders to boost their personal effectiveness and presence, while taking care of their health and happiness at the same time. She has coached a diverse range of clients from more than 20 nationalities on six continents, in a holistic style that engages clients in the three domains of intelligence: intellectual (language), emotional, and physical (somatic).

A highly personable coach, Clémence is known for her ability to make her clients feel at ease very fast, to cut through the noise of the everyday and get to the heart of the issue facing them thus giving them a clear structure to take positive action.

Creating Ecosystems for Exceptional Results

Maximising the Power of Diverse Perspectives

Eya Pagdanganan

with Roxanne Angela Pagdanganan Sicat

I am an ontological coach who believes in the importance of establishing robust support systems in all areas of our lives, allowing us to succeed in both the workplace and at home. Drawing upon 27 years of corporate experience, I support my coachees with my keen eye for identifying what makes great people tick and my principle of leveraging support systems to allow individuals to practise new, desired behaviours. By creating personalised support systems in my own life, I am able to bring the best out of myself as a business owner, coach, mother, and daughter.

Roxanne is my eldest daughter. She has grown up in multiple Southeast Asian countries as a result of my international career. Through these travels, Roxanne has grown to understand the importance of integrating diverse perspectives, especially across people, places, and cultures. She is currently pursuing graduate studies at the Imperial College London.

IT TAKES A VILLAGE

Oran a azu nwa is a proverb from Nigeria's Igbo people that translates to 'It takes a village to raise a child'.

I've always believed that humans are inherently social beings. Trying to achieve my goals alone has often left me feeling lonely and overwhelmed. The sense of isolation can be crushing, and it's during these times that I realised how crucial it is to have a support system around me. We are wired to seek connections and thrive in environments where collaboration and mutual support are present.

***

Furthermore, my experiences have led me to the realisation that it is incredibly challenging to try and achieve everything independently; doing so leads to burnout. As someone with numerous projects and limited time and energy, I have found that it is more practical to assemble teams of people and leverage their interconnected expertise towards a common goal. Not only is the load more manageable, but this allows me to extend my capabilities and maximise my potential by working with others. Building an ecosystem thus allows me to pool resources, knowledge, and skills, making it possible to reach multiple complex goals simultaneously. The resulting synergy is far greater than the sum of individual efforts.

* * *

It all started with a task at hand—something I wanted to accomplish that seemed daunting and complex. The journey was not just mine but intertwined with the life of my child, Marianne (not her real name). Marianne was born as a floppy baby. She was hypotonic, needing therapy from the tender age of six months.

Very quickly, I realised I couldn't do this myself. I was overwhelmed and underprepared for the myriad challenges we faced. In the midst of my struggle, a concept began to crystallise: Team Marianne. This wasn't just a catchy name; it represented a lifeline. Team Marianne was the embodiment of a supportive environment—a network of dedicated individuals, each contributing their expertise and care for Marianne's well-being.

Initially, I built Team Marianne with the approach of bringing together best practices. My instinct was to seek out existing expertise, believing that leveraging established methods was more efficient than starting from scratch. Our home became a revolving door of specialists: an occupational therapist, a physical therapist, and eventually, experts in speech, walking, talking, and even chewing.

In the beginning, my outlook was transactional: I needed help, so I sought it out, feeling burdened by the tasks I couldn't handle alone. But as time passed, something profound shifted. I began to see the true value of the team we had assembled. It was no longer about just needing extra hands; it was about embracing the collective expertise that these professionals brought into our lives. Marianne's therapists stopped being 'just' service providers. They became integral parts of Marianne's journey and our family's support system.

My approach can be summed up as follows. As Marianne's mother, I was able to bring to the table my own unique perspectives, strengths, and strategies. I began to see, however, that my perspective was just one of many. To get a robust breakdown of the problem at hand, I needed to draw upon the perspectives of a diverse group of people who naturally saw things differently. Put another way, the experts I had assembled brought more than just their knowledge, they also brought their life experiences and unique ways of seeing the world. This fundamental aspect of ontological coaching—the realisation that one's perspective is just one of many—has guided my approach to building teams ever since.[1, 2]

As an ontological coach, I often reflect on how my experience with Marianne reshaped my understanding of the importance of supportive environments. It taught me that forging great teams goes beyond assembling people with the right expertise; it is also about creating a nurturing space where everyone can thrive. By recognising and valuing the unique contributions of each individual and how they drive towards a common goal, we were able to enhance our collective ability to solve complex problems.[3] This is the essence of leadership: inspiring people to follow you because they believe in a shared vision.

In coaching, just as in life with Marianne, it's essential to build and maintain environments where support is readily available, expertise is valued, and collaboration is the norm. This supportive framework accelerates progress and leads to more sustainable and impactful results. Through Team Marianne, I learnt that supportive environments are the bedrock

---

1   Olalla, Julio and Rafael Echevarría. *The Art of Ontological Coaching.* Denver, CO, Newfield Network, 2017.

2   Olalla, Julio. *From Knowledge to Wisdom: Essays on the Crisis in Contemporary Learning.* Denver, CO, Newfield Network, 2004.

3   Olalla, Julio, and Terrie Lupberger. *Developing Your Own Emotional Awareness as a Coach.* Denver, CO, Newfield Network, 2017, p. 2.

of achievement. They transform daunting challenges into manageable tasks and turn solitary struggles into shared victories. All of this rests on a key insight from ontological coaching: each individual's view is just a perspective, and by combining different perspectives, we can explore more actions and achieve new results.[4]

WHY SHOULD WE CARE ABOUT ECOSYSTEMS

The Challenge of Individualism

In today's society, people often attempt to tackle challenges on their own. The absence of community and the supportive presence of others has become a norm, largely due to how society has evolved. As a result, many individuals do not want to ask for help. This tendency to avoid seeking help can be exacerbated by issues such as imposter syndrome. Many people fear that asking questions or seeking assistance will make them appear incompetent or insufficiently knowledgeable. They worry they might be judged as inadequate parents or professionals, plagued by thoughts of not being 'good enough'. Additionally, our education system often emphasises the importance of having the right answers and knowing everything, which can discourage the natural instinct to seek help and collaborate.

The breakdown of traditional friendship groups and the mobility of modern life also contribute to this challenge. People frequently move to new locations, leaving behind the wisdom and support of familiar communities and elders. This scarcity of natural support networks makes it even more crucial to intentionally create ecosystems of support.

---

4   Marsden, Marcus. *Start With Who: Reveal the Hidden Power of Identity to Create a Purposeful Life.* Singapore, Candid Creation Publishing LLP, 2022, p. 5.

The Value of Ecosystems

So why should we care about ecosystems? Humans are inherently social beings. By stepping back and acknowledging that our perspective is just one of many, we can see the value in finding like-minded individuals who share our goals or can be persuaded to join us in our pursuits. Establishing common goals doesn't require complete alignment; it's about moving in the same general direction and supporting each other along the way.

Imagine the power of reverting to a time when communal efforts were the norm, when people worked together to achieve shared objectives. This collective effort, which I refer to as an ecosystem, is intentionally designed to bring together diverse expertise and purpose, ensuring that all elements work harmoniously to thrive.

Creating an intentional ecosystem involves identifying and nurturing relationships with people who can contribute to our goals and whose goals we can support in return. It hinges upon the recognition that we don't have to navigate life's challenges alone. By fostering a community of support, we can leverage collective strengths and expertise to achieve more than we could individually. This approach not only helps us overcome individual challenges but also enables us to thrive in an increasingly complex and fast-paced world.

When crafting an ecosystem, it is essential to take ownership of the leading role. No matter how overwhelming building an ecosystem is, it takes the courage of putting your goals at the centre—and taking on the responsibility of seeing them through—that lies at the core of intentional ecosystems. By taking ownership of your needs, you will be able to begin creating a shared context, a common framework, or a set of mutual understandings that guide how you and your teammates will operate within this network. This shared understanding helps ensure that everyone involved understands the goals, values, and principles that underpin your collective efforts.[5] Not only will you enhance your ability to achieve your personal goals, but you will also strengthen the entire ecosystem, making it more resilient and adaptive.

ONTOLOGICAL COACHING MINDSET, SYSTEMIC, AND ECOSYSTEM THINKING

Before we delve into the steps of establishing an ecosystem coaching mindset, let's define a few words that will help us better understand what is required. These definitions will help us understand what an ecosystem coaching mindset is and how it can benefit us at work and in our personal lives.

Ontological Coaching Mindset

An ontological coaching mindset embodies openness, curiosity, and empathy, with a dedication to fostering growth and development in others.[6] It prioritises nurturing, learning, and encouraging personal evolution. This mindset is characterised by a sincere interest in others, an open attitude, and a supportive approach. Through attentive listening, insightful questioning, and constructive feedback, it helps individuals uncover their potential and achieve their goals, thereby enhancing their personal growth and confidence.

A Systemic Coaching Mindset

A systemic coaching mindset involves understanding and working with the interconnected parts of a team, organisation, or family. Imagine a

---

5   Clutterbuck, David. *Coaching The Team At Work.* 2nd ed., Boston, MA, Nicholas Brealey Publishing, 2020, p. 69.

6   Lupberger, Terrie. "The Coach's Imperative: Expanding Perspectives." *Professional Coaching: Principles and Practice*, edited by Susan English, Janice Manzi Sabatine, and Philip Brownell, New York, NY: Springer Publishing Company LLC, 2018, p.185–194.

harmonious system where every component plays a crucial role. In coaching, this means grasping the intricate relationships and dynamics within these environments to positively impact performance and outcomes.[7]

This approach focuses on understanding and harnessing the interdependencies within a system. By examining how these internal dynamics interact, coaches can foster positive transformation and growth. For example, a coach might help a manager see how team dynamics, communication patterns, and workflow processes are interconnected and how they collectively influence team performance.

An Ecosystem Coaching Mindset

An ecosystem coaching mindset builds on a systemic coaching mindset by recognising that everything is connected, like a vibrant, complex web that is always changing.[8] This includes the organisation, its partners, market conditions, community resources, and social factors. Understanding this big picture means seeing how each part, no matter how small, helps the whole system thrive.

A holistic perspective views an ecosystem as a vibrant, complex, vast, and ever-changing web of interconnected systems, both internal and external. This mindset also takes into account the various systems around us, both inside and outside the organisation. It understands that these systems are constantly interacting and changing. This approach stresses the importance of being flexible, understanding how different parts work together, and ensuring the impact lasts. It's essential to consider how outside factors like market trends and community resources affect success.

---

7   Hawkins, Peter. *Leadership Team Coaching: Developing Collective Transformational Leadership*. 4th ed., Kogan Page Ltd, 2021, p. 81.

8   Cavanagh, Michael and David Lane. "Coaching Psychology Coming of Age: The Challenges We Face in the Messy World of Complexity." *International Coaching Psychology Review*, vol. 7, no. 1, March 2012, doi.org/10.53841/bpsicpr.2012.7.1.75.

An Ontological Ecosystem Coaching Mindset

An ontological ecosystem coaching mindset builds on the strengths of the previously mentioned approaches by melding the principles of ontological coaching with the intricate dynamics of an ecosystem perspective. It begins with an acute sense of self-awareness and a commitment to continuous learning, recognising the inherent limitations in one's own capabilities and perspectives.

By fostering a space for intentional collaboration, this mindset appreciates the diverse insights and life experiences that each individual brings to the table. It seeks to create an environment where collective growth and mutual contribution are not merely encouraged but are the very fabric of the interaction.[9] This perspective champions the idea that effective communication and a genuine appreciation for others' contributions are pivotal. In essence, an ontological ecosystem coaching mindset is about crafting a context where everyone is empowered to thrive, leading to the co-creation of innovative and effective solutions. It is through this harmonious blend of self-awareness, continuous development, and collaborative spirit that true progress is made.

WHY AN ONTOLOGICAL ECOSYSTEM COACHING MINDSET MIGHT BE WHAT YOU NEED

Let's explore why embracing an ontological ecosystem coaching mindset can significantly benefit your professional and personal endeavours.

---

9   Flores, Fernando. *Conversations For Action and Collected Essays: Instilling a Culture of Commitment in Working Relationships*, edited by Maria Flores Letelier, North Charleston, SC, CreateSpace Independent Publishing Platform, 2012, p. 76.

Seeing the Bigger Picture

An ontological ecosystem coaching mindset encourages us to take a broader view, considering various factors that influence our outcomes. Cultivating a wider perspective helps us spot opportunities and potential challenges we might otherwise miss.[10]

Being More Adaptable

Flexibility and responsiveness are key in addressing many of today's challenges in the workplace and in our personal lives. An ontological ecosystem coaching mindset helps us build these habits into our routines. By considering both internal and external changes, we become better at handling new information and shifting conditions.

Creating Lasting Solutions

The best solutions are the ones that endure, as they address the core issue at hand rather than papering them over. An ontological ecosystem coaching mindset focuses on long-term sustainability, promoting resilience and lasting growth.

Encouraging Collaboration and Innovation

Quality collaboration often leads to great ideas. An ontological ecosystem coaching mindset encourages us to connect and work together across various systems and networks. By bringing together different perspectives and resources, we often find more creative and effective solutions, creating a symphony of ideas where each contribution enhances the whole.

---

10 Brothers, Chalmers. *Language and the Pursuit of Happiness: A New Foundation for Designing Your Life, Your Relationships, and Your Results.* Naples, FL, New Possibilities Press, 2005, pp. 1–3.

Making the Most of Resources

Through its emphasis on collaboration and synergy between different perspectives, an ontological ecosystem coaching mindset allows us to take stock of all the internal and external resources at our disposal. As a result, it allows us to ensure we are using all potential supports to reach our goals.

Managing Risks Better

In our ever-changing world, being prepared for risks is crucial. An ontological ecosystem coaching mindset helps us think about various external factors and their potential impacts, improving our ability to anticipate and manage risks. This proactive stance leads to better strategies that are sensitive to problems that may arise.

Understanding Interactions

Finally, an ontological ecosystem coaching mindset recognises the dynamic interactions between different systems. Understanding how changes in one area can affect others improves overall effectiveness and cohesion.

ADOPTING AN ONTOLOGICAL ECOSYSTEM COACHING MINDSET

In our rapidly changing world, navigating complexity is paramount to achieving our desired outcomes. Shifting to an ontological ecosystem coaching mindset can help bring us closer to our aims. By acknowledging the limitations of a single perspective and embracing the richness that comes from the interaction between diverse inputs, we can be better prepared for the challenges life throws at us. Creating a space where these diverse perspectives interact is vital for complex problem-solving. The journey begins with identifying a task or goal and acknowledging its complexity.

Perspective Exploration

- **Start with Perspective: Embrace Complexity**

  Understanding that your view of the world is just one perspective is vital. Recognising that your way of seeing or approaching a problem is just one perspective opens up the possibility of inviting others who naturally see things differently. Be open to exploring different viewpoints, encouraging continuous learning and self-reflection. Embodying this mindset helps foster an environment where everyone is open to growth and change, facilitating a culture of continuous improvement. This is the essence of an ontological coaching ecosystem mindset: understanding that we are part of a larger, interconnected system.

- **Promote Self-Awareness**

  Take the time to understand your beliefs, behaviours, and needs that guide your decisions and interactions with other people. Being able to identify the idiosyncrasies of one's own perspective makes it easier to identify the strengths and limitations of other peoples' approaches—this is why self-awareness is a cornerstone of the ontological coaching mindset. Engage in regular self-reflection and seek feedback from others to build stronger relationships within your ecosystem.

- **Navigating Complexity with Flexibility**

  Adopting an ontological ecosystem coaching mindset means embracing a 360° view, exploring all possibilities, and maintaining flexibility. It's about looking around and seeing the options available rather than getting stuck in a single point of view. This approach encourages forward motion towards goals, uplifted by values, faith, and hope, and connected to a higher purpose. It's about navigating around issues with a dynamic balance, staying centred, and moving onwards and upwards.

- **The Importance of Community and Asking for Help**

  Modern society often discourages asking for help due to fears of appearing inadequate. This tendency is compounded by factors like imposter syndrome, the breakdown of traditional community structures, and the isolation of individuals. Recognising that we are social beings, however, and intentionally creating communities or ecosystems where help and collaboration are encouraged can counteract this trend. We can create generative and supportive environments by finding like-minded individuals or convincing others to join in a shared purpose.

  Cultivate the ability to make specific requests and engage in meaningful conversations to enlist support. Normalise asking for assistance as a strength rather than a weakness. Clearly articulate your needs and show appreciation for the help you receive to build a robust support network. Mutual support is fundamental in an ontological ecosystem.

Intentional Creation

- **Design Enabling Environments**

  To proactively create environments that enhance your chances of success, identify the resources, tools, and structures that facilitate productivity and well-being. Tailor these systems to meet your team's unique needs, and continuously refine them based on feedback and evolving circumstances. An ontological approach ensures that the systems you produce are dynamic and adaptable to the ecosystem's needs.

- **Assemble Diverse Teams and Leverage Collective Strengths**

  Take advantage of the unique contributions of your team members to create a dynamic and effective ecosystem. Recognise and celebrate individual strengths and achievements. By harnessing the diverse talents within your team, you will be able to drive innovation and achieve superior results. Collective strengths are a vital resource in an ontological ecosystem.

As you assemble your team, you will see that beyond just knowledge, individuals bring their unique life experiences and ways of seeing the world. Even two experts with similar backgrounds will perceive and approach problems differently. Thus, intentionally seeking out individuals with varied experiences and expertise becomes critical. Encouraging open dialogue and ensuring everyone's voice is heard can lead to richer, more innovative solutions.

Create Nurturing Environments

The next step is to create an environment where these diverse individuals can thrive. It involves more than just bringing people together; it's about fostering a context where they feel comfortable and motivated to collaborate. This requires intentionality in building relationships—both between the leader and each team member, as well as among the team members themselves. This shift from transactional interactions to relationships based on common goals and mutual care enhances collaboration.

Creating this environment doesn't happen overnight. It involves fostering a space where ideas can be freely shared and mutual respect forms the foundation. People need to feel safe to take risks and learn from mistakes. Promoting a culture where feedback is constructive and aimed at collective growth ensures that everyone feels valued and supported. This ontological approach recognises that nurturing environments foster growth and development within the ecosystem.

- **Evaluate and Adjust**

  Regularly assess and refine the systems you've created to ensure they support your goals. Implement regular check-ins and feedback loops, making necessary adjustments to stay aligned with your goals and maintain momentum. Continuous evaluation and adaptation are key in an ontological ecosystem.

Embodied Leadership

- **Focus on Common Care**

  Unifying your team with shared goals is essential. Identifying interests and values that resonate with everyone helps create a strong sense of purpose. This common care motivates people to give their best, fostering a sense of belonging and mutual support. Leadership in this context is about inspiring people to follow a shared direction and creating a compelling vision that motivates people to go above and beyond.[11] In an ontological ecosystem, common care is the glue that holds the collective together.

- **Foster Team Collaboration**

  Ensure everyone understands their roles and how they contribute to the collective goal. Encourage cross-functional collaboration and open communication. By clarifying expectations and promoting a shared understanding of objectives, you can enhance teamwork and synergy. Collaboration strengthens the ecosystem.

- **Lead with Empathy**

  Connecting with team members on a personal level is crucial. Practising active listening and showing genuine interest in their well-being builds trust and loyalty. Empathetic leadership inspires the best

---

11 Poulos, Kelly, and Emily Liu. *Secrets to Winning*. Taipei, Taiwan, Commonwealth Magazine Co., Ltd, 2014, pp. 232–233.

efforts from your team. Ontological coaching emphasises empathy as a way to deepen connections and foster a harmonious ecosystem.

- **Build Resilience**

  Use the ontological coaching mindset to bounce back from setbacks. Shift your perspective, explore new solutions, and foster a growth mindset that views challenges as opportunities for learning. Equip your team with strategies to manage stress and maintain focus on long-term goals. Resilience is built through shared experiences and mutual support.

- **Maintaining Your Body Budget**

  Lastly, considering Lisa Feldman Barrett's concept of maintaining a body budget, creating an ecosystem supports our well-being.[12] By fostering environments that distribute the cognitive and emotional load among many, individuals can better manage their stress and maintain their overall health.

Our world today is characterised by volatility, uncertainty, complexity, and ambiguity (VUCA).[13,14] Unlike in the past, where there was more time and space to learn and achieve, today's fast-paced environment demands quick adaptation and collaboration. In this VUCA world, leaning on each other and creating supportive ecosystems becomes crucial. An ecosystem that serves a common purpose helps individuals achieve their goals more effectively; relying on the support of your ecosystem helps you remain flexible and responsive to change. The ontological

12 Barrett, Lisa Feldman. *How Emotions are Made: The Secret Life of the Brain.* Boston, MA, Mariner Books, 2018, pp. 232–233.

13 Mackey, Sr, Richard H. *Translating Vision into Reality: The Role of the Strategic Leader.* Carlisle Barracks, PA, US Army War College, 1992.

14 Bennis, Warren, and Burt Nanus. *Leaders: Strategies for Taking Charge.* New York, NY: Harper & Row, 1985.

approach helps you see the interconnectedness of all elements within the ecosystem.

In short, adopting an ontological ecosystem coaching mindset involves recognising multiple perspectives, creating environments where diverse views can thrive, fostering meaningful relationships, navigating complexity with flexibility, and reconnecting with community and humanity. This approach not only enhances problem-solving and innovation but also supports individual well-being in today's complex world. By integrating these elements into your approach, you can adopt an ontological ecosystem coaching mindset that helps navigate complexity, leverage diverse perspectives, and achieve meaningful success.

CRAFTING YOUR ECOSYSTEM FOR SUCCESS: A FINAL REFLECTION

Marcel Proust tells us that: "The true journey of discovery does not consist of searching for new landscapes, but in having 'new eyes.'"

As we close, I invite you to embark on the journey of applying these principles to your own life. The essence of what I wish to impart is encapsulated in the phrase 'Be, Do, Have.'[15] When you aspire to achieve something, especially if it appears daunting or complex, it's essential to step back and adopt a broader perspective—much like a drone soaring above, offering a panoramic view of the landscape below.

Visualise your objective from this elevated vantage point. It's not merely about observing the systems and interactions at the ground floor level or

---

15 Covey, Stephen R. *The 7 Habits of Highly Effective People: Restoring the Character Ethic*. New York, NY, Simon & Schuster, 1989, p. 51.

within a single building, as one might from a rooftop. Instead, it's about noticing the intricate web of connections that span the entire horizon. My invitation is to acknowledge the complexity and embrace it as an opportunity for deeper understanding and more effective action.

Remember, you're not alone. There are experts and allies who can support you on this journey. It's from this high vantage point that you can discern the myriad factors and elements at play, which may not be visible at ground level. This perspective reveals movement, the lifeblood of ecosystems. These interactions are dynamic, complex, and constantly evolving.

Adopting an ontological ecosystem perspective involves recognising that there's no singular 'right' way. Instead, it involves navigating through various forces and incidents, dancing with them rather than resisting. Hold a clear vision of your destination, but remain flexible in your approach, ready to adapt as circumstances shift.

The potential for feeling overwhelmed by this complexity is real. Yet, it's part of the journey. Appreciate the intricate interplay of elements and understand that certainty is elusive. Embrace the challenge with a spirit of experimentation and self-compassion. Recognise that you can't control everything, and that's perfectly fine.

This humility and acceptance foster a sense of connection and collaboration. Realise that others may have goals that intersect with yours, creating opportunities for mutual support and shared success. This interconnectedness can alleviate feelings of isolation, replacing them with a sense of community and appreciation for those around you.

In today's fast-paced world, recognising and valuing the contributions of others is crucial. Appreciate the elements and interactions within your ecosystem. By doing so, you increase your chances of success, feel less alone, and build a supportive network.

To start, define your desired outcome. Identify barriers and ride the metaphorical drone to gain an aerial view of the situation. Consider how to navigate from point A to point B, acknowledging all interacting dynamics. Reflect on the challenges, be kind to yourself, and remember you are not alone.

Effective leadership entails inspiring others to support you by finding common goals and building strong relationships. Break down your team's objectives, recognise their importance, and nurture these connections. Above all, care for the people involved, ensuring that relationships are at the heart of your efforts.

As you proceed, pause, connect with your ambitions, and explore your projects and goals from an ecosystem perspective. Embrace the complexity, practise leadership with empathy, and cultivate a supportive community around you. This approach will not only help you achieve your goals but also enrich your journey.

Remember, it takes a village.

Eya Pagdanganan ACTC, PCC, NBC-HWC
Partner and Executive Coach

Eya is an experienced executive, team, and leadership coach with over 27 years of corporate experience across Southeast Asia. She is an International Coaching Federation Advanced Certified Team Coach (ACTC), Professional Certified Coach (PCC), and a US Board Certified Health and Wellness Coach (NBC-HWC). Eya specialises in fostering leadership development, team dynamics, and well-being. Her career includes leadership roles at Unilever, Mead Johnson Nutrition, and Royal DSM, where she gained profound insights into managing multicultural teams and driving innovation.

Eya's coaching philosophy is rooted in ontological coaching, emphasising the creation of supportive ecosystems that enable individuals and teams to thrive. She believes in the power of diverse perspectives and intentional collaboration to achieve meaningful results. Her dedication to coaching is also reflected in her work as a Cancer Journey Coach, where she supports individuals navigating health challenges with empathy and expertise.

Eya's eldest daughter, Roxanne, co-authored a chapter in their book on creating ecosystems for exceptional results. Growing up in multiple Southeast Asian countries due to Eya's international career, Roxanne has developed a deep understanding of integrating diverse perspectives across cultures. She is pursuing graduate studies at Imperial College London, bringing her unique experiences and insights into this collaborative work.

In her personal life, Eya enjoys tranquil walks along Singapore's shoreline and prioritises meaningful connections with her adult children. Her work continues to inspire leaders to embrace the complexities of their roles with resilience and a collaborative spirit.

CHAPTER 12

Coaching as a Gateway to Our Consciousness

Opening the Door to Conscious Living Through Coaching

Nabil Mattar

WHAT IS CONSCIOUSNESS?

Consciousness is a topic that baffles many. I see it as a gift from the universe that is complex but beautiful and powerful. Most of us probably don't give it much thought and take it for granted, but it is something that has intrigued me for many years.

Consciousness is what differentiates human beings from other living beings on earth! Consciousness gives us our purpose, desires, and ability to question everything. As compared to animals or other living organisms whose primary drive is survival, they don't have goals or desires. This is a fundamental concept in biology and evolutionary theory. Because we are conscious, we question things, we question our lives, we question our purpose, and the world around us. This innate curiosity drives us to seek understanding and meaning in everything we encounter. We ponder our existence, our relationships, and the impact we have on others and the environment. Our consciousness pushes us to explore the unknown, challenge the status quo, and strive for progress and enlightenment. It is this relentless pursuit of knowledge and truth that defines our human experience and fuels our growth as individuals and as a society.

Till today, many philosophers and scientists are still trying to get to the bottom of consciousness for centuries. I came across this concept a decade ago as I was exploring meditation. I was taught that every human being has consciousness within us, and our consciousness can guide us to our life purpose. It was fascinating to me, but it was just a concept, until I started learning ontological coaching. As I began coaching others, I realised that I became a better coach when I expanded my consciousness in my life. As I became more conscious about myself, I was more aware about my daily thoughts, actions, feelings. I started becoming more curious, for example, about how I react to certain events or people, what the predominant thoughts are in my head, what my habits and my triggers are. It gave rise to a lot of questions about who I am and what my purpose was. And through such questions to myself, I was then better able to relate to my coachees. But before I share more on this topic, let's understand consciousness in a deeper level first.

CONSCIOUSNESS IS AWARENESS

Have you ever had a lucid dream where you know that you are dreaming? For example, in the dream, you dream that you are flying above the clouds but you are conscious enough to know that you are flying in a dream and that you are actually in a dream? There is a certain awareness in you and a distinction between your dream and reality. When you are conscious, you no longer get completely immersed in the events around you. Instead, you remain aware that you are the one experiencing both the events and the corresponding emotions and thoughts. You don't get lost in your emotions and thoughts.

Our consciousness has the ability to focus. It is part of the nature of consciousness. Awareness is the essence of consciousness and awareness has the ability to be more focused of one thing and less focused on something else. Think of a camera and its zoom function. You can choose to zoom out to have a bird's eye view or zoom in to focus on a subject. If a baby is looking at a toy in their hand and then notices something farther away, like a pet moving in the background, they may shift their focus from the toy to the distant pet. This demonstrates an awareness of spatial relationships. Nobody taught them how to do this. It was natural and intuitive.

Understanding consciousness is best done through our own experiences. Imagine you're reading a book. Suddenly, you realise you're no longer reading. Instead, your mind is flooded with thoughts. Maybe you're thinking about your next meal, an incident from the previous day, or wondering who sent you a message as your phone beeps. This scenario highlights a fascinating aspect of consciousness: its ability to shift focus. Whether it's a mental thought or an external object, our awareness can easily be drawn in different directions. This constant shifting of focus shows the active and fluid nature of our consciousness. When you're not aware, your consciousness tends to hop from one object to another. Sometimes, it gets so engrossed in a particular thought or distraction that you become completely absorbed, losing track of everything else.

Being aware means having more control over where your attention goes. It's like being the captain of your ship, steering through the sea of distractions with purpose and direction.

Consciousness is a dance of attention, constantly moving and changing. By becoming more aware of this dance, you can take the lead, directing your focus and finding a balance amid the distractions.

ARE WE EVER FULLY CONSCOIUS?

Picture yourself out on a boat, gazing at an iceberg. How much of it can you see? Only about 10% of the iceberg is visible above the waterline, while the remaining 90% lurks unseen beneath the surface.

Now, think about your consciousness. At any given moment, you're only aware of a small fraction of your thoughts, emotions, and physical sensations. Most of your mental and emotional life happens below the surface of your awareness, just like the submerged part of the iceberg.

Consider this: Every experience you've ever had, from before you were born up to this very moment, is stored in your memory. Studies have shown that with the right brain stimulation, you can recall every single detail of your life—every sight, sound, smell, emotion, and physical sensation. But how much of your past are you consciously thinking about right now? Almost none. If you were suddenly aware of all your past experiences at once, it would be overwhelming. Keeping most memories below the surface allows you to focus on the present, which is crucial for navigating daily life.

Think of your mind like a computer. It stores gigabytes of data, but only a tiny fraction appears on the screen at any one time. If everything showed up at once, the computer would be useless. Your mind operates similarly. Most of your thoughts, memories, beliefs, attitudes, and values stay below the waterline, out of your immediate awareness. You can access them, but most of the time, you don't need to.

What about your feelings? You're constantly experiencing emotions, but often you don't realise it. They happen below the conscious level. When you get angry, it's usually because you were already carrying some unconscious anger, and something triggered it. It's not that you suddenly became angry out of nowhere. The same goes for sadness or any other emotion. Many of us learnt as kids to hide our feelings, especially ones like anger, fear, or sadness. As adults, we often don't recognise the emotions we carry around unconsciously.

And your physical sensations? Are you aware of your breathing right now? Probably not until you started thinking about it. Your lungs handle breathing automatically. Are you aware of your eyes blinking or your tongue in your mouth? How about your heart beating? Occasionally, but usually, it beats without your attention. Imagine if you had to consciously keep your heart beating or your lungs breathing—you'd be exhausted. There are over 1,000 automatic functions your body performs to keep you alive: circulating blood, digesting food, regulating temperature. You can become aware of these functions, but most of the time, they happen without you even thinking about them.

So, more than 90% of what you think, feel, and sense physically happens outside your awareness. And that's essential for your survival. Embracing this understanding can help you become more mindful and aware of the vast, hidden depths of your consciousness.

OUR ILLUSION OF SELF

Imagine your mind as a television screen. Have you ever noticed how sometimes you become so engrossed in a TV show that you lose all awareness of your surroundings? You forget where you're sitting or what else is happening around you. Similarly, your mind constantly plays a movie of thoughts, memories, and future projections, drawing you in and often causing you to lose touch with the present moment.

This inner movie is made up of familiar thought patterns and emotions. Just like a director, your life experiences shape the scenes and themes of this movie. Our inner movie is created from past events and experiences. For example, consider a song that you associated with a past relationship. When you first heard it, it filled you with joy and love. It brings back all the wonderful memories of the time you were with your previous partner. But after a painful break-up, the same song now brings up sadness and a sinking feeling in your heart. All the wonderful memories suddenly turn into memories of pain and regret. Over time, you might develop beliefs like 'people can't be trusted' or 'it's safer to be alone', and these beliefs become part of your inner movie about relationships.

Here's another example. Consider a particular dish your grandmother used to make, which you loved as a child. It brought comfort, warmth, and a sense of being cared for. After her passing, the same dish might remind you of her absence and the void left in your life. The comfort food, which once evoked happy family times, now brings a bittersweet mix of fondness and grief, shaping your inner movie about family and loss.

Why does our mind create an inner movie?

Based on our past experiences, our brain builds models to simplify objects and events in the world. Everything we know is based on these models. It does not capture every detail, but just enough for the brain to determine appropriate responses.

When your inner movie takes over, you lose your centredness. Your consciousness gets absorbed in these patterns of thoughts and emotions, creating a false reality based on past experiences. This is what we call the illusion of self—identifying with the inner movie rather than your true self. And when we are in the illusion of self, you will find your consciousness becoming myopic, your awareness just focusing on certain events or objects, and you no longer have that separation from the inner movie and you. That's where your life becomes a repeated pattern of the inner movie that you created from the past. We might have recurring negative thoughts or emotional reactions to certain triggers. These mental and emotional patterns can become so ingrained that we don't even realise they're happening. The same goes for our interactions with others. We have habitual ways of responding to different situations and people. These responses are often automatic, shaped by past experiences and learned behaviours.

The key to breaking free from this illusion lies in awareness. And we are only fully aware when we are conscious about patterns, and the inner movie that creates our patterns. A conscious person can distinguish between themselves and their inner movie. Imagine watching a movie on TV, and when it ends, you switch off the television and suddenly become fully aware that you're sitting on your couch in the living room. You stop projecting yourself into the movie. This shift creates a space within you, and with space comes freedom—being free from your inner movie and being able to make a conscious choice.

In essence, our lives are shaped by a multitude of invisible patterns created by our inner movie. By bringing these patterns into our conscious awareness, we gain the ability to evaluate them and decide whether they align with our values and goals. This process of self-awareness and intentional choice is fundamental to personal growth and transformation. It allows us to break free from automatic behaviours and create a life that is more aligned with our true desires and aspirations.

THE OBSERVER WITHIN

When I began my journey to become a coach, I initially concentrated on the practical aspects—how to coach, the necessary skills, the competencies, and the questions. Although these components are crucial, I soon recognised that the true impact lies in the essence of 'being' a coach.

I understood that to contribute effectively to my coachees and to be an impactful coach, I needed to start with myself. Merely understanding the concepts of coaching intellectually wouldn't make me an effective coach. Being a coach means looking within, embodying the learnings, and applying them to my daily life. This is the essence of ontology—the study of the nature of being. Every day offers an opportunity for me to practise ontological coaching by tuning into my inner observer and noticing my body, emotions, and language. This is where consciousness comes into play—being aware of how I think, feel, and act in every moment.

I was intrigued and fascinated by how I could use these concepts and ideas to support deeper self-discovery. The distinctions between body, emotions, and language became very real to me. I started to connect the dots and uncover my patterns of behaviour and thought. With this understanding, I began aligning myself with my life's purpose, which sparked many profound questions within me:

- Who am I?
- What do I have to offer to the world?
- What is my purpose of existence?
- What's holding me back from living the life I want?

I also noticed how much richer life became through the new ontology distinctions I became aware of. These distinctions emerged when I allowed myself to slow down and tune into my observer. This was challenging for me, as it was counterintuitive to my logical, achievement-oriented mindset that prioritised learning to be a competent coach as quickly as possible. I then realised that this was my usual pattern in life—to always prioritise efficiency over everything else. I like to see the observer within me as a wise sage sitting atop a mountain, looking down with clarity and peace.

My invitation to you is to get familiar with your observer within. You can imagine yourself in a computer game and seeing yourself from a third-party point of view. From this perspective, you can start to see your thought patterns, emotional reactions, and the underlying reasons behind them. You begin to ask deeper, more profound questions about your life and purpose with a sense of non-judgemental curiosity. By staying present and aware, you can shift your consciousness and live more fully in the present moment, free from the grip of your inner movie.

It is easy to be caught up with all the distractions of the world but if you are able to tune in to your observer, you will be able to connect to your essence, the stillness, the peace within. One of the premises we hold as coaches is that the person who has the questions will also have the answers. As coaches, we hold that space for our coachees, so that they can tap into their consciousness, and discover the answers within. Likewise, I feel that as coaches, connecting with our observer within will allow us to expand our consciousness and to answer our own questions.

There are many ways to get familiar or to connect to our observer within through meditation, mindfulness practices, etc. The key is not to overcomplicate or intellectualise the process. The Consciousness Practice is a simple way to do it.

The Consciousness Practice

Find a quiet space to sit, and gently close your eyes.
- Take 10 deep breaths in and out and as deep as you can.
- On the last cycle, take a deep breath in and hold it for 10 seconds or more.
- Form a small 'O' in your mouth (as if you are whistling) and slowly exhale for 12 seconds.
- Go back to your normal breathing.
- Keep your eyes closed, feel the peace and stillness in you and begin to observe with no judgements. Observe the thoughts coming in and coming out of your mind. Observe your physical sensation. Observe your emotions.
- Use your breath as an anchor every time your mind starts to wander.

The more you practise being conscious, the more you can detach yourself from your thoughts and emotions and actions. And that's where you start building your observer muscle. You will start to go through your day-to-day life feeling more grounded, with more intent and focus. This, in turn, will create a deeper sense of presence and stillness as a coach to hold the space and contribute to our coachees effectively.

WE LIVE IN ANSWERS TO QUESTIONS WE NEVER ASK

Change begins with consciousness.

We can't recognise our patterns while we're stuck in them. This is why many people find change so challenging. They want change but are not aware of the unconscious 90% in them, what's below their waterline. Most people get so caught up with their inner movie and patterns in life that drain their energy and time, leaving them little room for creating change.

As coaches, we are supporting our coachees to lower the waterline of the iceberg, to see what's in the 90%—the beliefs, attitude, mindset, perspectives that are in control of how we see the world and show up in life. That's where most people get stuck in life; their 10% consciousness has an intention to go one way, but the 90% unconscious is pulling them the other way. But it's the 90% where the inner movie about how they see the world is playing. It is like an outdated computer program that keeps repeating over and over again, even though it does not serve a purpose to them. Most people have an illusion that this program is who they are and it's their reality. They remain unaware of the difference because they don't observe their own lives. Instead, they act as the programs of their lives, continually repeating the same patterns. It then becomes a game of survival which makes us no different to having the consciousness of animals!

To achieve lasting change, we endeavour to support our coachees to consciously look within. I like to imagine we coaches holding up a flame torch to support the coachees to illuminate their consciousness. Only when they can see what programs are keeping them stuck or holding them back, can they create their reality rather than replaying the old one. They will have clarity about the patterns they have, where they came from, and whether such patterns are serving them. Over time, this conscious creation will become their new program and their new reality. So, instead of being in a prison of their patterns, they have the freedom to choose.

For example, one of the most common New Year's goals that people have is related to losing weight. This is why gyms are often busiest at the start of the year. As the months go by, however, the gyms become less crowded as many people lose focus on their goal. This is where the 90% kicks in. The 90% refers to the underlying beliefs, attitudes, and behaviours that often sabotage their efforts. For many, it might be a limiting belief in their inability to lose weight as they have tried many times in the past but failed, or perhaps it's their work attitude taking precedence over fitness goals. Addressing this 90% is crucial. By understanding and working with these underlying factors, our coachees can achieve their desired goals and create a sustainable shift in their habits and lifestyle.

Understanding that the world is being created in the present, rather than something that was created by the past, is a rise in one's consciousness. We are the authors of our stories, we are the creators of our lives.

Exploring consciousness on a deeper level has also made me wonder: Is there a faster way to support myself and my coachees to illuminate our consciousness? In ontological coaching, there is a concept called break of transparency. As I shared previously, human beings live in patterns, and many a time, we repeat our patterns so often that it becomes invisible and transparent. The concept of a 'break in transparency' refers to a pivotal event or experience that disrupts our habitual patterns of thinking, feeling, and behaving, hence allowing us to see our lives and ourselves in a new light. This disruption often brings about a shift in consciousness, illuminating aspects of ourselves or our circumstances that were previously unseen or taken for granted.

I had a huge break in transparency in my life a couple of years ago when my wife passed away from cancer. The initial months after her passing were painful. It was a kind of pain in my heart that I have never felt before. It, however, illuminated a consciousness within me that was a catalyst to transform my life. Through that, I realised that I can expand my consciousness through voluntary self-introspection (building the observer within); and the other, often the more painful way, through the school of life, where I learn and grow from the challenges, adversities, and experiences that life presents.

I have always marvelled at how inspiring individuals manage to overcome the odds, fight through adversity, and rise above to become who they are today. Their journeys often include remarkable stories of resilience and triumph. Sometimes, I wonder: Do we need life to push us into a corner, with adversity staring us in the face, to awaken our consciousness? Is pain truly the greatest teacher in our lives? While I don't have a definitive answer, I have discovered that my courage to live life fully and accept whatever it brings certainly builds resilience and expands consciousness. I bring this perspective to my coaching, emphasising that every experience, no matter how challenging, contributes to the growth of our consciousness.

COLLECTIVE CONSCIOUSNESS

Every person I coach acts as a mirror, reflecting parts of my consciousness back to me. This helps me see myself more clearly, change, and grow in my beliefs about who I am, my relationships, and the world. The qualities I admire or dislike in my coachees are reflections of my own consciousness. Therefore, every coaching session is an opportunity for me to support another person and learn more about myself. Nothing in life is a coincidence, and every person I coach teaches me something.

As I grow as an ontological coach, I not only develop personally but also help others grow. This journey helps me expand my understanding and awareness. My role is not just about my own growth; it's also about helping others expand their consciousness. Each coaching interaction offers the potential for mutual growth. Every coachee brings a unique perspective, revealing hidden aspects of myself. This challenges me to integrate these aspects into my overall consciousness, creating a space for continuous learning and evolution.

Ontological coaching focuses on who we are as people. It helps us understand and change our core beliefs, emotions, and perceptions. By doing this, we improve our own lives and positively impact those we coach. I invite you, the reader, to join me in this exploration. Let's keep questioning ourselves and the nature of life, not because we want to get somewhere or achieve something, but to bring in a sense of wonder and curiosity. Because by doing so, we start living intentionally, guided by our conscious choices rather than old habits that no longer serve us.

The ripple effect of individual transformation extends far beyond personal boundaries. As we grow and evolve, we inspire others to embark on their own journeys of self-discovery. This collective movement towards greater awareness and understanding can lead to profound changes in our communities and society as a whole. By cultivating a deeper connection with ourselves and others, we can foster a world where empathy, compassion, and conscious living are the norm.

Together, we can elevate the collective consciousness and create a more harmonious and enlightened world.

Nabil Mattar, ACC
Partner, Trainer, and Executive Coach

With 15 years of experience in the derivatives brokerage industry, Nabil has held key regional and regional director roles, shaping client management strategies for major brokerages worldwide. His market expertise has earned him spots on *CNA*, *Bloomberg*, and *Money FM89.3*, where he shares insights on the financial markets.

Nabil's leadership approach, infused with performance coaching, has consistently driven high-performing teams to exceed their targets across continents. This passion for unlocking human potential led him to shift careers, becoming a leadership performance trainer and coach. Nabil is dedicated to helping others 'peel their onion', uncovering their core motivations and identity. His corporate acumen and results-oriented mindset have made him a sought-after coach for top leaders at companies like Prudential, PETRONAS, Shell, Accenture, Fonterra, Mekong Capital, VNG, and IG Group.

Always striving for growth, Nabil sought a deeper purpose beyond corporate success. He now focuses on helping clients align their talents and dreams with a meaningful life purpose.

Beyond coaching, Nabil is a certified meditation practitioner. He was featured in *The Straits Times* in 2016 for his unique approach to trading the financial markets, integrating meditation practices into his trading psychology.

Nabil's mission is clear: to lead with heart and inspire others to become their best selves.

Coaching for Life's Big Questions

Creating a Transformational Space for New Thinking

Terrie Lupberger

There's an old Buddhist proverb that says: 'Tend to the area of the garden you can reach.' For me, my garden has been personal transformation and executive coaching and how they intersect to bring out our best self. For as far back as I can remember, I've been interested in how we human beings can live more fully, with more aliveness, and with less suffering.

This deep curiosity and interest led me to coaching after running large projects and departments in big organisations in my earlier career. I saw the damage we inflicted upon each other at work and I wanted to learn how we could shift our mindsets and create healthier workplaces without sacrificing results.

I learnt an ontological approach to coaching, as you've been reading about in this book, and have been practising and teaching it for the last 25+ years. I was there at the beginning, helping steward coaching into a legitimate, credible, and potentially transformative profession.

I know wholeheartedly that coaching, when practised well, can root out and have us twist free from our outdated thinking, limiting beliefs, and old paradigms. We keep operating by these, doing more of the same but expecting new outcomes. So much more is possible and as a coach or a leader using a coach approach, at any level, the opportunity is to be a force for greater individual and collective positive change.

As we've explored so far, coaching expands the way you see and take action in your life. It supports you to achieve better outcomes for yourself, your team, organisation, family.

One way to think about coaching is that it helps you work with the content of your life—kids, spouse, career, health, finance, leadership, team, etc. It can help improve confidence, grow your emotional intelligence, support career planning and transitions, enhance your leadership capabilities, decision-making, and team effectiveness. It can aid you in creating and sticking to strategies to manage stress, build resilience and improve your well-being. It can help you improve your communication or conflict resolution skills, be a better parent and partner, and help you better adapt to and manage change.

From this perspective, think of coaching as a customised growth plan for your life and leadership with the added benefit of having a committed and non-judgemental partner in the coach to support you along the way and help you stay accountable.

LIFE IS NOT A SOLO SPORT

In addition to helping you better understand and manage the content of your life, coaching also helps you understand and navigate the multitude of systems that also influence your thinking, behaviours, and actions.

As a human being, you don't exist in the world by yourself. You are a living system yourself (respiratory, digestive, emotional, skeletal, sensory, cognitive, etc.) interacting with a multitude of other systems in various complex environments. From a systemic perspective, you are whole and complete and, at the same time, you are part of larger wholes—your family, organisation, community, nation, the human race, etc. You actually exist because of others. You achieve your goals with and because of others.

You even think the way you do because of others. The beliefs, values, opinions, and conclusions you've arrived at about who you are and what is possible have all been shaped by these systems—by your family of origin, by your schooling, by your places of work and your colleagues' thinking, where you grew up, your generation, gender, community, where you live now, etc.

All these influences had (and have) norms of behaviour and beliefs that have shaped your own. Most of these you unconsciously adopted or you consciously rejected (e.g. "I'll never behave that way to *my* children"). Good coaching is an opportunity to explore how these systems, and the beliefs that came with them, have influenced you and how they are supporting you or limiting you in the fulfilment of your aspirations.

Let me give you a simple example.

I was working with a female executive who felt like her career progression was stalling. She was considering leaving the organisation but also held a belief (among many) that she wouldn't find anything as fulfilling or that paid as well. She was stuck and couldn't make a move.

The coaching could have centred around the pros and cons of staying or leaving and what actions she would need to take for either step. By exploring the systems she had been influenced by, however, we were able to get to some underlying beliefs that were limiting her choices and undermining her confidence.

In our explorations, she shared with me that she was the first in her family to go to college. She didn't graduate because she went home to take care of a dying family member and never returned to college. She entered the workforce as an administrative assistant and worked her way up in this large organisation—from supervisor of a small section to eventually managing a large division. She was older than her counterparts and complained (but only to herself because she didn't want to 'make waves') that they were being promoted over her.

With more exploration, she said to me that she'd done really well for someone 'like her', with her background. She also admitted that part of her wondered if she was skilled or competent enough to lead in the C-suite and that she definitely felt like an imposter much of the time without her degree.

We discussed how her family's beliefs and the generation she grew up in might have influenced what she thought about herself and what she believed was possible for herself. We explored which beliefs were not serving her any longer and, most importantly, how to revise them.

As human beings, we all take on beliefs or stories about who we are and what we think we can and can't do. Because they are stories and not immutable facts, we can change them; which is what she did. She saw that her beliefs about herself weren't, in fact, true. She had proven herself over and over again in the organisation and, with a new-found story and confidence, had a powerful conversation with her boss about what she wanted next in her career.

In another example, I was working with a senior executive who was in serious 'burnout' (his words). In our sessions, he was focused on greater well-being and, as a result, began reducing his work hours and seeing a nutritionist. Those were good, foundational steps.

Equally as important, we also explored how the systems he was operating in might also be impacting his sense of burnout. At work, he had an extremely toxic team member that he hadn't dealt with for almost a year. He kept coming up with justifications as to why not, but he finally saw that his well-being, and that of his team's, was at stake by his inaction. Once he had the awareness, he could then move into designing actions to address it.

Coaching Note

This might be a good time for you to pause and consider what systems have influenced you the most. Consider these questions for yourself:

- Who influenced your own way of thinking the most? In what ways?
- What beliefs do you have which you inherited that might be limiting what else is possible for yourself? How does that serve you? How does that not serve you?
- What systems are you a part of now and how are they influencing what you do and don't do?
- Who would you be and what could you do if you freed yourself from your limiting beliefs?

It's important to note that when we explore the systems that have shaped us, we aren't doing so to blame them for how our lives are turning out. The toxic member didn't cause the executive's burnout. The family beliefs passed on to the female executive didn't cause her self-doubt. These people were surely influenced by the beliefs and stories of the systems they had been a part of, but once they saw the influences as well as the benefits and costs, they then had a choice as to what to do about it.

That's a key distinction we make in coaching. We human beings aren't condemned by our pasts nor are we fixed entities that can't change. We are always at choice. Even if we can't change the circumstances of our past or present, we do have a choice as to how we relate to and navigate them.

As a human being, you are always in an emerging process of becoming, evolving, and changing. With new awareness and new practices—which is what coaching offers—you can generate a new future for yourself.

THE META CONTEXT OF OUR LIVES

Beyond the systems unique to you, based on your own history and circumstances, there is also what I call the 'meta context' or the prevailing story of our times that is also shaping how you think, what you feel, and what you do, whether you are consciously aware of it or not.

In the current meta story, being a human being at this time on the planet is radically different from, say, hundreds of years or even decades ago. We find ourselves living at a time in which there are fewer and fewer simple problems left to address. The speed at which we are being asked to make decisions has greatly accelerated and the business landscape we are operating in more uncertain and chaotic.

In the backdrop of our daily living and leading are global, overarching challenges such as climate change, environmental degradation, pandemics, global conflicts, rapidly emerging technological disruption, polarisation and growing extremism of all kinds, bringing with them intolerance and dehumanisation.

At the same time, we human beings are interconnected in unprecedented ways we haven't experienced before—economically, socially, ecologically. Decisions in one part of the world have consequences for people and businesses on the other side of the world, often immediately.

Our interconnectedness is undeniable, yet the meta story of our times would have us believe that we are separate from everyone and everything else; that we don't rely on each other; that our individual actions don't have ripple effects all over this one planet that we all share.

This false but prevalent story drives our behaviour (often unconsciously) to be self-reliant and self-interested. It can perpetuate scarcity thinking that we have to get our own piece of the pie before the 'others' get theirs since there isn't enough for everyone. It can foster a sense of alienation and drive us to twist ourselves into knots to please others for fear of not being included.

Another facet of the current meta story that is influencing how we think and what we do is that we aren't enough nor do we have enough. This comes up a lot in coaching conversations and from very accomplished professionals. When you think about it, we are constantly bombarded with messages we get from a variety of sources that tell us that we need something else, something more, to be okay. We need a better car, partner, job title, salary, face, bank account balance, grade, ROI (return on investment), skill set, etc. to be successful; to feel good about ourselves (and, let's fess up, to make sure others 'like' us, literally and metaphorically).

In the current meta story, having more has become the measure for how we're doing in our own lives, in our organisations and families, and even in our nations.

Our perpetual quest for more can drive us to overwork, over-consume, to constantly compare ourselves to others, to over-criticise, and to overlook what's good about right now in favour of a potentially 'better' tomorrow. Yet, when we step back and take a breath, we know from our own experiences that we just can't achieve our way to happiness. You get the bonus or promotion, for example, and soon after you're looking for something more.

Unprecedented uncertainty, another element of the meta story running in the background of our lives, has us strain and strive for clarity and assurance. We cling to the outdated belief (maybe hope) that we can predict, control, and manage situations by knowing more, by filling in the gaps with information we don't have.

It makes sense we would look for more information to address our concerns. For most of us, our learning experiences in life (primary school, college, work trainings, etc.) have been about acquiring information to get the right answers. Useful, but also insufficient, rarely were we rewarded for asking thought-provoking questions, challenging the status quo, using our intuition, showing compassion, demonstrating social skills, being a better global citizen, having a strong somatic awareness or emotional intelligence, listening deeply. The predominantly singular focus on cognitive learning, on knowing information to apply it to problems, has led to our reluctance to admit when we don't know something, when we don't have an answer.

Information is actually a very small piece of what it means to lead or live a good life but admitting you don't know or are uncertain is often seen as a weakness. (That also comes up a lot in coaching.) Leaders in politics, business, environmental sciences, economics, etc. will often hesitate to acknowledge their uncertainty. We unfairly expect them to have answers, and we expect the same of ourselves. This leads us to solutions that are partial at best and quickly outdated. It leads to an oversimplification of the issues, reduces us to black-and-white/either-or thinking for expediency, an impatience with ourselves and others, and has us put too much trust in those who claim to have the answers.

The impermanence of our human existence—another element in the meta story that just comes with being human—also profoundly shapes how we think about and live our lives. This awareness often prompts a sense of urgency to accomplish our goals and leave a lasting impact in the fleeting time that we have. The deep knowing that our time is limited can either have us want to play it safe or inspire us to take risks and live authentically, rather than delaying our dreams for a distant future that may never come.

Facing our impermanence can also foster a deeper appreciation for the present moment. Recognising that everything is transient can heighten our gratitude for the beauty and experiences of everyday life. It can also cultivate resilience, as we learn to navigate the inevitable changes and losses that come our way, just by being a human being. Learning to embrace our impermanence (instead of resist or ignore or be afraid of it) can allow us to let go of the need for control and certainty. This is a topic that comes up in coaching often, usually for folks considering stepping into the next chapter of life.

Of course, there are other elements in the current meta story but these are some of the big ones. Like faint background music playing in a restaurant, we often don't even pay attention to it. But our resilience, our identity, the meaning of our lives, and even our sense of purpose is profoundly influenced by it.

Most of my clients come to coaching with a specific outcome in mind—a more effective team, a new job, better relationships with the Board members, etc. Very often, once we've addressed the immediate issues, the conversations eventually turn to the bigger questions and concerns in their lives. They want to talk about that background music. They have questions about meaning and purpose, about feeling inadequate to make a difference in the big hairy problems we're collectively living, about how to move more powerfully in their own life without fear.

COACHING CAN HELP WITH THE EXISTENTIAL CRISES OF BEING HUMAN

Author Ralph Peters said: "The great paradox of the 21st century is that, in this age of powerful technology, the biggest problems we face internationally are problems of the human soul."

One of the great paradoxes we're facing is the fact that while technology is immensely powerful and capable of solving many problems, it is not sufficient to address the fundamental issues rooted in human nature and society, in our human-beingness. We can build ships to outer space but can't get along in our teams. We can find cures for horrific diseases but can't find time to play with our children or sit in the garden and read a good book without feeling guilty that we aren't being productive.

The most significant issues we face are not technological but deeply human and they require from us qualities we didn't learn or haven't fostered such as deep empathy (for self and others), compassion, vulnerability, ethical consideration, compromise, collaboration, and a focus on human values that technology cannot provide.

I believe that's one of the major reasons that coaching emerged—as a response to our longing for safe space and authentic connection to reflect on the big questions of our lives. Questions on the best way forward when our traditional ways of thinking and doing are exhausted and our go-to solutions aren't working as we'd like.

Coaching, when practised well, is a safe space for our big wonderings—call them soul wonderings or existential wonderings—like: What is purpose? What is my life well lived? Whose life am I choosing to live? Who am I, really? What is my work to do here? It's a conversation in which you can wonder and reflect without fear of judgement and without fear of being converted to any belief system. The coach doesn't have an agenda for you, isn't trying to get you to believe what they believe, doesn't have a prescription for your life. The coach is there to challenge your perspectives and the habits you've fallen into that might be a source of your suffering or concerns. But it's YOU who decides how to move forward and what is best for your own life.

By the way, if you don't like the word 'soul', you can replace it with spirit or energy or the Divine or consciousness, or whatever word you have for the deep knowing that there is so much more to being a human being than we can possibly see or explain. Whatever you label it, it's who you really are beyond all the exterior trappings and titles, beyond your beliefs about who you think you are, beyond the layers of identity you have put on like coats of armour to stay safe in a seemingly less safe world, beyond your go-to strategies that you have on auto-repeat.

As Mark Borax and Ellias Lonsdale state in their book *Cosmic Weather Report: Notes from the Edge of the Universe*:

> We stand at an evolutionary crossroads.
> Fear and resistance are inevitable. Human
> nature stubbornly clings to the old even
> when the old is obsolete. But each of us has
> tremendous power packed within. Each has
> a core force that can be ignited to blaze a trail
> to a whole new era.

An ontological approach to coaching can create a transformational space to support you to blaze your trail.

YOU AS TRAIL BLAZER

We human beings are so much more than our beliefs, our thoughts, our emotions, the roles we play, our histories, the identities we have crafted. And that is so easy to forget while trying to keep up in our fast-paced, volatile, uncertain, day-to-day living and working.

As an ontologically-trained coach, you have the unique ability and skills to explore with clients, not just what they want to achieve but also the limitations of the self they think they are that has them draw lines and limits on what else is possible. That self isn't a fixed entity but rather a fluid and dynamic process of emergence that is capable of generating new futures, a new story, a new path.

You can help them understand how they have constructed their version of reality or life and to stretch and grow to new levels of awareness and broader perspectives. You can help reconnect them with their emotions and bodies, which are great sources of wisdom. You can help them identify the hidden assumptions and beliefs that are keeping them from fully experiencing life and finding greater fulfilment.

An ontological approach to coaching taps into all aspects of our human beingness, not just our thinking and reasoning skills which, while necessary and helpful to navigate in the world, are also insufficient on their own. Sustainable change requires a change to the whole self, not just a part of it; to the whole human being who is taking the actions; to the inhabitant of the consciousness trying to navigate this seeming reality.

Sustainable change also requires practice, in addition to new awareness. Learning a new theory or observing on the sidelines isn't likely enough to get you behaving differently. You have to try things out, and practise until the new behaviours come more easily. As Paulo Coelho, Brazilian writer and author of the bestseller *The Alchemist*, said: "The world is changed by your example, not by your opinion."

Blazing your trail also requires intent, which is often in short supply when you're in daily survival mode, trying to check all the things off your to-do list (only for it to fill up again the next day). Without intent, you are in danger of spending most of your time reacting to circumstances, acting mostly out of habit and unexamined assumptions. I call this being in the drift.

With intention, awareness, and practice, you blaze your trail by consciously deciding how you spend your time and with whom, where you want to put your attention and energy as a reflection of what matters most to you, what you want to learn, what you want to stop doing and start doing to move you along into the future you want to generate. I call this being in the design.

In the design, your life is about consciously choosing to take actions consistent with your values and your inner knowing.

In the drift, your life is more a result of just the way you've come to do things. It's a result of a million small and not-so-small decisions that you made out of habit or fear or justifications and reasons to accommodate to the circumstances.

In the design, you commit to the journey of self-discovery in which you examine how you've constructed your world view and perspectives and how that might be getting in the way of the highest and best version of you. You get more comfortable with not-knowing and uncertainty and, even if you stumble or fail, you know you are acting out of alignment and integrity with what matters most.

In the drift, you are more likely to blame your circumstances or others for how your life is turning out. You are also more likely caught on the treadmill of more as your measure of happiness.

In the design, you courageously relax your grip on the need for control and certainty, so that new thinking can emerge to take you in the direction you most want to go.

Coaching Note

This might be a good time for you to pause and reflect on where you are in drift and where you are in design in your life. Some questions for you to ponder:

- Where in your life do you seem to be drifting? (With your spouse, at work, with your own learning, with your health, with your finances, etc.) Is that okay with you?
- How would your future be different if you were intentional in the journey of discovery to generate a new future?
- What support do you need, and from whom, to help you with design?

Since I was introduced to the ontological approach to leading, living, and coaching many years ago, I've used it every single day in my personal life, as a leader in several organisations and as a coach. It's made me a better mother, partner, friend, professional, and, most of all, human being. It's helped me be intentional, in designing a career path and life I love.

In the design space, there are unlimited possibilities. Possibilities to generate kinder, more connected, more engaged places of work that still create successful outcomes. Possibilities to bring the best of our humanness to address the big hairy, scary social and global issues of our times. Possibilities to become a fuller version of ourselves with less fear, worry, or self-imposed limits.

Imagine a world where we are fuller expressions, full versions of ourselves. Where we are living more in alignment with what most matters to us, and more in harmony with the world around us. Imagine how that could positively impact our families, communities, organisations and the planet itself. By being able to hold transformational space for the bigger questions in life, all that is possible ... and more.

**Terrie Lupberger, MCC, ACTC
Director of Coach Training and Lead Trainer
with TCP**

In addition to her team coaching and talent development work, Terrie teaches coaching at the Healthcare Coaching Institute in the US, as well as in several programmes internationally. She also co-facilitates The Executive Sanctuary, a safe and supportive retreat space for non-profit leaders to work through their leadership challenges.

Terrie is contributing author to several books on coaching including: *The Handbook of Knowledge Based Coaching, A Coach's Guide to Emotional Intelligence*, and will soon publish her own book entitled *The Inner Work of Work* for leaders and coaches who want to have greater impact and success with less stress and suffering.

Terrie is considered a pioneer in the profession of coaching. She was a founding member of the Association of Coach Training Organizations, helped create the original core competencies still informing coaching professionalism today, and is a former Board Member of the International Coaching Federation.

Prior to coaching, Terrie's professional career was spent in various management and leadership positions, in both the private and public sectors. She was CEO of an international leadership and coaching consultancy, a former federal manager overseeing large scale initiatives, and director of a thousand-person outplacement programme. She knows first-hand what it takes to build teams, lead large-scale change, and navigate complexity. Her passion for people and her commitment to make a significant contribution to reducing suffering in organisations eventually led her to become an executive and team coach.

Terrie's international experience, executive coaching skills and more than 20 years' experience as an executive gives her a unique vantage point when working with her clients who want to play a bolder game without sacrificing their well-being.

Closing Thoughts

As you come to the end of this book, we invite you to pay attention to which chapters or segments have resonated most strongly with you. As mentioned in the introduction: "This book promises no easy answers, but it does promise challenging questions, provocation, and exploration."

Pay especial attention to the areas where you have the most opportunity to develop and grow. Very often, it is precisely those areas where you have the most to develop and grow; where your old habits might be keeping you stuck. Pay attention also to the areas that piqued your curiosity, as these may serve as invitations for you to explore more deeply and to guide your learning journey into new territories.

The provocations and challenges are there to stimulate you into new ways of seeing and new ways of interacting with the world. What new conversations have now become possible? In which relationships do you now see new possibilities? In explorations such as these, it is very common to become aware of areas that you have been taking people or things for granted. If that is the case for you, then what new possibilities now come into view? In what ways is your view of who you are in the world expanded?

The ontological approach is designed to help shine a light on you and how you are currently navigating your way through your life, physically, mentally, and emotionally. Beyond that, it is about supporting you to explore the limitations of the self you believe yourself to be. To explore who you can be beyond your created identities and external circumstances. In short, to create a powerful container for genuine and sustainable transformation.

This is not to say that your current way of being and doing is wrong, or faulty in any way. After all, it got you to where you are today. At the same time, it may also be the very thing keeping you from getting you to where you want to go next. What has happened is that your current way of operating (your 'mindset') has become *transparent*, and when you lose sight of it, you lose the power to make conscious choices about how you interact. You cannot change what you do not notice. Or put more eloquently:

"You cannot intervene in a world that you do not see."

Over time, the unnoticed mindset becomes 'just the way things are … just the way the world is … just who I am' … *but that's not true.*

The first step is to notice, and this book can serve as a catalyst in that process.

You might think of it as creating a *break* in the existing transparency. Once that break happens, you will most likely experience some discomfort, physically, mentally, or emotionally. It is, however, that very discomfort that will allow you to *expand* your current way of observing and interacting with the world around you.

The promise of this book is not that you become a better or somehow improved person because you read it.

The promise of this book is that it will offer you different points of view and different possibilities, along with invitations and provocations. What you go on to do with them, is and always will be, up to you.

A simple and specific example of how to move forward from here is to consider these four statements and how you would now honestly complete them:

- I am …
- Life is …
- Other people are …
- In the end, …

From here, then assess the extent to which these completed statements are productive and fulfilling for you at this point in your life, and the extent to which they are simply unnoticed remnants of past experiences and/or comforting old beliefs, that may now, in fact, be the very thing holding you back.

Once you have begun to notice (and to notice what you notice), the next steps are to take action, develop practices, and, very importantly, to build a network of support inside a like-minded community. In today's world, there is often a strong pull to think you need to do all this on your own, but nothing could be further from the truth.

Indeed, for many people, the strong desire to 'do things on my own' is one of the key elements that had existed, transparent and unquestioned in their current way of operating, and is now one of the biggest and most invisible barriers to the expansion of their world view.

In the 2020s, we are truly living in extraordinary times. The rate of technological advancement is challenging our very humanity.

As of today, there isn't a single human being on the planet who knows how Artificial Intelligence will impact the future of human beings, and how we will live our lives.

It is another paradox: The more that technology connects us, the more isolated we become.

What we do know, however, is that the ontological approach to coaching uniquely promises a way to navigate such uncertainty. It is an approach to life that transcends the simple transfer of information and knowledge and instead illuminates not only necessary conversations, but conversations about those conversations.

Get curious.

Enjoy the journey.

The Works Partnership

The Works Partnership (TWP) is a leading provider of high-impact experiential interventions to businesses and institutions worldwide. Our personal approach to development and growth has served to evoke new levels of excitement, commitment, and possibility in our clients for more than 20 years.

TWP has worked in partnership with organisations big and small across Asia, Europe, and the USA to further personal and organisational growth via the development of self-awareness, commitment, responsibility, leadership, and team development.

Based out of Singapore, with partner offices in Hong Kong, Taipei, Kuala Lumpur, Mumbai, and Jakarta, and coaches and trainers located throughout the world; TWP offers services in the areas of Leadership Development, Change Leadership, Line Manager Coach Training, 'Coaching Culture' work, Executive/Team Coaching, Influencing & Engagement, and Health and Wellness initiatives on a global basis. TWP interventions use the ontological 'start with who' process as a basis from which to trigger new levels of effectiveness for individuals and teams and thereby enable sustainable transformational change within their organisation.

Using an experiential process that begins with self-awareness and honesty before moving to trust, openness, commitment and responsibility, authenticity and contribution, TWP interventions challenge unproductive patterns of behaviour and conversation, while building genuine commitment to an organisation's vision and goals.

TWP challenges leaders to engage with their career, their team, their organisation, and ultimately their life, at a whole different level; to take responsibility for their results, to communicate authentically, to work in a cooperative spirit of partnership, and to have the courage to do, and be different.

TWP is dedicated to the excellence of individuals, companies, and communities and believes that it is only possible for a business to grow if its employees are also growing. TWP also owns one of the world's most respected coach training companies: **The Coach Partnership**.

The Coach Partnership

The Coach Partnership (TCP) is one of the world's leading transformational learning organisations. Founded in 2010, under the name Newfield Asia, the company was rebranded in 2019 as The Coach Partnership.

TCP uses the Newfield ontological coaching methodology to create world-class coaches via a nine-month ICF ACTP certified programme and a six-month ICF ACTC certification in team coaching, both of which are recognised as being the gold standard in coach training.

People attending these programmes come from all walks of life. Some are in the process of becoming Executive Coaches, but the majority of attendees are experienced leaders, managers, and professionals looking to become more adept in the domain of working with other human beings. Due to the nature of the work, wherever people come from, they invariably notice growth in their personal, as well their professional lives.

In recent times, TCP has added specialist certifications in Health Coaching, Parenting Coaching, Performance Coaching and (in partnership with Charles Feltman) Trust at Work. All programmes are designed to support individuals in a journey of discovery that initially challenges them to enlarge their own world view, take action aligned with what they care most about, and ultimately generate results consistent with their own deepest values.

Only when they have embarked on their own personal journey, does TCP begin to support them to be able to do the same with other people. Graduates of The Coach Partnership, therefore, authentically embody coaching as a way of relating to and conversing with other human beings, rather than seeing it simply as a methodology, a process, or a task to be done.

Suggestions for Further Reading

Chris Balsley *Stop Controlling, Start Leading: 27 Secrets for Effective Leadership at Work Home and Play*
"This book holds 27 leadership secrets that can change the actions you take in the world and take your leadership to the next level without your having to try harder. These strategies will inspire you to think and act differently."

Amanda Blake *Your Body Is Your Brain: Leverage Your Somatic Intelligence to Find Purpose, Build Resilience, Deepen Relationships and Lead More Powerfully*
"*Your Body is Your Brain* invites leaders of all stripes into a massive shift of their mental models, allowing them to access their highest and best selves."

Chalmers Brothers *Language and the Pursuit of Happiness: A New Foundation for Designing Your Life, Your Relationships, and Your Results*
"In this book, the author leads you on an eye-opening exploration of yourself, your language, your conversations, and their connections to your physical and emotional well-being. He introduces you to an emerging and thought-provoking way of thinking, one with very old and very new roots."

Chalmers Brothers *Language and the Pursuit of Leadership Excellence: How Extraordinary Leaders Build Relationships, Shape Culture and Drive Breakthrough Results*
"Drawing on conversations with thousands of CEOs, business owners, and senior leaders of all types over a decade, this book provides an eye-opening organisational blueprint, coupled with powerful, practical tools that leaders at all levels are employing to dramatically improve workplace relationships, shape culture, and drive breakthrough results."

Carol Courcy *Save Your Inner Tortoise!: Learn How to Cross the Finish Line Joyful and Satisfied*
"*Save Your Inner Tortoise!* shares step-by-step tools and includes great activities and exercises that showcase alternative life strategies to help tame the self-sacrificing, never-enough overachiever in you."

Angela Cusack *Discover the Matrix: Integrity—The True Mark of Leadership*
"This book delves into the pivotal role of integrity in leadership, proving it is the foundation for trust and long-term organisational success. It offers practical insights and real-world examples to help leaders understand that 'who they are is how they lead'. It provides a road map for leaders to explore their inner selves, aligning their core values with their leadership actions. By fostering a culture of trust and respect, leaders can inspire collaboration and innovation, ultimately building a brand rooted in integrity. This approach resonates deeply with employees and customers, cultivating lasting loyalty and a reputation for reliability and authenticity."

Croft Edwards *The Liquid Accordion: A Somatic Primer on Coaching In, With and Through the Body*
"For many coaches and leaders, somatic coaching seems great to do, but how do you do it? It is to answer this question that this book was written.

The book explores three fundamental questions around somatic coaching: Why we coach in, with, and through the body; Where/What we coach in, with, and through the body; and finally, How to coach in, with, and through the body. The book contains many high-quality diagrams, and ultra realistic images to paint the picture. Of note is the actual coaching moves and scripts that are included for the reader to be able to coach in, with, and through the body."

Charles Feltman *The Thin Book of Trust: An Essential Primer for Building Trust At Work (3rd Edition)*
"The book offers a framework that supports trust building as a workplace competency. It is based on the idea that building trust is a competency, a set of skills that can be learnt, improved, and practised. It will help you continuously improve your ability to build and maintain trust with others. It can also help you create and contribute to a high trust culture at work. The 3rd edition includes a new chapter on how to build trust in a team."

Aneace Haddad *Soaring Beyond Midlife: The Surprisingly Natural Emergence of Leadership Superpowers in Life's Second Half*
"Discover how midlife's inherent resilience, heightened self-awareness, and strategic thinking can naturally redefine and elevate your leadership. In this book, the midlife crisis is reimagined as a leadership rejuvenation, revealing six 'Midlife Superpowers' for transformative growth."

Aneace Haddad *The Eagle That Drank Hummingbird Nectar: A CEO's Tale of Midlife Rejuvenation*
"Dive into the transformative journey of Aidan Perez, a seasoned CEO grappling with personal loss and career uncertainty. This narrative blends novelistic richness with actionable leadership wisdom, offering a fresh perspective on embracing midlife challenges for profound renewal."

Kaylin Huang *Elevating Emotional Intelligence: A Guide to 10 Emotional Competencies for Career Success*
"Read the true stories of executives who resolved their career issues through understanding their emotions and developing their emotional competence, leading to breakthroughs in their careers. This book offers a complete guide to developing emotional intelligence and serves as a lifetime resource for you to turn to, as you face various challenges in the different stages of your career."

Terrie Lupberger *The Inner Work of Work* (coming 2025)
"Profound, practical, and actionable, this book offers coaches and leaders (at all levels) ways to get results and be a better human, without sacrificing well-being. Amidst these chaotic and uncertain times, we can't control external circumstances but we can learn ways to better navigate and respond. This book talks about the stuff we didn't get taught in school nor talk about at work. It offers a primer, a strong foundation upon which to build better leading and living."

Marcus and Sari Marsden *Fit To Lead: Transforming Your Leadership with the 5 Pillars of Performance*
"Frank and forward-thinking, *Fit To Lead* offers a dynamic new vision of leadership development that places the role of your physical body firmly alongside that of your thoughts and emotions. Written by husband-and-wife team, Marcus and Sari Marsden, the book combines the principles of personal development, executive coaching, nutrition, fitness training, and movement to provide you with a holistic system for transforming your leadership and producing breakthrough results for yourself and the people you lead."

Marcus Marsden *Start With Who: Reveal the Hidden Power of Identity to Create a Purposeful Life*
"In this book, the author demonstrates how the beliefs you hold about yourself not only produce your current reality, but also limit your future possibility. Transform your capacity to produce extraordinary results by examining the beliefs you hold about yourself."

Alan Sieler *Coaching to the Human Soul: Ontological Coaching and Deep Change, Volumes 1 to 4*
"*Coaching to the Human Soul* breaks new ground in the literature on coaching, as it provides a comprehensive coverage of what is probably the world's most advanced approach to Executive Coaching and Life Coaching. Ontological Coaching is based on a new understanding of human beings and human interaction."

www.ingramcontent.com/pod-product-compliance
Lightning Source LLC
Chambersburg PA
CBHW051303130726
47987CB00004B/1649